MW01054464

A Brave and
Lovely Woman

A Brave and Lovely Woman

Mamah Borthwick and Frank Lloyd Wright

Mark Borthwick

THE UNIVERSITY OF WISCONSIN PRESS

Publication of this book has been made possible, in part, through support from the Anonymous Fund of the College of Letters and Science at the University of Wisconsin–Madison.

The University of Wisconsin Press
728 State Street, Suite 443
Madison, Wisconsin 53706
uwpress.wisc.edu

Gray's Inn House, 127 Clerkenwell Road
London ECIR 5DB, United Kingdom
eurospanbookstore.com

Printed in the United States of America
This book may be available in a digital edition.

Library of Congress Cataloging-in-Publication Data
Names: Borthwick, Mark, author.
Title: A brave and lovely woman : Mamah Borthwick and
Frank Lloyd Wright / Mark Borthwick.
Description: Madison, Wisconsin : The University of Wisconsin Press, [2023] |
Includes bibliographical references and index.
Identifiers: LCCN 2022033654 | ISBN 9780299342906 (hardcover)
Subjects: LCSH: Borthwick, Mamah Bouton, 1869-1914. | Wright, Frank Lloyd,
1867-1959—Friends and associates. | Women translators—
United States—Biography.
Classification: LCC HQ1413.B665 B67 2023 | DDC 305.4092
[B]—dc23/eng/20220824
LC record available at https://lccn.loc.gov/2022033654

CONTENTS

Illustrations

PREFACE

The story of Mamah Borthwick's relationship with Frank Lloyd Wright began to appear in popular fiction nearly a century after it ended in tragedy. It is hardly surprising that the characters in these accounts bore little resemblance to who they had been in real life. This is not to say that a good deal of "fiction" was not written about Mamah Borthwick while she lived, much of it unflattering exposés of her affair with the legendary architect in the tabloid newspapers of the time. The *Ogden Standard* even quoted neighbors who pointed to the fire at Taliesin as "the strongest argument that the Avenging Angel still flies."[1] Of course, in some of the accounts, Borthwick's photograph was retouched beyond recognition to make her look the part of the seducer.

While certainly unkind and unreliable, these stories are a source of fascination to me personally because Mamah Borthwick and I are descended from the same Scottish immigrant, James Borthwick, who settled in the area of Albany, New York, in 1773. Separately, our family lines found their way to Iowa, settling in different parts of the state. In the parlance of genealogy, she is my second cousin thrice removed.

Growing up, I learned almost nothing about her from my family: my parents' generation observed a kind of radio silence on the subject, and my grandfather Borthwick seems to have known of her without knowing her personally. Families tend to avoid discussing their black sheep, not to mention topics like adultery, family desertion, and murder. In light of this, and since she has no surviving direct descendants, there initially seemed little hope of leveraging family ties to find out anything substantial about her. Furthermore, she left behind no love letters or thought-filled journals, in fact no personal records of any kind.

My own journey to this book has been lengthy, and I began to think of it as an archaeological expedition, digging through public records, libraries, newspapers, sorority and society archives, published works, family stories, and nearly forgotten items in distant relatives' attics and albums. On one occasion in 1989, I found myself in Brendan Gill's hideaway office in Manhattan. The well-known writer for the *New Yorker* had recently published *Many Masks*, his biography of Frank Lloyd Wright. As its title implies, the book surveyed Wright mythology and made as much of the masks as it did of the man. We spent much of our time pumping one another for information that neither of us possessed. The problem we both found perplexing was the absence of material about Mamah Borthwick in the massive archive on Wright. The once scattered collection has since been consolidated at the Avery Library of Columbia University, but it has not solved the lack of documentation on Borthwick. Only gradually did information start to emerge, and I embarked—like an archaeologist—on piecing together the shards I uncovered. Some of the fragments bear relationships to one another, and some fit together neatly, but inevitably the assemblage has cracks and gaps. I have taken some liberties in imagining Mamah's thoughts and feelings at times in an effort to fill some of those gaps, and I hope that the resulting picture adds to our understanding of her and the journey she made with Frank Lloyd Wright.

If I look upon both Borthwick and Wright with some sympathy, it is not because I entirely approve of their behavior. They were actors on a stage very distant from ours. The American Midwest leading up to World War I was full of tensions and changes that impacted all aspects of life, including gender and family politics, art, and technology. I attempt to approach their relationship with some humility for what we cannot know about how these events affected them and their contemporaries, and perhaps extend to them a bit of the sympathy that eluded them in their lifetimes.

ACKNOWLEDGMENTS

This book came about thanks to the support of many who provided information, advice, editing, and encouragement. It took shape in the Billiards Room of the Cosmos Club in Washington, DC, in conversations with James Conaway. His experience as a writer of nonfiction and fiction was invaluable; I only wish he had improved my game as well.

For editorial advice I am indebted to Jonathan Balcombe, Judith Robey, and Ralph Eubanks. Amber Cederström, acquisitions editor at the University of Wisconsin Press, provided especially critical guidance and editing.

The pandemic tested the mettle of all those who manage, maintain, or otherwise support libraries and archives. In no particular order I wish to thank those who responded generously when I asked for their help: Noraleen Young, Kappa Alpha Theta archives; Wendy Hall, Carnegie Library, Boulder, Colorado; Janet Curtiss, St. Clair County Library System; Jacob Nugent and Karen Wight, Bentley Historical Library, University of Michigan; Sharon Mitchell, Berea College, Hutchins Library; Liz Rogers, Marriott Library, University of Utah; Edward O'Brien, Oak Park Public Library; Trava Olivier, Pipestone County Museum; and at the Wisconsin Historical Society, Lee Grady, Susan Krueger, and Gayle Martinson.

From Sweden I received valuable assistance from Maja Rahm, Ellen Key's Strand; Ann-Charlotte Knochenhauer and Rasmus Lindgren, National Library of Sweden; Hedda Jansson at Stockholm University; Kirstin Strand of the Ellen Key Society; and Ronny Ambjörnsson. My special thanks to Filippo Fici in Italy and in Turkey to Mehmet Kentel, Istanbul Research Institute. I am also grateful for the help and expertise of Keiran Murphy, Anne Nissen, Mary Ann Porucznik, Janice Bardsley, and Andrew Gordon. Thanks to Kevin Abing,

Bob Drahozal, Terrie Johnson, and Alexandra Korey for pursuing research questions in their locales.

For illustrations and photographs I am very grateful to Rhea Higgins, James McIntosh, Douglas Steiner, Bill Hook, Grant Hildebrand, and Richard Guy Wilson. My thanks also to Sanford Wintersberger, Mike Jackson, Doug Carr, Eric O'Malley, Sarah McCormick Healy, Debbie Becker, Julie O'Connor, Jim Petrzilka, and Erin Greb.

I have drawn heavily on the work of accomplished historians, especially scholars of Frank Lloyd Wright and of the early feminist movement. Space does not allow me to name them all here but they are acknowledged, if inadequately, in the bibliography.

Finally, my thanks to my wife, Becky Lescaze, who served as first reader and judge of all my trial balloons. Her patient support and encouragement are testimony to my good fortune in having her in my life.

A Brave and Lovely Woman

INTRODUCTION

Mamah Borthwick was born on June 19, 1869, in Boone, Iowa. She was one of the rare women in the nineteenth century to earn a bachelor's degree, which she received from the University of Michigan in 1892. Even more unusually, she stayed for a master's degree, and she maintained a lively interest in literature and the arts all her life. Her skill in ancient Greek and interest in linguistics foreshadowed her acquisition of Swedish as an adult, which she learned for the express purpose of translating the writings of an important early feminist, Ellen Key. She is not remembered for her accomplishments or translations, however, but rather for her affair with one of America's most famous architects, Frank Lloyd Wright, and for her grisly murder at the hands of one of his employees on August 15, 1914.

Wright eulogized her in a local newspaper after her death, describing her as "a brave and lovely woman." For years afterward, little else about her appeared in print until his *An Autobiography* (1932). There and in later versions, he mentioned her mainly in reference to their life in Fiesole and her death and burial. His son John described her very briefly in his memoir of his father, *My Father Who Is on Earth* (1946).

Early Wright scholarship showed little interest in Borthwick. She is mentioned in passing in Grant Manson's *Frank Lloyd Wright to 1910: The First Golden Age* (1958). Much of the research on Wright that followed his death in 1959 occurred under the scrutiny of his widow, who controlled access to his archive. Unsurprisingly, Borthwick was not a welcome topic.

Daunted, perhaps, by Wright's extensive oeuvre over his long lifetime and the voluminous amount of material on him, none of Wright's biographers have discussed Borthwick in any significant detail. The first extensive primary research that revealed new information about her was done by Anthony Alofsin

3

in his 1987 Columbia University PhD dissertation. Focusing on Wright's European experience, it was later adopted for publication as *Frank Lloyd Wright—the Lost Years, 1910–1922: A Study of Influence* (1993). In *Wright Studies*, vol 1, *Taliesin 1911–1914*, edited by Narciso G. Menocal (1992), Neil Levine makes the case that Borthwick was a central inspiration for Wright's house, Taliesin. Ron McCrea's *Building Taliesin* (2013) draws on her life with Wright in Italy and provides details of her publishing efforts on behalf of Ellen Key. Their time in Florence and Fiesole is covered in depth by Filipo Fici in his article "Frank Lloyd Wright in Florence and Fiesole, 1909–1910." In *Death in a Prairie House* (2007), William Drennan describes Borthwick's murder but leaves many questions unanswered.

The above discussions are primarily concerned with Wright's life and work. The first scholarly research to focus exclusively on Mamah Borthwick and the implications of her relationship with Wright was the pioneering MIT master's thesis by Anne D. Nissen, "From the Cheney House to Taliesin: Frank Lloyd Wright and Feminist Mamah Borthwick" (1988). The discovery of Borthwick's letters to Ellen Key led to three scholarly articles. The first, Lena Johannesson's "Notes on the Historiography of Non-existing History" (1995), introduced the letters, and a second, Alice T. Friedman's "Frank Lloyd Wright and Feminism" (2002), included letter excerpts with useful commentary and notes. Lastly, Barbara Miller Lane updated this work with respect to chronology and Key's aesthetic ideas with "An Introduction to Ellen Key's Beauty in the Home" (2008).

In addition to these academic publications, there have been more fanciful adaptations, such as Nancy Horan's novel *Loving Frank*. This is a work of historical fiction and not a useful source, though it unfortunately is occasionally cited as such.

If Mamah has been the mystery woman of the Frank Lloyd Wright saga, it is partly because of Wright's tendency to eclipse those around him. It is also because of her identification with the early feminist movement, which itself had little to do with architecture. Further, as a translator, whose writings were not her own, she occupied a somewhat liminal space. But it was not for this reason that she receded into the background. Her achievements in translating the works of the Swedish feminist Ellen Key were lost in the cultural wormhole created by the catastrophe of World War I. What emerged on the other side was a changed feminist movement that marginalized Key, and by extension Mamah.

Mamah Borthwick was full of contradictions. Although a disciple of Ellen Key, the world's leading champion of motherhood, she left her children. Gracious and intelligent, she loved a vain showman. Born on the frontier prairie, she held a master's degree. Given how few personal records she left behind, she seems nearly out of reach as a subject. As part of the early feminist movement, she was, like many remarkable women of that time, largely forgotten, despite having provided the link between Wright and Ellen Key. The three of them together formed a spiritual triangle that bolstered Wright in an important way during their sojourn in Europe.

Wright tried to give the impression that his creativity was influenced only by Nature. He wished to be seen as an independent creative force. This posturing notwithstanding, both he and Mamah were products of their time. They saw themselves as actors on the stage of a dawning new era. As they prepared to translate their ideas into action, pursuing their ideal of living truthfully, abandoning their families and homes in the Chicago suburb of Oak Park for Europe, they became reckless, somewhat naive, and arrogant. Wright was little humbled by their experience abroad, but Borthwick confronted the implications of her decision.

Upon returning, they found that they would always have America, but America would not have them. They bestowed on it a national treasure called Taliesin, where they tried to live on their own terms but never achieved social acceptance or the peace they sought. Still, the place would be recalled for the sense of promise it held before World War I as something grand and original that seemed to signal a new beginning, not just for them but for American architecture. Appearances were deceiving. It was not the right time. And yet the time itself is worthy of focus. The tension between modernism and a late nineteenth-century sensibility informed the couple as much as it did Taliesin, their redoubt in Wisconsin.

PART I

CHAPTER I

WOMAN OF THE HOUR

On April 27, 1908, the meeting room of Unity House was nearly filled with round tables set for lunch. The annex adjacent to Frank Lloyd Wright's masterpiece, Unity Temple in Oak Park, Illinois, was often used for secular events. On this occasion it was to host the annual meeting of the Nineteenth Century Club, the women's group that represented the Chicago suburb's female establishment.[1] They usually met in the community center, the Scoville Institute, but on this occasion, they required additional space, a fact made obvious by an improvised stage that crowded the tables.

The meeting's attendees wore elaborate hats, a carryover from the club's namesake century, when hats were still worn indoors on such occasions. Some members may have unpinned and removed them, taking their cue from Chicago doyen Mrs. Lydia Avery Coonley-Ward. In 1900, she had notoriously upended the city's millinery trade by riding hatless in a carriage in Lincoln Park. But the reason for removing hats on this occasion was to ensure that everyone had a view of the stage.

The play to be performed, *Woman of the Hour*, was written mainly by one of the club's new members, Mamah (MAY-mah) Borthwick Cheney, who also had top billing in the role of Victoria Lawson, editor in chief of the play's all-woman newspaper.[2] The script, said to have been written by a few "kind contributors," shows every sign of having been written mostly by Borthwick: its sarcastic view of courtship and marriage testified to her unhappy marriage to Edwin Cheney.

At this point, her love affair with Frank Lloyd Wright was still unknown. Reports that later circulated about them riding about in Oak Park in his car at this time, flagrantly displaying affection in public, are untrue. Both were married with children and held in high esteem by the community. One of

9

Wright's studio employees had become suspicious, but they kept their relationship secret for most of their time in Oak Park.

In October 1907, Borthwick had finally joined the Nineteenth Century Club after years of resistance. Membership had long been open to her, and many of her friends and acquaintances had belonged for years. Wright's wife, Catherine, was a member, his mother was a club founder, and Mamah's University of Michigan classmate Julia Herrick had joined soon after their graduation in 1892. It is unclear why Borthwick held back until she was thirty-eight years old.

Equally puzzling was the fact that just after joining, she made a joint presentation with Catherine Wright on the poet Johann Wolfgang von Goethe. Their audience is commonly believed to have been the Nineteenth Century Club, but it was in fact something called "the Study Group," an informal group of women who met regularly to prepare for a series of lectures on drama or literature. Until then the group had not included Catherine, so it is likely it was Borthwick who arranged for them to make the presentation together. If in return Catherine had convinced her to join the Nineteenth Century Club, it would mean they had become close just when one would have expected Borthwick to seek distance from her.

Said to have been beautiful, Mamah Borthwick did not always photograph well. Her photographs at a younger age are unflattering. Her deep-set eyes and dark hair sometimes gave her an aura of gravity, which she dispelled with a mischievous sense of humor and infectious laugh. This paradox of gravity and laughter can be seen in *Woman of the Hour*. Written when she was betraying both her husband and her friend Catherine, its humor suggests that she had not yet confronted her dishonesty. No one who saw her that day at Unity House could have imagined that she was having an affair. A prominent member of the nation's first national sorority, Kappa Alpha Theta, she had very recently been the banquet toastmistress of its national convention in Chicago. Yet, in a few years, her reworked image would appear in newspapers across America as a simulacrum of a brazen seductress.

Some of the women of the club had known her since childhood. One was Grace Hall Hemingway, Ernest's mother. With her husband, Clarence, she had graduated from Oak Park High School two years behind Borthwick. Grace and Mamah had recently begun to rehearse with an all-woman cast for a benefit performance of *As You Like It* in support of the Wellesley College gymnasium fund.

Edith Winslow, from nearby River Forest, was another member whose interests overlapped with Borthwick's. She, too, lived in a house designed by Frank

Lloyd Wright and was a fellow member of the Study Group. They cochaired its subcommittee on the modern German playwright Gerhart Hauptmann.

Borthwick's next-door neighbor Lulu Belknap is also likely to have been at the luncheon. Sixty years later, her nine-year-old daughter, Margaret, would publish a memoir in which she claimed to have peered down from the second floor of her home to spy on Borthwick and Wright regularly "making love."[3] For reasons discussed in chapter 10, this is nearly impossible. The only contemporary adult to leave an eyewitness account of the drama in Oak Park in the first decade of the 1900s was a British woman, Janet Ashbee, whose husband, Robert, was Wright's close friend. Her journal has proven to be fairly reliable in describing the deterioration in Wright's marriage.[4] Catherine knew that something was wrong with her marriage and later claimed to have suspected Mamah, but all indications are that she only learned the truth in August 1908. Certainly neither Margaret Belknap nor her mother, nor any other attendees at the April meeting, would have been likely to have any knowledge of the forthcoming scandal.

Never had an annual meeting of the Nineteenth Century Club included a performance like *Woman of the Hour*. If Borthwick had resisted joining the club because she considered its agendas to be boring, the play certainly livened things up. She had experience performing her own words, having given a speech at the University of Michigan commencement in 1892. But while she had there poked good-natured fun at people she knew, this time her words contained a scarcely concealed edge.

According to a description of the performance provided by the much-amused editor of *Oak Leaves*, the local newspaper, the setting was "a daily newspaper office of the yellow type."[5] In an allusion to Oak Park's provincialism, the newspaper was said to be serving a rural community. The actors occasionally read news items aloud to the audience as parodies of rural life, each an insider's joke about life in the Chicago suburb. One of the first news items read aloud revealed Borthwick's authorship:

> There was a great excitement out on the East Road the other day. The Cheneys saw a band of savages with war clubs on the hill north of their place. They quickly raised the drawbridge, let the portcullis fall, and fled to the inner courts of the castle, where they passed a sleepless night. They feel sure that but for these precautions they would all have been slain. The next morning the savages had disappeared, but the family feel thankful that they have these defenses, living in so isolated a spot. The Cheney motto is, "In times of peace prepare for war."

The audience knew that "the East Road" referred to the Cheneys' address on North East Avenue and that the description of their Frank Lloyd Wright house as a fortified castle referred to its perimeter wall and fortress-like appearance. More difficult to interpret is the so-called Cheney family motto, "In times of peace prepare for war." There is no such Cheney motto. Perhaps we can read it as the author's veiled warning of trouble to come? The play's next message was less subtle. A poem, "To Phineas," had been submitted to the newspaper and was read aloud. It was said to have been written by a woman to her husband "on leaving home for a visit."

> I am going to leave you,
> But wherever I roam,
> I shall always remember
> That I'm there
> And you're home.

> I am going to leave you,
> But do not despair,
> I shall never forget
> That you're here,
> And I'm there.

The cold sarcasm could not have been a coincidence. Borthwick's marriage to Edwin Cheney had reached a crisis whose extent escaped the notice of her cool, collected husband.

Having included the Cheney name in the play's script, the Wright name had to appear as well. The review in the play, read aloud by the theater critic, included an aside in which she lamented the color of the Warrington Theater's stage curtain, calling it "far from Wright." Apparently, the famous local architect had declared it to be ugly. His iconoclasm in matters of taste, including even the appropriate color for the stage curtain, was well known in Oak Park. The women of the Nineteenth Century Club would have caught the pun when his name was spoken with emphasis.

The critic also read her review of a play titled *The Wishing Hour*, an allegory about the norms of courtship and marriage in which Borthwick's authorship is again discernible. The main characters, a woman named Rudbeckia and a man named Fussmore, fall in love and become engaged, but a "jealous spinster" tells Rudbeckia that Fussmore has an unworthy past. He has been seen "eating onions in a cheap restaurant."[6] When Rudbeckia accuses Fussmore, he confesses, forcing her to confront a dilemma: "Shall she choose life with Fussmore and onions, or life without either Fussmore or onions? She knows that a man who has had a past can have no future. Who can blame her if under the strain of emotion she is unable to endure either alternative? She chooses the simple middle course: She and Fussmore each devour a poisoned onion and expire."

In this play-within-a-play, the character of Fussmore represented the fussy, controlling Frank Lloyd Wright. Borthwick's character, Rudbeckia, was willing to put up with "life with Fussmore and onions" rather than endure life without him. Indeed, the ultimate solution of eating poison onions with Fussmore declared the hopelessness of their situation. Whether it was an expression of frustration, a warning, or both, it suggests that Borthwick understood her dilemma. The statement "a man who has had a past can have no future" reflected the reality that a scandal would probably ruin Wright's reputation and certainly hers.

We cannot know what, if anything, lay behind the choice of the name Rudbeckia, the genus name of the black-eyed Susan flower. According to the "floriography" in popular use before World War I, Rudbeckia symbolized justice. This matched the name of her character, Victoria Lawson, but if intentional it was inapt for her situation.

Exploiting word allusions and puns, she in fact gave most of the characters aptronyms: Dottie Fanted, the nervous city editor, was always on the edge of fainting; Madame Placid was the calm managing editor; Hyacinth Gear was the sporting editor; Fluffy Ruffles was the society editor; Grace Ossip was in charge of personals; and Helen Troy, who was apparently very pretty, was the typist. By contrast, Borthwick's character had a serious name. Even the name of the man addressed in the "I am going to leave you" poem may have held a meaning, since Phineas was the name of a blind seer in Greek mythology. Could this be the oblivious Edwin Cheney?

The only character whose name was more direct in its meaning was the poetry-reading Sappho, described in the program as "loved and sung."[7] A fluent reader of classical Greek, Borthwick thus saluted one of the ancient Mediterranean's most famous poets, whose work was recited to the accompaniment of a lyre. The Greek poetess's love poems were expressed to other women rather than men, reflecting perhaps Borthwick's feminist inclinations.

The lighthearted performance of *Woman of the Hour* concealed its author's complex feelings. Her situation seemed hopeless. By joining the Nineteenth

Century Club, she may have been making a doomed and perhaps short-lived effort to live virtuously and repair endangered relationships. When Wright received an invitation to go to Berlin in 1908, a key development, he did not immediately seize the opportunity. When he finally did, it was likely with Borthwick's encouragement.

The people of Oak Park thought they knew her. No one suspected how profoundly discontented she had become. If she appeared to be a so-called New Woman, it did not mean she was a feminist as the term later came to be understood. A photograph taken of her six years later suggests a woman transformed, but that image alone does not convey how far she had come.

To understand the transformation she must have undergone, we must look to her family's beginnings on the half-settled prairie of Iowa in the mid-nineteenth century. Her parents embodied the era's divisions: her Southern mother married her Northern father as the Civil War began. That internecine conflict may have appeared in the family's dynamics in ways that can only be imagined. What is clear is that her parents valued education for women and made it a priority for her. Little is known about her mother; more is understood about her father. Marcus Borthwick was a pioneer, an inventor, and a builder. If such traits suggest something of Frank Lloyd Wright, so does Marcus's experience as a young man leaving home. He left Albany, New York, to make his fortune nearly forty years before Wright left Madison, Wisconsin. Both men set their sights on Chicago.

CHAPTER 2

HEARTLAND

In 1850 it was routine for the express train from Albany to arrive in Buffalo just before the steamboat *Niagara* departed for Chicago. The 245-foot Great Lakes "palace steamer" was built specifically for the four-day run from Buffalo, the largest port of the eastern Great Lakes, to the much smaller but growing port of Chicago in the west. The *Niagara*, along with two dozen other palace steamers, carried passengers in relative comfort, creating a pleasant beginning for twenty-two-year-old Marcus Borthwick as he started his pioneer journey from his home in Albany. It was also inexpensive: the fare from Buffalo to Chicago was only ten dollars. Many of his fellow passengers on the ship would have been immigrant families headed for Wisconsin and the so-called forty-niners, men of all ages headed for the California Gold Rush. His destination was Iowa, where his sister Cordelia and her husband were farming near the city of Davenport.

Chicago was the seat of the grain trade, with its own kind of gold stored in tall, slate-roofed elevators near the lake. They were the first buildings he would have seen in the distance as the steamboat approached the low, sprawling city of wooden houses, hotels, and shops. Only as the ship drew closer would he have been able to make out the array of fine homes on the lakefront. Facing the water, they stretched south along a tree-lined promenade. Still farther south, an uncluttered shore reached all the way to the boundary of the city, a legacy of the far-sighted city founders who had resisted the despoilment of the water-front by commercial development.

His first task upon arrival was to find the depot of the Chicago and Galena Union Railroad, the single train line stretching west from Chicago. Located near the Chicago River at Canal and Kinzie Streets, it was a two-story wooden building that doubled as offices for the railroad executives. A west-facing "captain's watch" surmounted the second floor so that the company's president, John B. Turner, could keep a lookout for approaching trains with a mariner's telescope. Spying one, he would lean out his window and announce its imminent arrival to the crowd below. Turner's railroad would soon merge with another called the North West Company, and in a few years, it would grow to become Marcus's lifelong employer, the Chicago and North Western Railway. In 1850, its rail line had only been completed as far as Elgin, Illinois, a forty-two-mile stretch.

Aboard the train to Elgin, his first stop was a town called Oak Ridge, also known as Oak Park. In December 1848, a farmer named Mellican Hunt had herded his hogs onto a construction car of the train when it stopped in Oak Park on its way to the city, bringing the first freight shipment by rail to what Carl Sandburg would one day call the "hog butcher for the world." Seeing Oak Park for the first time from the train, Marcus may not have taken much notice. Thirty years later, it would be the place he chose for raising a family.

In Elgin he transferred to the Frink & Walker's stagecoach line for a fifty-mile journey on to Rockford. Although in summer the dirt roads and trails were in better condition, it was slow going on the prairie. Stagecoaches passed through towns at a gallop as the drivers blew their horns to make a show and drum up excitement, but most of the way they spared the horses by traveling at a walk. The trip to Rockford was thus an overnight journey. He would have had dinner at a coach stop inn, probably giving him his first taste of "prairie chicken," the once abundant variety of grouse that is now nearly extinct.

From Rockford, he completed the rest of his journey on the Rock River. Barely navigable to the Mississippi, its commercial traffic was limited to flatboats and small steamboats. The Rock River entered the Mississippi within a few miles of his destination, Davenport. At his journey's end, he could claim to be a pioneer like his sister.

Thirty-one-year-old Cordelia Borthwick Davidson had arrived in Iowa with her husband, Garrett, in 1847. Married in Albany, they had no children until they were settled near Davenport. Soon after Marcus Borthwick arrived, their six-year-old daughter, Mary, died. Marcus would one day commemorate her by giving his third daughter her name. His Mary, however, would come to be known as Mamah.

With no intention of emulating his brother-in-law by becoming a farmer, he moved a day's ride north to the river town of Lyons in the expectation that the railroad would soon cross the Mississippi there. He thus assumed the town had a future, even if in 1850 it was little more than a hundred low buildings facing the water.

The youngest of ten children, Marcus had left Albany with a small financial stake to be used in the purchase of land. If the first railroad bridge across the Mississippi would be at Lyons, it made sense to buy land there. Finding land for sale was no challenge, but he needed a partner who was a veteran of the Mexican-American War (1846–48). A land rush was underway as a result of the issuance of military land warrants. Each veteran of the war had been given a military bounty warrant entitling him to at least 160 acres of prairie. The guarantee of land rights with a term of enlistment had created, in effect, an army of mercenaries. Many of them wanted to cash out quickly by transferring their warrants to buyers at below-market rates. In April 1853, Marcus used such a warrant to buy 160 acres of level, open prairie not far from Lyons. Worth $700 at the time he bought it, its value had increased to $5,000 ($155,000 in today's currency) when he moved away in the 1860s. He did not try to improve the land or to make his living by farming it. Instead, he began to work in Lyons as a carpenter.

A local building boom was underway, driven by the ready availability of lumber and a strong influx of settlers. Massive log rafts, some nearly a mile long, floated for hundreds of miles down the Mississippi from the vast forests of Minnesota and Wisconsin. Small gangs of men lived on them in huts and delivered them to river towns along the Upper Mississippi, where lumberyards were becoming the world's largest. Few locations on the Iowa side of the river were as ideally suited to the congruence of the railroads and the lumber trade as Lyons and its neighboring town, Clinton. Together they grew rapidly, merged, and were consolidated into a prosperous small city, Clinton, overseen by the families of the lumber barons.

Meanwhile, the railroad companies pressed westward from Chicago. The Chicago and North Western Railway finally arrived in Clinton after buying out some of the Illinois competition. While the design of the new bridge on the Mississippi needed immediate improvement, it served well enough to enable the railroads to move new rolling stock across to Iowa. Railroad cars were in short supply, especially cars in good repair. Possessing mechanical as well as carpentry skills, a combination much in demand by the railroads, Marcus soon found work with the Chicago and North Western Railway as a builder of railroad cars.

One of the first new institutions to emerge in the fast-growing Clinton-Lyons community was a college for women. By then, the University of Iowa had become the first public university in the United States to admit both sexes on an equal basis. The founding of the Presbyterian-affiliated Lyons Female

College further reflected the state's favorable environment for women's education. When its doors opened in 1858, the city founders welcomed it as an attraction for new settlers and a chance to educate their daughters. Lyons was a private school, however, and much like its counterpart, Iowa's Dubuque Female Seminary, it made itself available mainly to young women from prosperous families. The curriculum comprised classical languages, vocal and instrumental music, drawing, painting, and some natural sciences.

Marcus Borthwick and his sister Cordelia Davidson were so impressed with the college that they persuaded their brother Alexander Borthwick to bring his daughter Lizzie from Albany and enroll her. For the next three years, Marcus looked after his niece until she graduated from Lyons and went on to receive language and vocal musical training in Europe. Lizzie's own children would die in infancy, but she seems to have played a maternal role to Marcus's children, her young cousins, after both families found themselves living in Chicago. The educated, multilingual Lizzie Borthwick Felton almost certainly served as a role model for Marcus's daughters. The fact that he named his second daughter Lizzie confirms their closeness. In all likelihood she was the one who introduced Marcus to her classmate at Lyons Female College, Almira Bocock, the woman he would eventually marry.

The Bococks were a prominent Virginia family known for its strong ties to the Presbyterian Church. That affiliation might have been what led them to send Almira to Lyons Female College, where she could receive the kind of finishing school education that was believed to enhance a Southern upper-class young woman's marital prospects.[1] Born in antebellum Charlottesville, Almira was twelve years younger than Marcus and only a few years older than Lizzie Felton.[2]

Marriage to a Northerner is not likely to have been what Almira's parents had in mind when they sent her to Lyons College. To complicate matters further, she accepted Marcus's proposal of marriage in 1861, just as the Civil War was breaking out. Fort Sumter's surrender on April 13, 1861, was followed by a few weeks of calm, just enough time for them to marry. They took a steamboat to Memphis (which was in competition with Richmond to become the capital of the new Confederate States) and married on April 27.

Almira's family name, Bocock, connected her to Thomas S. Bocock from Virginia, Speaker of the Confederate Congress.[3] This spelling of her name appeared in the Memphis marriage registry, which must have been completed in Almira's presence. However, the name on her gravestone in Illinois is spelled "Bowcock." If, as seems likely, the marriage register contains the correct spelling, she may have changed the spelling of her family name as a defensive step

Gravestone of Marcus and Almira Borthwick. Mamah's mother's name was spelled Bocock on her marriage registry but Bowcock on her gravestone. The change may have been a result of Almira's wish to disguise her family connection to a prominent Confederate political leader, Thomas Bocock. Photograph by Debbie Becker.

during the Civil War to avoid the appearance of having Confederate sympathies. Marcus Borthwick had to have known her actual maiden name, but whether or not his children also knew is unclear; the grave's spelling of her name is, ultimately, a mystery.

Within a year of marriage, Almira Bocock Borthwick gave birth to their first child, Frank, followed shortly by daughters Jessie and Lizzie. In 1867, the family moved to a town in central Iowa where the Chicago and North Western Railway was establishing a center of operations. After a railyard, roundhouse, hotel, and maintenance center had been added, the town's name was changed from Montana to Boone, the name of the county.

The American frontier had moved further west, but a trickle of pioneers still crossed Iowa on the Mormon Trail. Jesse James began building his reputation for recklessness by robbing a train outside nearby Adair, Iowa. The last of the great herds of bison were also a train ride away to the north or west.

With an additional speculative purchase of farmland, this time near Humboldt, Iowa, Marcus's finances continued to improve as land values rose at a rate of 25 percent annually. The 1870 census suggests that his household wealth was comparable to that of local merchants in Boone. With his prospects steadily improving, his last child, Mary Bouton Borthwick, was born on June 19, 1869.

No baptismal record exists, but the federal census records of 1870 and 1880 confirm that her given name was Mary. By the time of the 1890 census, however, it had changed to Mamah. The nickname for Mary, especially in the nineteenth century, was Mame or Mamie. Mamah may have been derived from a fond memory of an early childhood mispronunciation, "MAY-muh." Whatever the origin of this nickname, it soon became her preferred name. By the age of sixteen, Mamah was the only name she was known by. It seems that from an early age, she defined herself on her own terms. The widespread notion that her given name was Martha is without foundation.[4]

The origin of her middle name, Bouton, must have been through a connection to the Bouton family in the Albany-Rensselaer area of New York. As prominent as the Borthwicks, the Boutons ran successful commercial enterprises of various kinds that resulted in their mutual cooperation and friendship, evident in a photograph of a Bouton & Vine grocery store located within the Hotel Borthwick in Albany.

For Marcus Borthwick, whose livelihood depended on the railroads, the year 1869 was a banner year. The completion of the transcontinental railroad at Promontory Summit, Utah, in May 1869 signaled that he had chosen a promising field. More important, in building railroad cars he had developed

Hotel Borthwick, 1897. Mamah's middle name may have derived from her family's friendship with the Bouton family, whose Bouton & Vine grocery store (*lower right*) was part of Hotel Borthwick in Albany, New York. Courtesy of Friends of Albany History.

skills suited to his ambition. In 1869, he received US Patent No. 96542 for an "Improved Railway-Car Brake."

Slowing or stopping a train was a daunting technical challenge. The equipment and methods for doing so were crude and unsafe. Brakemen atop the cars had to scamper up and down the length of a train applying individual brakes in response to signals from the conductor. As the number of accidents grew, so did the urgency to develop an alternative. Marcus's brake invention solved a significant problem by connecting the brakes on each car by means of articulated rods. The system could be "operated at either end or at any intermediate point."

But his timing was poor. He received his patent just as the New York inventor George Westinghouse patented a different train brake design. Considerably more advanced than Marcus's brake, it used compressed air to simultaneously apply pressure to the brakes in all the cars. It became the standard system used by railroads around the world.

Notwithstanding his invention's immediate obsolescence, Marcus's patent indicates that he was a man with practical ideas who was capable of delivering a workable design. In an era full of get-rich-quick schemes and frivolous inventions, he demonstrated significant abilities by targeting a fundamental problem for his industry, engineering a solution, and obtaining a patent. There can be little doubt that Marcus was forward-looking, ambitious, and entrepreneurial.

He also appears to have been progressive on the subject of women's education. In this respect, his attitudes toward gender roles may have been influenced by his surroundings. Not only were schools like the University of Iowa and Lyons Female College proving that women could be educated; at nearby Iowa Agricultural College in Ames (now Iowa State University), a young Carrie Chapman Catt, a future champion of women's suffrage, was organizing military drills and leading debates. Women in Boone would later make history by staging one of the nation's first suffrage marches.

Boone's growth was driven by more than the railroads. The discovery of shallow coal beds in central Iowa gave the economy yet another boost. As the number of mines multiplied, so did the opportunities to work in them, which resulted in the arrival of Swedish and German immigrants. One small community near Boone, composed entirely of Swedish immigrants, came to be known as Swede Bend.

Swedes and Germans became a major part of the Boone community, and census records confirm the common presence of young, female domestic servants from Sweden in households like the Borthwicks' in Boone. Thus, during Mamah's early years she is likely to have been exposed to some spoken Swedish, especially if any of the young women were working in her own household. She would have heard German spoken by playmates. She would come to use both languages in adulthood.

The census records from Boone indicate that Marcus was a railroad car builder. At the time, railroad cars in the Midwest included US Postal Service cars built to strict specifications. As the Chicago and North Western Railway developed into the largest railroad network in the Midwest, it became the first in the region to manufacture postal cars (1865), placing them in service in 1867. Used for sorting mail, the postal car also provided a senior postal employee a small bed and closet in a long room of shelves with a series of casement-like windows, often with small clerestory windows. It is easy to imagine Mamah in Boone, later in Chicago, admiring her father as he worked on such a car with its sweeping linearity, undecorated wood, and built-in furniture. These elements of what became modern design perhaps influenced her own sense of style. In the early 1900s, when the Borthwick genealogical record was compiled in consultation with the scattered family members, Mamah is the likely reason why "architect" appears beside her father's name.[5]

Marcus's unsuccessful patent must have impressed the railroad's senior management, because he was called to Chicago to be a foreman in the "car shops" where the company's railroad cars were designed, built, and repaired when Mamah was four.[6] Arriving in Chicago's Central Station by train, her family is likely to have encountered a melee of waiting passengers and piles of stacked luggage. The Iowa prairie was now far away, replaced by the noise and acrid smell of Chicago. Only recently, much of the city had burned to the ground in the Great Fire of 1871. Central Station was damaged, but it had mostly escaped; only a few final repairs were still being made. An engraving of the era depicts a train station scene in Chicago with its tumult of passengers and general sense that change was in the air.

GREAT RAILWAY STATION AT CHICAGO—DEPARTURE OF A TRAIN.

Great Railway Station at Chicago—Departure of a Train. Wood engraving, 1871. U.S. National Archives and Records Administration.

CHAPTER 3

DAKOTA TERRITORY

Fire was not finished with Chicago. In July 1874, just after the Borthwicks arrived, another fire started near where the earlier one had begun and swept north and east. It consumed a slum area and threatened the business district, doing a great deal of damage, but the absence of wind spared most of the city. Rebuilding started anew and became almost as famous as the Great Fire itself. Desolate, burned-out areas were soon reconstructed, while areas untouched by the fire expanded with new growth. Lady Duffus Hardy, a British novelist and journalist in the 1880s, expressed her surprise at the pace of progress. Upon visiting Chicago, she wrote, "Phoenix-like the city has risen out of its own ashes, grander and statelier than ever."

But with a third of the population made homeless, the pressure for new housing became intense. In response, city leaders erected temporary barracks for workers but soon tore them down, replacing them with eight thousand small, individual houses for rent beyond the city limits. The idea was to relocate propertyless workers away from the neighborhoods of the wealthy and ameliorate fears of disease spreading from the lower classes. To reinforce the boundary, Chicago's aldermen instituted so-called fire zones to regulate the number of single-family dwellings inside city limits. Effectively a zoning ordinance, it prevented the building of small individual wooden houses.[1] As a result, large areas near what is now the Loop became populated with two- and three-story masonry buildings.

The Borthwicks' arrival and settlement in Chicago is likely to have been assisted by Marcus Borthwick's niece Lizzie, now living there with her husband. After graduating from Lyons Female College, she had studied in Europe and then married her childhood sweetheart, Charles Felton, a successful executive with a railroad company. Felton's biography describes her as a linguist.[2] Close to Mamah's mother from their days at Lyons College, she may have encouraged Mamah in her linguistic aptitude and helped with funding her university education.[3]

Marcus found a rental flat just north of the Chicago River on State Street, in the heart of what is now the Near North Side. Later he moved the family to a flat on Wells Street in the same area. It was common for a family to rent the entire floor of a small, three-story apartment building in small neighborhoods that combined commercial with residential use. The same pattern can still be observed in neighborhoods of Chicago that are well preserved, such as Old Town. The 1880 census shows the Borthwicks surrounded by middle-class professionals like grocers and accountants. Everyone shopped and worked near where they lived. Marcus had easy access to the rail yard located close to the downtown area.

Lizzie Borthwick Felton. Mamah's older cousin, described as a linguist, married the wealthy businessman Charles Felton. She and her husband were living in Hyde Park when the Borthwicks moved to Chicago in the early 1870s.

Chicago was crowded, dirty, and noisy compared to Boone, Iowa, but it offered a similar mix of languages. German and Swedish dominated the neighborhood Mamah lived in, and she may even have spoken German in the classroom.[4] Education was to be had where it could be found, and although language was a subject of nearly constant debate in the early education system of Chicago, in this case, the German immigrants on the Near North Side had sufficient political power to insist that their children be taught in German. They exercised a similar dominance in neighborhood commerce. Many transactions in small family grocery stores were done in German and must have constituted part of Mamah's ongoing, informal language training whenever she did the shopping for her mother.

When in 1880 the Chicago and North Western Railway moved its repair and manufacturing operations beyond the city limits to the town of Cicero, Marcus Borthwick decided to follow. His was one of countless decisions with far-reaching implications for the region's real estate, itself a major Chicago product. In the late nineteenth century, undeveloped land stretched westward from Lake Michigan without interruption, while to the north and south more territory beckoned. Oak Park, then a part of Cicero, enjoyed a strong connection to the downtown through a new streetcar line, the Chicago, Harlem, & Batavia "dummy" line running approximately along the present-day Eisenhower Expressway. It was called "dummy" because its trains used miniature steam locomotives with a false cladding to conceal the moving parts and thus avoid startling horses. Places that ten years earlier had seemed like remote villages now offered quiet, safe, uncrowded environments with reasonable home prices and easy access by rail to the city. The mass, middle-class migration to the suburbs had begun, encouraged by industries moving to the city outskirts.

Oak Park was far removed from the rich, textured life of Chicago. The busy, crowded world of two- and three-flats in the Near North Side neighborhoods brought together in close quarters a mix of languages, classes, age groups, and small businesses. In contrast, the suburbs effectively isolated families in houses on long, quiet streets. Whether or not Mamah missed Chicago as a young girl in Oak Park, she would one day feel the difference in her twenties, when she lived in her parents' home as a single woman.

For Marcus Borthwick, Oak Park offered the advantage of being a better place to educate his children. While Frank at age eighteen had already completed high school and preferred to work for the railroad, his three sisters attended the Oak Park schools. The high school sent many of its graduates to the best universities in the Midwest. It was an ideal springboard for Mamah.

Oak Park consisted of about two thousand people scattered across 480 acres. Its streets were unpaved, the stores scattered and relatively few in number. The Cicero Water, Gas and Electric Light Company had not yet begun to supply electricity. The few trees that lined the streets were young. Open space was plentiful. As late as 1899, the village sought to pass an ordinance to prevent people from pasturing their cows next to their neighbors' houses.[5]

A stable for boarding a horse could easily be found, and Marcus is likely to have done so since his daughters became experienced riders: five years after moving to Oak Park, two of them even joined a summer excursion that involved riding and hunting in the Dakota Territory, the vast region that would soon become North and South Dakota. Sending a sixteen-year-old Mamah and her twenty-two-year-old sister Jessie to the eastern part of the Dakota Territory in 1885 testifies not only to Marcus's broadmindedness but also to the independence and prowess of the two young women, who set off to ride, hunt, and fish in the Territory with a group from Chicago, as noted by the local Cicero newspaper.[6]

Urban dwellers in the 1880s considered the Dakota Territory to be a rough frontier, no place for women of refinement. The Great Sioux War had officially ended only eight years earlier, leaving its bloody stain on American history. Tensions remained, but the threat of outright violence was mostly dormant at the time; the outrage of the massacre of the Sioux at Wounded Knee would not occur for yet another five years. Much of the vast Dakota Territory remained unsettled by white people. Towns along the excursion party's intended route were only just emerging. Their first destination, the remote town of Pipestone, Minnesota, on the edge of the Dakota Territory, did not even exist seven years earlier. From Pipestone they would travel to the twin cities of Moorhead and Fargo, then further north before turning back to complete a journey of over eighteen hundred miles.[7]

Even though this excursion was officially a fishing and hunting party, its choice of Pipestone as a jumping-off point suggests that for some of the men in the group, the expedition involved more than just sport. The itinerary took them across regions where intense railroad competition was underway and opportunities for route investments were still to be found. That made it inadvisable for those scouting out such opportunities to advertise their real purpose. This aspect of the trip and the fact that there is no record of other women in the party make Mamah and Jessie's involvement an extraordinary fact and an unsolved puzzle.

When Mamah and Jessie boarded a westbound train with the excursion party in Chicago, they left their sister Lizzie, their parents, and everything familiar behind them. Crossing the Mississippi at Rock Island, they continued as far as Iowa City before heading northwest across the low hills of northern Iowa, where the farms became more scattered. Great hay barns loomed protectively near small houses. Gradually the fields of wheat, corn, and pasture gave way to open prairie as they entered Minnesota and drew close to Pipestone. An early photograph of the town reveals a cluster of low buildings dwarfed by a flat, unbroken landscape. Mamah and Jessie disembarked with the rest of the party onto a main street populated by two-story buildings. It was a more substantial town than they might have expected, many of the buildings constructed from the distinctive red stone from the nearby quarry.

After settling in the Calumet Hotel, they would have learned that hunting for foxes and wolves and riding to hounds, however incongruous that may seem

Jessie Octavia Borthwick. Mamah's oldest sister. Higgins family photograph.

Pipestone, Minnesota, ca. 1885. The town was barely visible on the horizon of the tallgrass prairie when Borthwick stayed there prior to entering the Dakota Territory. Northern History Publishing Company.

on the prairie, was an organized sport in Pipestone.[8] Its sponsors were probably the Close brothers, wealthy land investors from England with an office in Chicago. The brothers were land speculators who encouraged excursion groups. They might have personally welcomed the party to Pipestone.

For Mamah, the prairie would have been but a faint memory from her childhood in Boone. In Pipestone, she encountered it again, this time with the matured sensibilities of a young woman. Newcomers often found the unforested beauty of the tallgrass prairie spellbinding. From the train it had seemed like an endless sea. Up close it assumed greater definition, varieties of grass mixing with what seemed like a tangle of weeds and flowers named by the pioneers: Indian grass, prairie blazing stars, Great Plains ladies' tresses, prairie dropseed, and big bluestem. To stand in silence at sunrise or sunset amid its splendor on the outskirts of the town would have been to know the prairie's changing light and orchestration of birdsong and what a young midwestern architect would one day call its "quiet level."[9]

Few details of the journey are known except that they did a good deal of riding and hunting. This raises the question whether the Borthwick sisters had to ride sidesaddle. If they had English hosts who offered sidesaddles, they might have used them, but for much of the journey, a sidesaddle would have been impractical and perhaps not an option. The ubiquitous Western-style saddle provided an opportunity to learn to ride astride in a place where standards for women's riding apparel were more relaxed. Accounts by women of that era about their experience riding astride for the first time confirm that it was a liberating experience.[10] In contrast to the Victorian sidesaddle, which was uncomfortable for both rider and mount and dangerous to boot, riding Western-style with a split skirt quite literally opened up new possibilities for women.

Travel by rail from Pipestone to Fargo and Moorhead in 1885 is likely to have involved delays, schedule uncertainties, and workaround routing because of cutthroat railroad competition. Upon drawing near the twin cities of Moorhead and Fargo, the traveler encountered the Red River, cluttered with barges and small boats. At least one steamboat was always tied up at the Moorhead landing, where the town of white frame houses and barns was becoming a small city. The newer houses were of obvious high quality. The mansion of the prominent attorney Solomon Comstock is still on display. If Moorhead had thrived on the Minnesota side of the river, Fargo on the Dakota side had fairly boomed. By 1885, according to a city directory, it had grown to a size of "8,000 inhabitants, twelve hotels, seven churches, four banks, and five newspapers (two dailies and three weeklies) two public halls, [and] a new opera house."[11]

In the midst of the so-called Dakota Boom, the bustling city of Fargo presented a chance for Mamah and Jessie to catch a glimpse of the vanishing frontier theater, a surprising specialty of the city in the 1880s. Mamah was a talented actor and speaker by the age of sixteen according to mentions of her in local Cicero newspapers.[12] She would have been thrilled by the diverse, tumultuous theater world of Fargo, where vaudeville was big business. Shows of all kinds ran in theaters six days a week.

Women were not supposed to attend vaudeville because of the loud, raucous audiences, but Mamah and Jessie were a long way from Oak Park. We can imagine that these two intrepid young women managed to sneak a peek at a number of acts, which, according to Fargo historian James Browning, included "boxing, contortionists, gymnasts, acrobats, club swinging, and knife juggling, instrumental soloists, orchestras, trapeze, tight ropes, loose ropes, right wire, character artists comedians, Scandinavian dialectician, fire-eating, magicians, rifle marksmanship, female impersonation, and knife throwing."[13] If the rough audiences kept them away from vaudeville, they could always attend theatrical performances in the small opera house or the substantial

Coliseum Theater, which offered ballets, acrobatics, full-length dramas, plays, musicals, and burlesque.

The excursion party had opportunities to fish and hunt locally out of Fargo, but they eventually continued northward with a more distant objective in mind, the area around Devils Lake, where a rail line had just opened. Fifty miles from the Canadian border, formed from an ancient glacial lake, the area around Devils Lake offered ideal conditions for fishing and hunting. It took less than a day on the train from Fargo to reach it. The first sign of civilization as one approached Devils Lake was a small town in the distance. At first glance, what seemed to be a giant, snow-covered haystack on its outskirts came into focus as a mountain of white buffalo bones. The gruesome spectacle, a product of the great slaughter of bison still going on in the West, was repeated elsewhere around Devils Lake. The bison had retreated, driven from their ancient routes in the Red River Valley, leaving behind wide, vacant pathways, dust wallows, and, ultimately, countless bones. Despite their massive numbers, the bones were a valuable, sought-after commodity. Dried and charred, they produced a substance called bone black, which was used to filter impurities out of sugar-cane juice to process white sugar. The buffalo bone trade, just like the slaughter itself, was a boom-and-bust business. It flourished in the 1880s, but the bone mountains grew smaller until eventually they, too, disappeared.

Fall was in the air. The summer's final cutting of hay lay drying in the fields to be piled on racks and taken into barns. In Minnewaukan, on the other side of Devils Lake, the Lakeview Hotel was advertising for a "first-class dining room girl. None other need apply." Thanks to the railroad, the area anticipated a greater influx of visitors. The excursion group, having come there to hunt ducks, was not disappointed. The local newspaper reported that one hunter had easily bagged forty canvasbacks in a day. Perhaps teasingly, the women were told there would be an opportunity for them to go fishing, using just pitchforks. In fact, the local farmers were renowned for their success in fishing with pitchforks. The enormously plentiful Northern Pike on occasion would lurk near the surface in numbers so vast that they could fairly easily be speared and hauled out with a pitchfork. But such a feat was possible only in the icy waters of winter, when the fish congregated near the surface and were sluggish. Jessie and Mamah professed to be greatly disappointed at their poor timing.[14]

In early September, they boarded a train and headed back toward the southeast. Their next destination, Lake Minnetonka, Minnesota, was a conventional stopover, a welcome chance to enjoy resort life for a day or two in a place that attracted summer vacationers from across the country. When they returned to Oak Park, the *Cicero Vindicator* reported that the two "Misses Borthwick" stepped off the train "loaded down with beautiful specimens, ruddy complexions, and wonderful stories."[15]

It was a formative experience for Mamah, an adventure rarely afforded a young, urbanized woman in the 1880s. Returning to high school in Oak Park afterward is likely to have been a letdown, but her life was full of activity. Regularly called upon at social events to give a "recitation," she seems to have enjoyed acting, and certainly showed some real talent. This much is evident from a day in December when her high school class performed scenes from Shakespeare for the public. Mamah played Lady Macbeth, her performance earning praise from the *Lake Vindicator*'s editor William Halley:

> Shakespeare Day at the Oak Park School occurred Wednesday afternoon, and a large audience assembled to listen to the literary beauties compiled by the Bard of Avon. Miss Mamah Borthwick's rendition of the instigation scene from "Macbeth," where that worthy's wife incites him to strike the blow that would give him kingly honors, was exceedingly well rendered, and therefore deserves special mention.[16]

The so-called instigation scene is a challenging role for a mature actress, not to mention a sixteen-year-old girl. She must have played Lady Macbeth with gusto, goading Macbeth to commit the murder that would make him king and her queen. Her enthusiasm for the theater at an early age foreshadowed the importance it would hold for her in adulthood.

Frank Lloyd Wright settled in Oak Park the year Mamah left it for the University of Michigan. It is highly unlikely that they would have met at that time, and they would not have had much in common. Before moving to Oak Park, Wright had arrived in Chicago from Madison, Wisconsin. According to his autobiography, he wandered the streets applying for work with architectural companies. Hired first by the firm of J. L. Silsbee, he soon moved to that of the great Louis Sullivan and rose quickly to the position of head draftsman. Almost simultaneously, he rushed into an engagement to Catherine Tobin, an ingenue two years younger than Mamah from Chicago's fashionable Kenwood area. Thanks to a generous loan from Sullivan, Wright was able to build a house for them in Oak Park in 1888.

In early October of that year, as Mamah prepared to leave for the University of Michigan, escorted by her father, an urgent telegram arrived for him from Dixon, Illinois. Her brother, Frank, then working as a brakeman on the Chicago and North Western Railway, had been injured. He had been helping to unhitch a damaged locomotive from a freight train when it suddenly shifted backward, crushing him against a car. Marcus rushed to the scene to find his twenty-eight-year-old son in critical condition from internal bleeding and broken ribs. The timing of the accident prevented Marcus from accompanying Mamah on the train trip to Ann Arbor, but after her adventure in the Dakota Territory, she had proven herself capable of making the journey on her own.

CHAPTER 4

THE PROPHECY

Upon arriving in Ann Arbor, Borthwick stepped from the train into a medieval-looking station mobbed with students. Writing about it in an 1889 article for *Cosmopolitan* magazine, her classmate Edith Sheffield described the scene.

> There stands a sophomore. Oh, how we envy her!—oh, how she looks down upon us! See the hacks fly away bearing sophs, juniors, and seniors to the rooms which await them. We poor little freshmen are left behind to take care of ourselves as best we may, and we follow the crowd up the long street, shaded by majestic oaks and maples.[1]

It was not a long walk to the campus, and it usually underwhelmed upon arrival. From the northwest corner, Borthwick would have seen only an unkempt mass of trees, bushes, and grass that half hid the scattered buildings. As one undergraduate described it, "Here and there within the classic fields of learning there grazed a meditative cow, as stolidly indifferent to the outside world and its hustle and bustle as any German professor. For long these quadrupeds served as the only lawn mowers."[2]

As Sheffield noted, the immediate task for a woman was to find housing—and a roommate. In the absence of dormitories, this was a greater challenge for women than men. Female students lived in private homes and boarding houses, while many of the men found quarters in fraternities. Borthwick found a room in a boarding house on the corner of Thompson and Jefferson Streets, just a few blocks from campus. It was to be her residence throughout her time at Michigan. The identity of her roommate during the first year is unknown, but from the start of the 1889 school year, she was joined by Martha "Mattie" Chadbourne from Vinton, Iowa, a freshman for whom the University of Michigan

The University of Michigan, late 1880s. Bentley Historical Library, © Regents of the University of Michigan.

was a family tradition.[3] Mattie's older brother Ted was a medical student. Her cousin Tom Chadbourne studied law and was the star of the football team. The two women became close friends and remained roommates for the rest of Borthwick's time at Michigan.

Each incoming freshman had a personal meeting with the university president, James Angell, one of the outstanding college presidents of the century. A kindly looking man with a wispy beard, Angell was popular with students even if they found their first meeting with him to be rather perfunctory. Students had to stand in line for one or two hours in order to receive his personal stamp of approval, after which they were formally admitted. Only then could they pay their tuition at the university treasurer's office. The order in which they did so was recorded and often used to assign classroom seating.

The members of the class of '92 came to know one another through various first-year traditions. One tradition, called the "rush," was a massive, free-for-all game resembling football, played between men of the sophomore and freshman classes. More than one hundred on each side nearly filled the field. The rules were not codified, and there was often disagreement. In the end, the game seems to have involved kicking the ball as much as it did carrying it, interspersed with episodes of tackling, wrestling, and even boxing. Sufficient numbers of injuries occurred on both sides in the rush of 1888 to make it one of the last to be held at Michigan. The female students were expected to look on and cheer with the official class of '92 yell: "Ninety-two, Ninety-two, Rah-Rah-Rah, Hobble-gobble, Razzle-dazzle, Fizz! Boom! Ah!"

Whatever she may have thought of these antics, Borthwick must have relished her new freedom and the intellectual environment that Michigan offered. In the perennial experience of all new college students, those at Michigan found themselves suddenly free of parental supervision. Sheffield reported that she found it liberating.

Women like Mamah Borthwick who majored in arts and literature had an easier time of it than women enrolled in the medical and law schools, where they received chilly receptions from their male classmates. This was especially true of the medical school. Coeducational medical instruction was considered problematic in courses like Practical Anatomy, in which it was considered undesirable for the two sexes to be taught together. But despite such limitations of the professional schools, female students were not looked upon as a curiosity. Their right to a university education had become firmly established by the 1890s.

The chairman of the literature department, Professor Edward L. Walter, admired Borthwick's abilities. In a letter of recommendation, he wrote that she was "uniformly counted among the best members of the class . . . with an active mind . . . unusually quick in the mastery of languages . . . clear in expressing herself."[4] John Dewey, chairman of the philosophy department, was another one of her teachers. Busy establishing a national reputation through his writings on philosophy and education, Dewey still managed to find time for students outside of the classroom. One of the most popular and admired members of the faculty, he often took part in social activities such as those sponsored by his church, the First Congregational Church of Ann Arbor, where Borthwick was a member.[5]

The male editors of the student newspaper the *Chronicle* gave women's interests limited, condescending attention. Although they kept track of each new issue of Oscar Wilde's newly named *Women's World*, such interest was fleeting. Wilde's early modernism otherwise drew scant attention. Like any traditional college of the Midwest at the end of the nineteenth century, Michigan's campus society adhered to social conventions.

The inseparable Mamah Borthwick and Mattie Chadbourne were perceived by their friends as a couple. This closeness was not, however, considered
unusual. Victorian social restrictions on women's relations with men encouraged
female friendships.[6] Little is known about Chadbourne except that her English
literature professor praised her "earnestness and enthusiasm in the pursuit of
literary studies" and her "good sense and ladylike bearing and character."[7]

Under the watchful eye of the administration, students supported the school
enthusiastically with raucous shouts and chants at the football games. Nevertheless, at the time of the class white-tie event known as the senior reception,
the sedate customs of the nineteenth century prevailed. Courtship practices,
highly regimented, required a man to call on a woman at her residence prior
to being seen with her in public. The practice depended especially on the
woman's place of residence and whether the house had a parlor for receiving
callers. For a rooming house to be in want of a parlor, as some were, was considered a serious deficiency.

Borthwick's boarding house may have had a parlor, but the man who would
appear in it, Edwin H. Cheney, was nowhere in sight during her first year.
Arriving from Detroit in the fall of 1889, Cheney did not enroll until the start
of Borthwick's sophomore year. He was technically a member of the class of
'93, not '92, but on the basis of advanced credits and perhaps some summer
school, he was able to advance and complete his studies in time to graduate as
a member of Borthwick's class with a bachelor of science degree in electrical
engineering.

An avid sailor and first tenor in the Glee Club, Cheney had few interests
that overlapped with Borthwick's. He showed little interest in languages and
literature, devoting himself mainly to technology and electrical engineering.
As she would later reveal, he enjoyed singing into that new invention, the
telephone, and presumably he serenaded her that way. But in those days young
women's relationships with men lacked the spontaneity and emotional intimacy
of their ties to close female friends.[8]

The earliest known image of Mamah Borthwick appears in the photograph
of the graduating class of the Department of Literature, Science and the Arts
in 1892. Edwin Cheney sits just a few feet away, looking slightly off balance
and, as usual, unhappy. In keeping with the customary manner of posing,
almost no one smiled. Barely recognizable alongside her later photographs,
Borthwick looks wonkishly serious. In a photograph taken the following year
with her Kappa Alpha Theta sorority sisters, she has doffed the mortarboard
cap to be as stylish as them.

University of Michigan class of Literature, Science and the Arts, 1892. Circled, Mamah Borthwick and Edwin Cheney. Bentley Historical Library, University of Michigan.

As the first Greek-letter society organized by and for women in the United States, Kappa Alpha Theta had been established for a decade at Michigan before the local chapter abruptly withdrew from the national organization. It objected to the sorority's readiness to establish chapters at lesser-known schools. Several Michigan members who had not wanted to leave the organization created a placeholder group in hopes that the chapter could be reinstated. They asked Borthwick and Chadbourne to join to assist their cause. Borthwick must have regretted the lateness of this invitation because "Theta," as it was known, would one day become her single most important social network, but at the time the offer was extended, it was too late for her to enjoy campus life in the sorority.

In her junior and senior years, she increased her focus on her academic work. Special rooms were reserved in the library for the more advanced seniors like her, who were expected to demonstrate their abilities through seminars and essays. Borthwick was what students called a "lit," short for literature major, a liberal arts nerd. By the time of graduation, she had taken eighteen courses in Greek and Latin, earning twenty-four credits in each. She added another twenty-five credits in French, fifteen in German, four in Italian, and six in English. With her master's degree she received a teaching certificate with specialties in Greek and French.

Sheffield wrote that she found the lits to be a bit full of themselves, but there is no evidence that Mamah was arrogant. Her popularity with her senior class peers led them to honor her with the title Class Seer. According to the university's *Michigan Book*, to be named the "Seer or Prophet [was] a leading honor in the senior academic class." One reason was the Seer's traditional responsibility to write and deliver an oration at commencement known as the Prophecy.

Unlike most speeches that dominated the typical graduation exercise, the Prophecy was something to look forward to, a classmate insider's take on who they were and might become, an unserious forecast of their futures. The Prophecy could sometimes be sentimental, but to succeed, it had to be perceptive, witty, and intelligent. Her classmates knew Borthwick well enough to hope that she would produce something different from the prophecies of previous commencements. In that, they would not be disappointed.

Commencement was an all-day affair. The *Inter Ocean* newspaper in Chicago sent a reporter who claimed that three thousand people were present. The ceremony began with a prayer, a welcome from the university president, and the class oration. The latter, by graduating senior William Dellenback, on the merits of "international arbitration," took at least forty-five minutes. Next, Borthwick's classmate from Oak Park, Julia Herrick, read the class poem. According to the *Inter Ocean*, she stood "clothed in pure white, her hair arranged in curls of striking originality. She read as though she knew [the poem's] merits and did not mean to lose any valuable opportunities of bringing them out."[9]

The long poem took almost as much time to deliver as the class oration. A luncheon followed, after which the ceremony moved outdoors to a lawn area shaded by a great oak. It was called the Tappan Oak, in honor of Henry Phillip Tappan, the university's first president, who had opposed the admission of women on the grounds that the work would be too taxing for them. When it came Borthwick's turn to deliver the Prophecy, the audience knew to expect something tongue in cheek. Mamah proved Tappan gloriously wrong beneath his eponymous oak, and gave the audience all the inside jokes and gentle ribbing they could have hoped for, doubtless with the confident aplomb of a seasoned young actress.

Prophecies of prior years had attempted to use rhyme. Borthwick opted for a twenty-three-hundred-word free-verse poem. As Class Seer speaking on behalf of Apollo, the Greek god of inspiration and art, she presented herself as standing "far on the heights by Castalian's spring" in the person of the high priestess Pythia, Oracle of Delphi, to provide a vision for the class.[10] A parody of Greek oracular rhetoric was just right for the Literature, Science and the Arts class of '92, which had been required to read extensively in the classics. The reference to Castalian's spring, a sacred place near Delphi, gave a nod to the Michigan literary publication *The Castalian* and perhaps reassurance to the faculty that she intended no disrespect. After all, the classics were a hallowed subject at Michigan. The use of parody was a bit of a gamble, but everyone knew it was in good fun. With frequent insider jokes, references to Michigan landmarks, and crossword puzzle–like hints, the Prophecy would not have been understood by many people other than members of the class. From her supposed vantage point in the twentieth century looking back, she presented them with their futures.

Only in recent years had it become acceptable for a woman to address such a large, mixed gathering. Susan B. Anthony, who twenty years earlier had been arrested for voting, remarked that a man once told her, "I would rather see my wife and daughter in their coffins than addressing a public meeting."[11]

Lucy Stone, invited to write a commencement address for her graduation at Oberlin in 1847, had refused on the grounds that she would not be allowed to read it.[12] But by 1892, it had become acceptable for a woman to speak at graduation. Even so, the Prophecy was expected to be an inoffensive description of people's futures. Borthwick's skewering of a few male egos, lighthearted though it was, must have caused some consternation (and perhaps a few laughs).

In 1892, the term "New Woman" had yet to appear, and Ella Dixon had not yet published her novel *The Story of a Modern Woman*. And yet here, before the Michigan class of '92, stood a woman who not only spoke as an equal of men; she seized the chance to poke fun at several of them. Take, for example, this stanza halfway through her poem:

In 'o1 McKnight took up his labor
And still they say "He hasn't done anything since."
Carpenter and Barnum always write
The letters F. R. S. beside their names[13]
And are prime movers in the Sons of Rest.

Further along she dryly predicted that the class football star would continue to be "carried from the field disabled."

Not everyone she named was in for a lesson in humility. The class was too large to name each person, but several of those she selected achieved a degree of success that she seems to have sensed was coming. From the vantage point of the future, she declared:

The favorite scriptural verse of Warner Bishop,
In later years has truly been fulfilled,
That all the land whereon his feet have trod
Is his, and his alone forever more.

Bishop became a famous librarian who organized the Vatican Library. She announced that Robert Wolcott's "great museum has there combined more rarity and worth than in the largest library in the West." As it turned out, Wolcott became a distinguished scientist and ornithologist of the American West. Glen Chapman became a Detroit newspaper reporter and editor. She predicted he would be someone who "grinds his editorials out with frightful waste of paper, pen and ink." Uncannily, she also singled out Wilhelm Miller, destined to become a nationally recognized landscape architect whose signature designs were associated with the work of Frank Lloyd Wright. Miller would one day draw Wright's ire when he called his landscapes Prairie Style.[14]

Finally, she came to Edwin Cheney, who sat among the graduates. One imagines him cracking a rare smile when she teased:

> Ed Cheney sings in Allen's telephone
> To advertise its merits far and near,
> And even when at college in Course I
> In physics where he earned his credits-lip.

After graduating from a Detroit high school, Cheney had applied himself to the study of electricity and electrical equipment. Fascinated by the nation's newly emergent electrical grid, he was destined to become the senior manager of an electric utility. Even if Borthwick did not necessarily find him electrifying as a person, she must have enjoyed him as a companion whom she could tease and with whom she shared an enthusiasm for all things modern.

The University of Michigan had been a natural home for her. As one of the nation's foremost land-grant institutions, it had admitted women by the score, sending some to fill positions in medical schools and the faculties of other institutions. No wonder her poem expressed a sense of wonder at being a "chosen one." The idea must have resonated with her fellow graduates who felt fortunate to have been admitted to Michigan and to have survived four years of grueling work. More than half the original class had dropped out, or, as Borthwick put it, bolted. She, on the other hand, could not get enough of the place. She would remain another year at Michigan to earn a master's degree.

With its glib language and insider knowledge, the Prophecy reveals little of her inner life except when expressed with a wink, such as the perennial problem of men and marriage:

> Miss Zuell Preston still is heard to murmur
> In palliation of abased mankind.
> "Well, all men have their peculiarities,"
> And so she quite forgives their many faults.

Of the 172 undergraduates receiving bachelor's degrees in the Department of Literature, Science and the Arts, 46 were women. Her predictions about them were uniformly optimistic, notwithstanding a few wry allusions to loneliness, courtship, and the burdens of marriage. She gave a nod to the fine intellects of some and predicted that one would invent an electric burglar alarm. Two, she said, would publish their own successful, independent magazines. Here she may have been expressing an ambition of her own. She even described some of her female classmates as having escaped to future creative lives in Italy, articulating another dream she perhaps entertained for herself. She gave an appreciative nod to two reform-minded women, one "not only for her eloquence, but for the mighty wrongs she strives to right," the other for how she "labors hard to reconstruct mankind." Still, the female graduates did not enjoy the range of employment opportunities available to men. Most of the women were, as she put it, "inquiring for a place to teach"—as she herself would shortly do.

The Prophecy reveals Mamah Borthwick at the age of twenty-three as someone charming and casually witty. Her characterizations of her classmates were endearing and mostly flattering. As the Seer, she was expected to declare what the next century would bring them, but she was not allowed to predict her own future. If her perspective was thus at times wistful, it may have been because she lacked a vision for herself. She had no noble purpose like that of the Oracle of Delphi, who had been tasked with "the greatest, noblest work Apollo ever gave [her] to perform." Eventually she would find such a purpose, but at great cost. Her farewell, slightly abbreviated here, foreshadowed her destiny with her future Apollo.

And now my sovereign master, dear Apollo,
Receive me back into thy sweet oblivion.
. . . .
Ne'er shall I speak to mortal man again,
For ne'er will equal like to thee arise.
Farewell forever, great and noble class,
For thee alone I have awaked,
For thee again I seek pathetic dust.

CHAPTER 5

❦

A NOBLER WOMANHOOD

The conclusion of the commencement ceremony was the signal for the graduates to rush off and prepare for the evening's celebrations. Their final days on
campus provided an opportunity to reflect on the end of an important stage
in their lives, as Borthwick undoubtedly did, even though she would remain
on campus without her classmates for another year to earn her master's degree.[1]
Sheffield's conclusion may well have echoed her sentiments: "Commencement
Day, with its throng of spectators, college graduates in class hats, professors,
flowers, music, and diplomas, is like a curtain falling before our eyes. . . . We
think of leaving all the dear friends. . . . We wonder, indeed, if we will ever
have so good a time again—wonder if any four years in the future will ever be
as full of joy as these past years have been. We visit all the familiar haunts in
loving and tender farewell."[2]

Edwin Cheney headed for Chicago to begin employment with the Chicago
Edison Company, while Mamah remained in Ann Arbor. Whatever his feelings for her might have been, Borthwick seems to have no intention of marrying him, or perhaps anyone. Half the women graduates of Michigan never
married, in fact. In contrast, her friendship with Mattie Chadbourne remained
deep and strong. In late April 1893, she and Chadbourne visited a friend in
Pontiac and then continued to Port Huron, where they successfully applied
for a pair of teaching positions in the public high school.

They graduated in June, Chadbourne with a bachelor's degree, Borthwick
with a master's, and together they boarded a train to Chicago. After visiting
Mamah's family in Oak Park, they spent considerable time on the South Side of
Chicago at two events, the national convention of Kappa Alpha Theta and the
1893 World's Fair. The latter was known formally as the World's Columbian

Exposition, a celebration of the four hundredth anniversary of Columbus's first encounter with the New World. An expansively ambitious undertaking even for Chicago, it exceeded the size and scope of any exposition held anywhere in the world. Covering over six hundred acres, drawing a total of twenty-seven million visitors by the time it closed in October, it left a lasting impression on American society and culture. Chicago took pride in having been selected by Congress over New York to host the fair. It drew on a wide range of talent, with overall responsibility for its development given to architect Daniel Burnham. He was not above recruiting established architects from New York, with the result that the fair's appearance partially bore their stamp. But under the direction of Frederick Law Olmsted, the Jackson Park area had been transformed with vast landscaping that achieved grandeur beyond all expectation.

Thousands of workers had assembled the main buildings at a frenetic pace made possible by applying shaped stucco surfaces over substantial if temporary frames. Uniformly whitewashed, they presented a scene that came to be known as the "White City." Louis Sullivan lamented what he considered a lost opportunity. He felt that the designs based on Beaux Arts classicism had set back civic architecture in America, but few joined his complaint. His Transportation Building stood alone in declaring an alternative vision with its magnificent arched entrance.

That summer, no Americans outside New York had ridden an elevated train like the new "L" in Chicago. Borthwick and Chadbourne would have ridden it to and from the fair, starting near the Loop alongside thousands of others. The screeching iron wheels on the curves were unsettling, but the tracks ran mostly straight along the lake. With far more to be seen at the fair than even a few days would permit, a priority for them would undoubtedly have been the Woman's Building. Designed by architect Sophia Hayden in the Italian Renaissance style, the four-hundred-foot-long structure held inspirational exhibits celebrating the achievements of women. Battles had been fought within the Board of Lady Managers over the exhibits, some of which were criticized for displaying bourgeois notions of femininity. But for the two young women who had just graduated from a university, the building's very existence must have seemed like a harbinger of change. Kate Field, publisher of a national weekly newspaper, had declared earlier in the summer that a Woman's Building was unnecessary, but by the time Borthwick and Chadbourne arrived, she had changed her mind. "If all the world were enlightened, the Woman's Building would have been a wasteful endeavor," she wrote, "but the least understood being on earth is woman, even to her own self. She needed a revelation and has had it."[3]

In the Prophecy, Borthwick had envisioned women in her class as artists, writers, editors, and inventors. She is likely to have been drawn to the displays of female accomplishment in the Woman's Building. One that loomed high above her as she entered the great atrium, a large mural by Mary Cassatt, was titled *Modern Woman*. Its central panel, "Young Women Plucking the Fruits of Knowledge or Science," is remembered for its strong composition and depictions of women working together. An expatriate living in Paris and one of the finest of the Impressionist painters, Cassatt left no doubt of her intentions in creating the mural. In a letter to Bertha Palmer, president of the Board for the Woman's Building, she wrote, "An American friend asked me in rather a huffy tone the other day 'Then this is woman apart from her relations to man?' I told him it was."[4]

The Woman's Building occupied a prominent position on the fair's large lagoon. When Borthwick exited the building onto its grand terrace, she would have looked across the water to a wooded island with traditional Japanese buildings. Whether or not she took the time to visit the so-called Ho-o-Den (Phoenix Temple), it is likely that Frank Lloyd Wright did. Louis Sullivan had just fired him for moonlighting, giving him time to assimilate the design and craftsmanship he would later extoll. Wright and Borthwick had yet to meet, but the proximity of the Woman's Building and the Ho-o-Den symbolized the way their worlds were converging. At the fair, each gazed across the water at a building that represented the other's future.

The Woman's Building included two wings on either side that served important functions. One was a kind of hotel with temporary overnight accommodations for single women. The other was a large daycare facility replete with kindergarten classes. Both were overwhelmed by demand. Additionally, the Woman's Building included a room where members of any of the national sororities could meet and relax. It is there that Mamah and Mattie are likely to have first encountered some members of Kappa Alpha Theta.

The sorority had invited a delegation from the University of Michigan to its tenth biennial national convention on July 24–29 at the South Beach Hotel on the outskirts of the fair. One of its purposes was to heal the breach described earlier with the university's former chapter. Losing the membership of Michigan, one of the most highly regarded universities in America, had been a setback for Theta. Reinstating it was a priority for everyone involved. Tempers had cooled, and they expected to resolve the matter amicably.

Lagoon, 1893 Chicago World's Fair. The Woman's Building, rear, faced the Japanese pavilion, the Ho-o-Den, located on an island in the lagoon. Archival photograph courtesy of the Chicago Architectural Center.

Generally overlooked by historians, the "women's fraternity" movement of the nineteenth century played a significant role in women's education. Institutional support for women was sorely lacking on nearly every campus. In midcentury, a female student was often on her own, isolated even in her boarding house. As the number of female students grew, so did the imperative to create "women's fraternities." Sororities, as they became known, improved the quality of college life for women who would otherwise lack social networks. The challenge was to establish sorority chapters, with selective recruitment of members being the priority. It could not be left to inexperienced students whose focus was on their studies. Instead, each sorority's dedicated alumnae were tasked with building their organization's national presence.

Borthwick and Chadbourne were recruited with this in mind. As recent graduates, their role would be to support the development of the Michigan chapter. They welcomed the chance to do so since it enabled them to remain engaged with a network of college-educated women. Mamah Borthwick in particular was seen to be someone who could help attract new pledges. In a letter to a colleague prior to the convention, a Theta member observed specifically of Borthwick that "she will be a help in sending us new members and in making us known and creating a favorable impression for us abroad."[5]

Sororities were growing rapidly in conjunction with the number of women who were attending college. The founding purpose of sororities was more than social. They sought to build and maintain an unassailable position for women in the venues of higher education. Borthwick met her Theta friends for the first time at the convention that summer. She would have known about some of them in advance. One, Alice Freeman Palmer, had been the first female president of Wellesley College and had just become Dean of Women at the newly founded University of Chicago. A graduate of the University of Michigan, Palmer had made speeches in Ann Arbor, so she and Borthwick may have already met. She was the cofounder of the American Association of University Women and an inspirational figure for the Thetas.

A goal of the convention was to reinstate the Michigan chapter and give it a new name, "Eta." As with all sororities and fraternities, their initiation ceremony was secret, but the principles the organization espoused were not. To accept membership in Theta was to agree to uphold its high standards of behavior. In the ritualized ceremony, each Theta pledged her loyalty "in the name of a nobler womanhood" and was instructed that henceforth her words, actions, and behavior would be regarded as a reflection of her personal character and the entire sorority. She received a silver link with her Greek name engraved on it. As part of the ceremony, she added that link to the chapter's chain, thereby "binding" herself in the chain of the sorority.[6] If Borthwick felt no hesitation in binding the reputation of the sisterhood to her own, it would one day weigh upon her heavily.

Their teaching obligations in Port Huron would not begin until September, allowing Borthwick and Chadbourne to stay longer and see more of the fair. They may have taken the opportunity to ride the gigantic Ferris Wheel, an engineering marvel unmatched in size for a century to come. It carried passengers in large cars the size of Pullmans that hung on gimbals and took ten minutes to reach a height of 264 feet before returning to earth. At the peak of the great wheel's cycle, one gained a vast view of Lake Michigan to the east

University of Michigan Initiates, Kappa Alpha Theta, 1893. Mamah Borthwick is on the far left. Dodge, *Sixty Years in Kappa Alpha Theta.*

while below the fair's buildings became toy-like. To the north, the Loop disappeared in the distant haze. To the west, the stockyards loomed, announcing their presence through their odor on the breeze.

Just outside the fair's boundary, Buffalo Bill's Wild West Show was led by the great impresario himself. Crowds flowed constantly between the show and the fair. Even Chief Standing Bear had ridden the Ferris Wheel in full headdress regalia. Near the Wild West Show, lines of railroad tracks fanned out from a train station to the west. Chicago had become more than a gateway to the West; it was an exemplar, a prototype of the modern city, with all the pluses and minuses that implied.

Their remaining weeks of the summer are likely to have been spent with Borthwick's parents and sisters in Oak Park. Like everyone in Chicago, they would have been excited by the fair and probably visited it multiple times. The entrepreneurial, adventuresome Marcus Borthwick, a pioneer in his youth, embodied the American character that historian Frederick Jackson Turner saw as having been shaped by the frontier.[7] His much-disputed thesis, given as an address during the fair, seemed to fit people like Marcus. At the same time, Turner declared that the frontier had disappeared, promoting a national nostalgia for it.[8]

Marcus must have had difficulty in deciding which to see first, the exhibits of train locomotives, which represented the future (and his own profession), or Buffalo Bill's Wild West Show, which represented the past—or at least a mythic construction of it. Although the performances of the latter are recognized today as largely based on racist stereotypes, they were crowd-pleasing spectacles and largely taken as historically realistic at the time. A telling episode arose with a standoff between Susan B. Anthony and a church leader who thought she should join him in opposing the fair's being open on Sundays. When he asked Anthony if she would approve of a son of hers attending the Wild West Show on a Sunday instead of going to church, she replied, "Yes, he would learn far more." After Buffalo Bill (William F. Cody) heard about this exchange, he invited Anthony to attend the show and provided her with tickets for seating in a special box. One of the women who accompanied Anthony, Anna Howard Shaw, later described the occasion: "When the performance began, Cody entered the arena, rode to the boxes, and swept his hat to his saddle-bow in salute. Aunt Susan rose, bowed in return, and for a moment enthusiastic as a girl, waved her handkerchief at him."[9]

"The significance of the moment escaped no one," historian Erik Larson notes. "Here was one of the greatest heroes of America's past saluting one of the foremost heroes of its future. The encounter brought the audience to its feet in a thunder of applause and cheers."[10]

One can only hope that Marcus Borthwick was there to see it. An unfailing supporter of women's education, he had high hopes for Mamah. If Susan B. Anthony represented the future, so did his clever, courageous youngest daughter. But Anthony represented only half the equation. The Woman's Building revealed the divide between those who would focus on the legal rights of women and those who would stress women's importance in the home and through their capabilities. The latter perspective resonated in Mary Cassatt's mural. One of the fair's most popular venues and a tribute to the leadership of Bertha Palmer's organizing committee, the Woman's Building also represented the challenges facing the international feminist movement. In showing the extraordinary range of accomplishments of women around the world, it implicitly relegated them to a separate sphere. The building itself was destroyed in a fire two years later, and its architect, Sophia Hayden, was never fairly compensated for her work.

With the exception of Louis Sullivan's Transportation Building, the fair lacked a modern appearance. And yet it had a modern feel in the way it signified the dawn of a new era. The Wild West Show's relegation to its periphery had to do with its representation of the past: on the whole, the fair looked to the future, with technological innovation on display everywhere. The very electricity that transformed it at night into a wonderland was made possible by Nikola Tesla's innovative alternating current. Thomas Edison's direct current system, which until very recently had seemed destined to rule the grid, was clearly out of date. The significance of this would have escaped most people, but not Edwin Cheney. The newly minted electrical engineer had arrived in Chicago at a key moment in the history of electrification. With his aptitude for business management and electrical engineering, he would thrive at his new employer, Chicago Edison, then move up the corporate ladder in a succession of positions with companies related to Chicago's electrical infrastructure. His progress in wooing Mamah Borthwick would be much slower. She continued to discourage his hopes for marriage.

Remaining at Michigan for a master's degree enabled her to continue to live with Chadbourne and then move with her to Port Huron. It had the added benefit of keeping Cheney at a distance. She didn't appear to find him especially objectionable, but like many women who had recently graduated from college, she was not ready to undertake marriage and motherhood. Married life may have looked as constraining as the whalebone cage of her corset.

CHAPTER 6

MRS. JARLEY AND
MRS. CHENEY

Mamah Borthwick and Mattie Chadbourne arrived in Port Huron in the pleasant weather of late summer to find it filled with the sounds of a growing city. Bells tolled from church steeples while the steam whistles of ferries competed with those of the trains. A walk up the major thoroughfare of Huron Avenue and away from the wharf led into a quieter world of horse-drawn vehicles. The crackling overhead wires of a passing electric trolley might have unsettled the horses, but pedestrians could still stroll in relative peace along the storefronts. The awnings on Huron Avenue were said to have formed such an unbroken procession that one could walk down the street on a rainy day and stay dry.[1]

Huron Avenue, Port Huron, Michigan, ca. 1910. Kirby Company.

A compact city of ten thousand, Port Huron had prospered from the convergence of rail and water to become an important commercial center in what Easterners still called the "Northwest." Since Port Huron was oriented to Lake Huron and the St. Clair River on the one hand, agriculture and forests on the other, its investors had taken full advantage by building lumber mills, railroad yards, shipyards, and a ferry terminal.

The city was welcoming to visitors. It boasted a variety of hotels, four railroad depots, seven steamship lines, and four wharves. Impressive downtown buildings in the Richardsonian Romanesque style had sprung up. In residential areas, fine houses stood for decades until new owners indifferently razed them. It was a city of societies that included any number of lodges: the Odd Fellows and the Templars of Temperance; St. Patrick's Society and various literary associations such as the Ladies' Library, the Shakespearean, the Lotos Club, and the Literary and Debating Society; and even a military order known as the Port Huron Guards.

Borthwick and Chadbourne's arrival coincided with the departures of summer visitors, making it relatively easy to find lodgings. A boarding house on Military Street not far from the high school became their first home. Within a year, they moved to a boarding house on Seventh Street where other schoolteachers lived. From the outset, they were among the highest-paid teachers in the school, teaching languages and other subjects.

Mamah Borthwick is described in most Wright biographies as having been a librarian in Port Huron, but the city had no public library when she was there. She may have been a member of the Ladies Library Association, a club of women overseeing a repository of donated and purchased books. Throughout the country after the Civil War, women's organizations in local communities collected library resources for the benefit of public education. Thanks to the Port Huron Ladies Library Association, the supply of books grew until it exceeded the capacity of the high school's temporary storage. Borthwick and Chadbourne may have informally served as librarians until the collection could be transferred to the city's first public library.

The Port Huron community embraced both women. Borthwick joined the Congregational Church and within a year was elected vice president of the Young Women's Club, joining in its discussions and presentations. She might easily have met eligible men through the church, but if Edwin Cheney had a rival in Port Huron, there is no sign of it. He is said to have made repeated trips from Chicago to see her. Secure in his position with the Chicago Edison Company, he had moved to Oak Park in part because her family lived there.

After first taking up residence in the suburb's fashionable Plaza Hotel, he moved in with his parents and sister in 1895 after they moved to Oak Park from Detroit.

Borthwick was in no hurry to join him. She signed a contract to teach for another year and with Chadbourne made occasional trips to Ann Arbor to visit their friends in Kappa Alpha Theta. They clearly intended to remain in Port Huron, but Chadbourne became gravely ill. Whatever the nature of the illness, it was serious enough to cause her to resign her position. Once it became clear that Chadbourne would leave Port Huron, Borthwick, unwilling to remain there alone, also resigned from her teaching position before the start of the new school year in 1896.[2]

It must have been a difficult departure. She had come to know and enjoy the city. Years later, the *Times Herald* of Port Huron observed that she had "made many friends in and out of school circles. She was beautiful, talented, and unusually refined."[3] Weeks later in Chicago, she and Chadbourne parted company and the latter proceeded to Iowa to live with her parents in Vinton. In time she recovered sufficiently to begin teaching in Cedar Rapids, but her frail health would haunt the two women at a critical juncture in the future.

When Mamah moved back in the fall of 1896, her sisters, Jessie and Lizzie Borthwick, were still living with their parents. The house must have seemed crowded after her arrival, even though her brother, Frank, had moved out. Having recovered from the serious injury he sustained when he was a brakeman, he had moved to Chicago to work as a switchman with the Chicago and North Western Railway. His disappearance from the historical record after that is a mystery.[4]

Borthwick soon found a job teaching high school in the suburb of Riverside, a planned community designed by landscape architect Frederick Law Olmsted and Calvert Vaux. Six miles from Oak Park, its new school building was architect Charles Whittlesey's tribute to his teacher Louis Sullivan. The arcade-like windows and massive, semicircular entrance must have reminded her of Sullivan's great "golden door" in the spectacular Transportation Building at the 1893 Columbian Exposition.

She earned a seventy-five-dollar monthly salary, which rose to eighty-five the following year, well above the school system average of fifty-eight.[5] Because most of the student population made up the lower grades, the high school's classes were relatively small. Her immediate challenge was the commute from Oak Park. Public transport between the suburbs was almost nonexistent, and going by horseback was not an easy option. The best solution, a bicycle, required

Central School, Riverside, Illinois. Architect Charles Whittlesey's building (1897) where Mamah Borthwick taught high school was a salute to his mentor Louis Sullivan's Transportation Building at the 1893 World's Fair. Village of Riverside.

her to cross yet another implicit boundary for women. Typical of the period, the Woman's Rescue League in Washington had just passed a national resolution condemning the riding of bicycles by women.[6]

This hardly posed an obstacle for her: more and more women were riding bicycles, especially on the level suburban streets paved with close-fitting cedar blocks. Maria Ward, the author of *Bicycling for Ladies* (1897), reminded women that the bicycle was a metaphor for their empowerment: "Mounted on a wheel, you feel at once the keenest sense of responsibility. You are there to do as you will within reasonable limits; you are continually being called upon to judge and to determine points that before have not needed your consideration, and consequently you become alert, active, quick-sighted, and keenly alive as well to the rights of others as to what is due yourself."[7]

Remembered for the thespian talent she had shown in high school, Borthwick was recruited by the First Congregational Church to play the part of Mrs. Jarley in a series of benefit performances of *Mrs. Jarley's Waxworks*. It may even have been her idea. The local newspaper described her as "a capital Mrs. Jarley," the character inspired by the Madame Tussaud–like character in Charles Dickens's novel *The Old Curiosity Shop*.[8] Performed in playhouses all over America, the farce featured an outlandish female huckster, Mrs. Jarley, giving a tour of her famous wax museum. Each scene parodied the *tableaux vivants*, or "living pictures," popular in the 1890s. Silent actors, arranging themselves in frozen poses, were made up to look like wax figures of famous personages such as Captain Kidd, Napoleon, or Lord Byron. Each figure would wait its turn to be wound up like a mechanical device, after which it would move with the jerky movements seen in the crude motion picture machines of the 1890s.

Mamah embraced the role of the brash Mrs. Jarley with the same gusto she had displayed as a teen when she played Lady Macbeth. Perhaps she saw it as a chance to be part of the vaudevillian world she had witnessed in Fargo. The script and stage directions called for her to be dressed in a "black stuff dress, chintz skirt gaily trimmed; gaudy shawl, fan and duster; huge bonnet." As the curtain rose, she stood center stage with the living "statues" of famous personalities arrayed around her.

> Ladies and Gentlemen! You here behold Mrs. Jarley! one of the most remarkable women of the world, who has traveled all over the country with her curious Collection of Waxworks. These figures have been gathered, at great expense, from every clime and country, and are here shown together for the first time. I shall describe each one of them for your benefit, and shall order my assistants to bring some of them forward, so you can see them to advantage. After I have given you the history of each one of this stupendous collection, I shall have each one of them wound up, for they are all fitted with clockworks inside, and they can go through the same motions they did when living. In fact, they do their movements so naturally, that many people have supposed them to be alive but I assure you that they are all made of wood and wax, blockheads every one.[9]

The audience knew all the actors as friends and neighbors, so lines like this were part of the fun. At the rear of the stage, two men in livery with powdered hair waited, holding tools and oilcans. Their role in each scene was to grasp a statue by the elbows, carry it forward, pretend to oil its parts, and wind it up with a loud, winding noise that came from backstage. Occasionally, they would pretend to drop a statue accidentally while carrying it, creating mock consternation. The first one Borthwick introduced was Captain Kidd:

> You here behold the first privateer and the first victim of his murderous propensities. Captain Kidd, the robber of the main, supposed to have originated somewhere Down East. His whole life being spent upon the stormy deep, he amassed an immense fortune and buried it in the sand along the flower-clad banks of

Mrs. Jarley. The boisterous stage character of Mrs. Jarley was familiar to audiences across America in the late nineteenth century. Mamah Borthwick played the role in Oak Park in 1897. Look & Learn, Ltd.

MRS JARLEY

Cape Cod, by which course he invented the Savings Bank, now so common along the shore, having hidden away so much property, which, like so many modern investments, never can be unearthed.[10]

Between each scene, a small chorus may have added a Gilbert and Sullivan–like song, with Borthwick joining in. How many in the audience knew that the boisterous lead performer in the play held a master's degree from the University of Michigan? Edwin knew, and he seems to have redoubled his efforts to court her. Meanwhile, Mamah's sister Jessie began to enjoy the attention of her own suitor, a man named Albert Pitkin.

A lively, popular figure in Oak Park, Mamah Borthwick was not the "reclusive" person imagined by Wright biographer Meryle Secrest.[11] And yet it is difficult to gauge her depth at that age. An undated photograph of Borthwick taken in Oak Park by her friend Lily Wiltberger offers little help. Wiltberger

Mamah Borthwick, ca. 1898. Higgins family photograph.

started as a professional photographer in the late 1890s using a room in her mother's home. The old-fashioned cameo portrait provides barely a hint of the impishness that led Mamah to play Mrs. Jarley. Her only jewelry is the all-important Kappa Alpha Theta kite pinned at her neckline.

In January 1898, her mother died at age fifty-nine. The cause of death is unknown. Borthwick experienced a further shock months later when her former mentor, Professor Edward Walter, went down with the SS *La Bourgogne* when it collided with another ship on its way to Europe. These sad developments at the end of the century signaled the end of Mamah's carefree years. Her grief was perhaps compounded by the disappointment of finding herself in her late twenties living with her sisters and father in his home. They were close as a family, but she was adrift. Whatever future she had dreamed of, living in her childhood home and risking a reputation as an "old maid" was probably not it.

Edwin Cheney, by contrast, was rising in his profession. After serving as a senior executive in the construction department of the Chicago Edison Company, he became the director and treasurer of the Mutual Electric Company of Chicago.[12] When the company sold its interests to Chicago Edison, he would have been compensated in the buyout. He was soon named secretary-treasurer of the Illinois Maintenance Company. His only shortfall as he saw it was his unmarried status. While later newspaper reports said incorrectly that he practically carried Borthwick back from Port Huron, it is clear that he persisted in pressing his suit with her. He offered her a prosperous, comfortable future, and she knew it. At some point, perhaps as late as January 1899, she finally agreed to marry him. It may have been no coincidence that she was about to turn thirty.

Seven years earlier in Ann Arbor, with Edwin Cheney in the audience, Borthwick had extolled her relationship with Apollo. A lighthearted jest at the time, in hindsight it reads like a subliminal plea to the gods to spare her from an ordinary marriage. This prayer went unheard. Edwin was no Apollo. While he enjoyed sailing and music and was a credit to his profession, his face in every photo is more than the sober mien typical of the era's photography; he looks frankly unhappy. Perhaps he believed that Borthwick could make him happy, but we know little about him. Meryle Secrest interviewed an Oak Park woman, Verna Ross Orndorff, who was seven when Cheney was forty. The interview, conducted when Orndorff was in her late eighties, offers only hearsay about Cheney after he had left Oak Park. She described him as "a prince of a man . . . middle-aged, dark-eyed and bald. You could hardly

Edwin H. Cheney,
1902. Witherspoon,
Men of Illinois.

call him a Don Juan, but he was so charming and gracious that he didn't have an enemy."[13]

Apparently sober, constant, and determined, to judge by his years-long courtship of Borthwick, he lacked the vivacious spark she herself nurtured on and off stage. Probably none of the men in her class measured up to her standard, but she no longer had the luxury of time. With no sign that their relationship had changed, the free-spirited Mrs. Jarley consented to become Mrs. Cheney.

CHAPTER 7

WESTWARD HO

Borthwick selected a gown of white silk grenadine with lace trimmings, but we can assume she kept it out of sight until her wedding day, June 15, because her sister Jessie was to be married in a far more modest gown to Albert Pitkin on June 8 in a private ceremony. Mamah's wedding was large and included fifteen of her University of Michigan classmates. They heartily approved of her choice of colors, Michigan's maize and blue. Friends and family were undoubtedly relieved for the sake of both women, who were considered dangerously old. Their ceremonies took place a week apart in the parlor of their father's house.

Arriving from Iowa to be Mamah's maid of honor, Mattie Chadbourne must have seen through her friend's false cheer and bravado. With bridesmaids Jessie Pitkin and Lizzie Borthwick, she looked on sympathetically as Mamah entered, carrying a bouquet of roses. A group called Thomaso's Mandolin Orchestra played the wedding march from *Lohengrin* while Edwin Cheney and his best man, a tall Detroit dentist named Archie Diack, stood with the minister. After a reception for two hundred guests, the newlyweds left on a train for New York and from there embarked on a two-month honeymoon in Europe. Returning via Muskegon, Michigan, to attend the wedding of close friends, they arrived back in Oak Park in late August. They lived briefly in Edwin's flat on South Boulevard before moving to a small, seven-room house at 410 Wesley Avenue.

The reluctance she felt at becoming a suburban housewife can be inferred from the importance she assigned her university connections. As Kappa Alpha Theta's corresponding secretary for the Chicago area, Borthwick kept in touch with the "Eta Girls" of the Michigan chapter, but she sought to meet initiates from other campuses as well. Within weeks of her wedding, she traveled to Ann Arbor to attend the initiation of new sorority sisters. In November 1899, she invited all the Eta women in the Chicago area to a luncheon in her home. The colors of the beaded curtains she hung all around it were the University of Michigan's maize and blue. Thoughtfully, she added the colors of Edwin Cheney's fraternity, Phi Gamma Delta. Finally, as Christmas approached, she planned with the local alumnae to celebrate the season. Networking with other college-educated women provided the social environment she seems to have craved. For the same reason, she became a charter member of the Chicago College Club, comprising only women college graduates. We have no indication that she looked down on women in Oak Park who had not attended college, but she thrived in the company of those who had, and would travel as she needed to participate in that society. Over the next few years, she would seize opportunities to attend events hosted by Theta chapters at various schools in the Midwest, but especially the ones in Ann Arbor.

Urban historian Elaine Lewinnek has observed that cities and suburbs do not evolve naturally: they are socially produced spaces.[1] As the membership of the Oak Park Club in the 1880s reflects, Oak Park had evolved as a broadly egalitarian community. Many young families were members. They congregated for dinners and parties in the large clubhouse, presumably with little attention given to social status. But as Oak Park's population grew in the 1890s, the settings for socializing diversified beyond the suburb. Community leaders began to realize that it needed an additional, different kind of club.

Golf provided an organizing theme for America's upper-middle-class suburban society in a way that satisfied a combination of needs. Men's clubs and sports clubs in the city centers played a role, as did rural resorts and health spas. The new term "country club," invented by Bostonian Murray Forbes in 1882, when he founded the Country Club of Brookline, foretold this development. Residents of the wealthier suburbs wanted resort-like facilities that were close to home and that offered outdoor recreation for both sexes and opportunities to socialize. The answer in most cases was a club where members could play golf.

The Chicago Golf Club, with members from socially prominent families like the Marshall Fields, the McCormicks, the Deerings, and the Palmers, created America's first eighteen-hole course in 1892 in the suburb of Downers Grove. Other suburbs around Chicago responded almost overnight by establishing golf clubs of their own. By the turn of the century, there were twenty-six golf clubs or courses surrounding the city. One of them, River Forest, one-upped its neighbor, Oak Park, by commissioning Frank Lloyd Wright to design its clubhouse. For the thirty-one-year-old Wright, it was a great opportunity. What better place for finding new clients than a golf club?

In all likelihood, this happened thanks to the industrialist William H. Winslow, Wright's first major client as an independent architect. Winslow's company supplied the wrought-iron grillwork for Sullivan's Auditorium building. Winslow had come to know Wright through their collaboration on the grillwork designs. Having commissioned the young architect to design his house in River Forest, he is likely to have recommended him for the River Forest Golf Club project, giving Wright entrée not only to the golf network but also to the River Forest Tennis Club, which would one day also invite him to design a clubhouse.

Meanwhile, municipal leaders in Oak Park were determined to have a golf club like River Forest, but they lacked the required open space. They soon settled on an area called Galewood in the north part of the suburb with a large meadow enclosed by dense native timber on one side and extensive prairie on the other. A mansion next door would serve temporarily as a clubhouse until they could build a new one. A golf course designer was hired along with a Scottish golf pro, David E. McIntosh, but they lacked a name for the club. Wishing to avoid sounding too much like the existing Oak Park Club, they chose to call it Westward Ho after a famous club in England. Within a year, *Western Golf* magazine heralded it as a club that "seems destined to become one of the most powerful clubs in the west."[2] The *Oak Park Reporter* gushed at the club's inauguration in 1899: "The grounds of the Westward Ho Club, although still new, are among the finest in the country, comprising 165 acres of high, rolling meadowland laid out with 18 holes, extending over a course of more than 3 miles."[3]

Chicago organizations that enjoyed relatively high status found recognition in the equivalent of a social register known as the *Blue Book*. For a suburban club to appear in the *Blue Book* signaled that its membership enjoyed significant social standing. Within a year of its founding, Westward Ho was listed in it. Oak Park's women's group, the Nineteenth Century Club, did not appear in the *Blue Book* until 1905.

Westward Ho offered membership to couples and individuals and provided a socially active scene. Lizzie Borthwick, Mamah Borthwick (now Cheney), and Edwin Cheney joined in 1900.[4] The sisters may have felt encouraged by the skill of their fellow club member Bessie Anthony, who went on to win the 1903 U.S. Women's Amateur championship.[5] Winner of the championship the previous two years, Genevieve Hecker, published the first instructional book on golf geared exclusively to women.[6] Like cycling, golf offered women healthy exercise and liberation from heavy, restrictive clothing. For serious women golfers, fashion may not have held importance on the links, but stylish golf clothing added to the sport's allure. The well-known illustrator Joseph C. Leyendecker depicted women as serious golfers. A rival illustrator, Charles Dana Gibson, essentially invented the brand associated with the New Woman, the so-called Gibson Girl, as someone often found on the links with a golf club in her hand.

Still, Westward Ho's leadership was men only. They held their meetings at the Scoville Institute, the stone Romanesque building that served the community as a library, art gallery, and meetinghouse. It is likely to have been at one of those meetings that Edwin Cheney met Frank Lloyd Wright, a Westward Ho charter member. Early club officers were Arthur Heurtley, who would soon live in a Wright-designed house, and George Furbeck, who already did. The significance of Westward Ho as a possible source of clients for Wright has gone unnoticed despite his charter membership and the fact that he designed houses for at least ten of its members, houses known by their names: Gale, Martin, Furbeck, Heurtley, Pitkin, Williams, Moore, Waller, Copeland, and Cheney.[7]

Westward Ho distinguished itself by erecting a large clubhouse where it held social events in a large assembly hall and dining room on the first floor. A second floor was devoted to women's locker rooms and sleeping rooms. A broad covered veranda wrapped around three sides, offering expansive views of the golf course.[8] This grand clubhouse burned to the ground in November 1901, but until then Westward Ho was known for its social events. It is not known which one served as the occasion for the pivotal moment when Frank Lloyd Wright and Mamah Borthwick met, but according to Wright, it came during an evening social event, most likely at the Westward Ho Golf Club. One can easily imagine Edwin Cheney spying his new acquaintance across the room and bringing Mamah over.

"Frank, I don't believe you've met my wife."

PART II

CHAPTER 8

～⚘～

MODERNS IN TRANSITION

The meeting never is to be forgotten by either of us. It was electrical! The effect was one that I had not thought possible. From that night on, Mrs. Cheney was indifferent to her husband, and I to my wife.

　　—FRANK LLOYD WRIGHT, quoted in *Chicago Examiner*,
　　December 30, 1911

The time and place of Wright and Mamah Borthwick's first encounter has been a matter of speculation.[1] Strangely enough, no Wright biographer has mentioned his description of it. In 1911, the reporters to whom he told the episode quoted him differently, but they all agreed that Wright identified Edwin as the one who introduced them at an evening social event and that the effect on both of them had been "electrical." He seems to have presumed that he could speak for Borthwick about her feelings, but we have no direct testimony from her on the subject. Perhaps the Delphic priestess of Michigan knew she had met her Apollo in this charismatic, good-looking man, but his assertion of their immediate indifference to their spouses sounds overstated. It does seem likely, though, that the growing disappointment she felt with Edwin would have been magnified when they socialized with Frank and Catherine Wright. The specific course of the affair is unknown but is unlikely to have developed rapidly. It took years for them to break from their families, and not until late in the drama was the characterization "reckless" generally applied to them. Until then, they were cautious as they navigated the limitations imposed by their circumstances.

Wright made a good first impression on many women. Janet Ashbee, the wife of the British architect Robert Ashbee, a close friend of Wright's, intuitively understood his appeal but eventually became disillusioned with him. Upon first meeting him in 1900, she described him as "a strange, delightful soul— a radical original thinker working out his ideas consistently as an artist in his architecture. . . . He has big ideas, and is gloriously ruthless in sticking to what he believes."[2]

Frank Lloyd Wright,
ca. 1900. Photographer
unknown. The Wright
Library, Wright
Portraits, http://www
.steinerag.com/flw/
index.htm.

Her view of him had changed considerably by the time she wrote to her
husband in 1916, having spent more time with Wright by then. "I really do
dislike the man," she wrote, "and his poses and all his talk and gas, and parade
of it all. The theatrical is always a bit disgusting. . . . Catherine [Wright's wife]
evidently hashed it all up but I don't think as a nature apart from his work that
he is worth bothering about. How silly of her not to divorce him."[3]

For Mamah Borthwick, the bloom clearly never entirely came off the rose
with Wright. She had a tolerant, forbearing nature that enabled her to remain
loyal to him. And yet Mamah's graduation prophecy demonstrates that she did
not readily defer to men and was willing to subject them to irony and sarcasm.
She seems to have been amply equipped to handle Wright's well-documented
narcissism and limited capacity for self-reflection.

Her mother's death in 1898 may have been unexpected, but the much greater
shock came with the death of her father two years later. Marcus Borthwick had
been in good health until a bout of pleurisy. He was gone in just three days. No
one had played such an outsized role in her life. An inventive, resourceful man
and the agent of the family's fortunes, he had been an enthusiastic supporter

of her education at every stage and, as the Dakota Territory episode demonstrates, had had every confidence in her and her siblings.

A second blow fell a year later. At the age of thirty-seven, Jessie died after giving birth to a healthy daughter. Her husband, Albert Pitkin, had been living with her in the house left by Marcus Borthwick. Upon her death, he moved out and lost his moorings in Oak Park. An aspiring writer-poet, he had none of the business instincts of his brothers and began a precarious existence. Placing his child in the care of Mamah and Edwin, he moved away and was rarely seen again in Oak Park, even by his daughter.[4]

Jessie's funeral took place in the home of Albert's brother, E. H. Pitkin, a client of Wright's who lived nine blocks from his house.[5] Wright may have been present at the service, looking on in sympathy as Albert gave his baby daughter, Jessie, over to Mamah. In a single tragic stroke, Mamah and Edwin had become parents, a situation she could not have imagined years earlier when she and Jessie had shared adventures in the Dakota Territory. They moved to a house on South Scoville Avenue. Mamah's sister Lizzie moved in with them, and they hired a nanny. Even so, caring for a newborn child must have been a major adjustment.

In June, she and Edwin traveled to Vinton, Iowa, to visit Mattie Chadbourne, who had also recently lost her father. They stayed several days in Vinton in the large house where Mattie's mother lived. Mattie had become engaged to a childhood friend, Alden Brown, a graduate in mining engineering from the University of Iowa. Within a year, she and Alden would marry in a small, private ceremony and move to Boulder, Colorado, where he would work for a mining company. It meant that the two women would be living even farther apart. They agreed to try to spend summers together whenever they could.

The trip to see Mattie had been a morale booster, but Mamah needed more time away from Oak Park. The Cheneys decided on a European vacation. Leaving the infant Jessie in the care of Lizzie, the nanny, and Edwin's mother, the couple sailed in late July from New York on the steamer *Kaiser Wilhelm*.[6] Edwin's passport provides no other record of the trip other than the name of their ship's final destination, Bremen. If they spent time in Germany, it would have been an opportunity for Mamah to hone her language skills and to gain exposure to modern German society.

They returned to a Chicago experiencing its usual tumult of change. The stockyards, soon to be made infamous by Upton Sinclair's novel *The Jungle*, continued to expand as their odor became detectable farther north. Streets were still crowded with some ten thousand horses, but eight hundred new automobile licenses had been issued. New elevated railway routes competed with numerous trolley lines to carry the growing workforce to and from the city.

Customs were changing in ways that some found shocking. Saloons opened dance halls for young working-class women so they could meet men more regularly. Unescorted women in dance halls seemed all of a piece with women riding bicycles in unflattering bloomers. Mores were changing, but a more modern outlook did not immediately extend to all areas of life. For example, the daring Theodore Dreiser novel *Sister Carrie* (1900) found few buyers. About a country girl in Chicago who went from being a man's mistress to becoming his superior as a famous actress, it is recognized today as a pathbreaking classic. For Chicago at the start of the twentieth century, it was simply too outré.

And yet Chicago considered itself modern. Ever since the 1893 Exposition, its leading citizens had used the word with enthusiasm, albeit more in reference to business and technology than art. In general, the word "modern" had a positive connotation. A crude measure of its importance in the public mind is evident in the frequency with which it appeared in the *Chicago Tribune* in comparison with the *New York Times*. Little used in the 1870s, it became increasingly common, always appearing with greater frequency in the *Tribune* than in the *Times*.[7] While this does not necessarily indicate a greater interest in things modern in Chicago than in New York, it reflects Chicago's eagerness to be seen as on the cutting edge and its readiness to receive what Frank Lloyd Wright would offer.

Chicago was a young city, but this did not make it a promulgator so much as a proving ground for the new. In July 2004, the now-defunct Terra Museum of American Art in Chicago announced an exhibition, *Chicago Modern, 1893–1945: Pursuit of the New*, assuming correctly that people in Chicago would know intuitively what that meant. Focused on painting, not architecture, it illustrated Chicago's role as a test bed for the creative class. Chicagoans like Wright and his friend the writer Hamlin Garland believed there was something special about the Midwest's creative output. (On the other hand, Willa Cather—who did not much like either Garland or Chicago—was not so sure.)[8] Talented Chicago artists like Pauline Dohn (1865–1934), who would have known Mamah Borthwick's sister Jessie through their studies at the Art Institute, were less concerned with the idea of a uniquely midwestern creativity than with the new Impressionist style of painting.

Wright and Garland had spent their formative years on midwestern farms. Only men from that era, perhaps, could be sentimental about a boyhood spent working behind a horse-drawn McCormick Reaper. That environment had exposed them daily to the forces of nature and profoundly shaped their understanding of how such forces related to their work.

Wright was a man of action, a builder, and someone with vision. The more Borthwick saw of him, the more she must have felt admiration for his dynamic and uncompromising artistic idealism. For his part, he seems to have been excited by how she restored, rejuvenated, and apparently inspired him. Equal to her intellectually, he does not appear to have been insecure in the presence of her advanced education (he had but a brief stint at the University of Wisconsin). If anything, all indications are that he admired her education and did not hesitate to make use of it. Eventually, he would support her translation efforts by adding his talent for poetic expression. In this sense, their relationship was modern. He treated her as an equal and with a measure of respect that he did not always extend to others.

Her specific influence on his work is ultimately unknowable. He considered himself a singular creative force, and to an extent that was true. Instead, she engaged him in ideas beyond the world of architecture. Having come of age in the nineteenth century, they shared a resistance to its cultural restrictions, but they did not reject its intellectual legacy. They were influenced by the New England Enlightenment and shared similar tastes in literature and art. Where she differed from him was in her way of engaging "the new." Enthusiastic about the benefits of machinery but openly disdainful of what the Renaissance had bestowed to architecture, Wright rebelled against cultural conventions and traditions. As her prophecy suggests, Borthwick did not, at least not right away. She welcomed modernity but was less inclined to see it as a revolt against the past.

A hint of how she affected Wright appears in the form of a sculpture he commissioned not long after they met. Referred to as *Flower in the Crannied Wall*, it was inspired by Tennyson's poem of that name, which was engraved on its back.

Flower in the crannied wall
I pluck you out of the crannies
Hold you here root and all
In my Hand
Little Flower
But if I could understand
What you are

Root and all
And all in all
I should know
What God and Man is.

Initially, Wright tried to explain his concept to the sculptor A. L. Van den Berghen but eventually fired him in frustration. He turned to his friend Richard W. Bock, a sculptor who eventually completed the work in 1904. His specific instructions for the sculpture are not known, but the result is a female figure engaging with an architectural form. When Bock finished the work, Wright is said to have exclaimed, "You have done it Dicky, you have done it!"[9]

The feminine figure in the sculpture contemplates the cube she holds in her hand. It seems to come from the architectural pillar before her. Made to grace the entryway of Wright's Dana-Thomas House in Springfield, Illinois, where it now resides, the sculpture had complex, layered meanings for Wright. More than representing simply the Muse of Architecture, it expresses wonder at the process of creation and the emergence of artistic abstraction from a reified Nature. The installation of a copy of the sculpture, which was commissioned soon after he met Mamah Borthwick, years later in the courtyard of Taliesin, the home he built for her, is significant. So is the fact that he felt it so important for the sculpture to feature a woman that he brought Bock into his Oak Park studio to work from a nude model.[10] His use of Victorian poetry demonstrated an overlapping interest with Borthwick, who loved the poems of Robert Browning. If they discussed such poetry, it is possible that he shared his ideas for the sculpture with her and even brought her into the studio to see it. Bock's design was modern but the poem was not, a reflection of its cultural amalgam of the two centuries.

To describe either Wright or Borthwick as modern, premodern, or even out of phase with the modern would be a disservice to their complexity. Conceptions of a modern outlook differ depending upon context. Borthwick represented what historian Lucy Delap calls the "feminist avant-garde," that is, women who were concerned mainly with individualism and identity.[11] Wright, certain of his identity, explored new forms, ideas, and expressions; a definition of modernism. He must have impressed Borthwick as someone who embodied a modern outlook more than anyone she had met. He had the same effect on his peers in the profession, who had begun to give him the kind of attention usually accorded someone older. An illustrated article on his work had appeared in *Architectural Review* around the time he began sharing office space

Flower in the Crannied Wall, *by Richard Bock.* Commissioned by Frank Lloyd
Wright for Dana-Thomas House, Springfield, Illinois. Photograph by Mike Jackson,
FAIA.

downtown in Steinway Hall with three young, up-and-coming architects. The three men—Robert Spencer, Dwight Perkins, and Robert Hunt—were becoming known for work inspired by the Arts and Crafts movement led by, among others, the architect Charles Ashbee in England. Brimming with the confidence that characterized Chicago's city fathers, the three men were rather full of themselves. Or at least they were until their idol, Charles Ashbee himself, visited Chicago.

CHAPTER 9

୧ฺ୬

LOCAL HERO

On the evening of December 5, 1900, a reporter for the *Chicago Tribune* covering a lecture at the Art Institute of Chicago saw an unexpected story develop.
Midlecture, several young architects of the Chicago Architectural Club had
become incensed and stalked out of the room and down the institute's lion-
guarded steps into the night. Now, a small group of more sober-minded men
remained to escort their guest speaker, the British architect Charles Robert
Ashbee, to the clubroom in the institute's basement for drinks and further discussion. No one seems to have objected when the reporter tagged along as
they descended the stairs.

It was to have been a cordial reception after Ashbee's speech, but instead it
had become a showdown of the sort that only a group of young, ambitious,
but touchy architects could have produced. Ashbee had insulted them, they
felt, and not only them but Chicago. "How, in a city like Chicago," he had
said, "am I to appeal for history to a people that have none? Or beauty, to a
people that know none, not at least as we in the East conceive it? The New
Englanders and we in Britain claim kinship more intimately. We have the
same traditions. Their art is ours, their ethics the same as ours. But in these
great cosmopolitan cities, how are we to touch these great bear cubs of democracy? How can we clip their claws or trim them?"

As if this had not been enough to rile his audience, he went on to describe
a "nameless" city that most of those present assumed had to be Chicago. "This
city," he said, "typifies all that a city should not be. Her citizens are all that true
citizens should not be. Her two rivers are covered with the slime of factory
refuse. They make their fortunes and then move to a pleasanter place. New
York or some other city."[1] It was around then that many in the audience had
walked out.

Downstairs in the rooms of the Architectural Club, the men stood awkwardly among scattered tables and austere wooden rockers. The president of the club, reserved Hyde Park architect Henry K. Holsman, opened the conversation by asking Dwight Heald Perkins to give his opinion of Ashbee's speech. The dark-haired, boldly mustachioed Perkins shared an office with Wright in Steinway Hall. He was an outspoken, progressive architect, but that night he was unwilling to confront his idol, Ashbee. His comments were vague. Holsman turned to James Galloway of the powerful Chicago Real Estate Board.

"Jim, how do you think the Real Estate Board would respond to Mr. Ashbee?"

As he would indicate later, the usually reticent Galloway did not welcome the opportunity to speak in front of a reporter. He addressed Ashbee in a manner described by the *Tribune* reporter as "crisp."

"I find that I have misunderstood the purpose of your presence here, Mr. Ashbee," he began, and proceeded to deliver a withering put-down of Ashbee's attempt to interest the club in preserving "old ruins in England dear to the British heart." Galloway assured him that "we have a history and we have plenty of art within our city limits." Placed on the defensive, Ashbee disclaimed having had any intention to raise money from his audience. The "unnamed city" of his remarks, he explained, had been Pittsburgh, not Chicago. His peace offering was accepted skeptically.

There is no record of Wright having been part of the group that evening. Although not a member of the Architectural Club, he was featured in many of its shows. He and Ashbee had bonded over dinner the night before at Hull House, the renowned community development center founded by Jane Addams. The scene at the Architectural Club would have made for an awkward beginning to their friendship.[2] The next day, undaunted by the chilly reception, Ashbee addressed a group at the University of Chicago with the same uncompromising, haughty complaint. Again, he sniffed at Chicago's lack of history and art and chastised the city leaders for not having planned sufficiently for the future.

The people of Chicago are so busy in industrial pursuits that nobody finds time to give attention to the new ideas which are presented to them. Here in Chicago, you have not done nearly as much as you ought with your opportunities. The city is just growing now, and this is the time for you to make those improvements which will be needed so badly in later years. Chicago is far behind London in

Charles R. Ashbee.
Ashbee's note on the back of the print (reproduced below the photograph here) confirms that Frank Lloyd Wright took the photograph in November 1900. © Guild of Handicraft Trust, UK, http://www .courtbarn.org.

this respect. You praise up the few things you have done and think that is enough. You say, "Just look at Lincoln Park, the boulevards, and the Art Institute," but those things are not a fleabite to what should have been accomplished.[3]

It seemed strange to his listeners that he should throw down a gauntlet in a city that considered itself more modern than London. Franklin MacVeagh, president of the Municipal Art League, said Ashbee was "way off the track in many of his remarks, though of course there was some truth in his criticism of our lack of historical spots and of art conditions."[4]

Ashbee's attitude could be attributed to his having arrived in Chicago in the worst seasonal weather, the dreary winter of 1900. But it is likely that his scathing critique of the city was further influenced by the views of his wife, Janet. Her journal entry sums up her reaction:

> When a man has finished with Hell, says a proverb, he is sent to Chicago; and when you first arrive you endorse this statement. Smoke, darkness, noise, the clashing of car bells, engine bells, steamer bells, the grating of endless trolleys as they dash along the streets, the shriek of the American voice trying to make itself heard above the uproar. The rattle and thunder of the elevated railway, the unearthly buzzing of electric cabs and the thudding of power houses that shakes a whole street. To the east stretches the gray sea of Michigan with its tides and storms and breakwaters. And along its edge, the dreary Park, flat, and gray too in its wintry dress, with dreary houses of the wealthy, horrid little pretentious castles of money, along the side.[5]

Wright was not put off by these views of the Ashbees, and to some extent he shared them. Looking ahead, he knew he would need contacts abroad like Robert Ashbee. The two men were of one mind on many aspects of architecture. He invited the Ashbees to stay with him for a few days in Oak Park prior to their leaving Chicago. In doing so, he may not yet have grasped Ashbee's half-kept secret. His wife of two years, who was accompanying him on his trip to America, was providing cover for him so that he could hide his true sexual orientation. To Wright, the Ashbees were a conventional couple. It is not clear how soon he learned how unusual their relationship was.

Janet knew the truth about her husband by 1900, accepted it, and had begun to jointly make entries in a journal with him. She wrote about Wright's wife, Catherine, with keen perception, noting that she was delicate, youthful, and strongly opinionated. "Every tone of her voice rings with fearless honesty—almost a defiant cry against sham—compromise and all disloyalty." It was an aspect of Catherine's character that would make her a formidable opponent for Mamah.

On April 22, 1901, the *Chicago Tribune* published Ashbee's report of his visit to Chicago. He paid several compliments to the city, but it was not enough to placate Holsman, who complained that he had singled out Wright for praise without thanking the Architectural Club for its hospitality. And certainly when Wright spoke before the Chicago Arts and Crafts Society at Jane Addams's Hull House nine days later, he basked in the light of Ashbee's accolade. It may have helped him shrug off the frosty reception he received when he delivered his speech, "The Art and Craft of the Machine." Considered one of his most significant essays, its counterintuitive argument about the potential benefits of "the machine" demonstrated his growing self-confidence as a philosopher-architect. What he meant by "machine" was not always clear, but he did not find machines alienating. "All machinery makes some recurrent noise sound clack or beat above the hum," he wrote in his autobiography, "a rhythm that is the obvious poetry in the mathematics of this universe." In this sense, he saw the machine not in conflict with Nature but as a potential aid to art. He admonished his Arts and Crafts audience not to forgo the benefits of machine-aided production.

The much-analyzed speech requires no further elaboration here except for its subtext, the implication of the architect as a hero. Long before novelist Ayn Rand wrote *The Fountainhead* (1943), creating an archetypal heroic image of the architect (some say Wright was the model), he declared that the machine could enable the architect to regain the stature he had lost since the Middle Ages. That loss, according to his reading of Victor Hugo, had occurred when the printed book replaced architecture as the chief means of transmitting culture, a perspective derived in part from his former teacher and mentor Louis Sullivan. Although Sullivan dismissed the idea of the architect as an "artist," he messianically told his colleagues that they were the chosen, the poets and interpreters of the national life of their time.

Wright's address set teeth on edge among members of his Arts and Crafts audience, who were deeply ambivalent about machines. The idea that an artisan should rely on a machine to create more and better things went against their traditions and instincts. Wright's lay audiences, on the other hand, were taken with his eloquence. They were persuaded that an architect could be heroic. This appears to be the light in which Borthwick saw Wright.

To many of his Oak Park neighbors, Frank Lloyd Wright was a hero. In 1901, he impressed the community with an interview he gave to the *Oak Park Reporter* about a model community to be built in the suburb. Skilled in spinning a story that overpromised on schedule and underestimated on cost, he alleged that a two-block area north of Chicago Avenue and west of Oak Park Avenue would become the site for eight houses of an unusual design. He even led the newspaper to believe that they were already financed: "Work will begin in a few days, and before fall the houses will be ready to be occupied, but Mr. Wright does not expect to have the grounds in correct condition before next spring when the full beauty of a whole neighborhood built on one artistic plan will be unfolded to all who care to visit Oak Park."[6]

Wright declared that "money sufficient to carry out the plan has been obtained" when in fact no such money existed. The entire Chicago area had been suffering from a decade of declining rates of investment in construction. Described by the newspaper as "Mr. Wright's colony," the plan was nevertheless innovative. It is remembered today as his Quadruple Block Plan, for which the article was effectively a marketing tool: "Everything will be in harmony and nothing offensive to the eye shall exist. Each house will cost about $6,000 or $7,000 and will be built as a part of an artistic plan for the whole two blocks. Mr. Wright believes the suburban resident spends too much on his house and too little on his ground."[7]

Assigning more of a property's cost to the land in this way only made the plan impractical. Real estate agents were determined to squeeze the average lot size well below Wright's proposed half acre. Worse, houses that were virtually indistinguishable from one another were not what upper-middle-class buyers aspired to.[8] Typical of Wright the idealist, urban planner, and creator of grand schemes, the proposal was his vision for change in the suburbs. Americans would become better neighbors and citizens in his egalitarian community, he declared. The usual messes they created would not sully the houses and landscapes in his design. He would prevent their owners from doing that: "Parkways will take the place of streets, there will be no alleys in this neighborhood and the discouraging prospect presented by the usual backyard fence will also be eliminated, but the washtubs and clothes line which the high board fence is expected to shield from public view will not be in evidence in Mr. Wright's colony. Those homely but necessary articles will be safely stowed away in niches to be built in the basements. . . . The houses will be constructed on lines to harmonize with the prairie, with low terraces and broad eves."[9]

The low, clean, uncluttered look, the essence of the Prairie Style, graced the large illustrations of the *Ladies' Home Journal* in February 1901. Titled "Home in a Prairie Town," the article helped burnish Wright's reputation. The association of his modern design with the prairie supported his idealization of the Midwest.[10]

The local newspaper concluded by noting that "residents of Oak Park are pleased with the prospect, for Mr. Wright is held in high esteem by his neighbors." But the highly esteemed Mr. Wright had made promises he could not keep. It is not clear why he made them in the first place. If he was trying to preempt his neighbors' possible objections to his plan, at least his concern was prescient. High esteem or no, they resisted his project and forced a delay. It was not realized until two years later on a much-reduced scale in a different part of Oak Park.

The episode illustrates how Wright could be a hero to some while to others he was an annoying self-promoter. In 1902, he caused the first of several rifts in the Chicago Architectural Club by being featured prominently in its annual exhibition although he was not a member. Had it not been for the advocacy of his colleagues like Dwight Perkins, he would have been excluded from the exhibition altogether.

One Chicago architect had no need to exhibit and could make the thirty-four-year-old Wright look diminutive. Daniel H. Burnham was more than a hero in Chicago—he was a legend. While Wright was trying to sell his neighbors on a barely existing Quadruple Block Plan, Burnham was designing the world's largest department store. With a floor space of seventy-three acres (300,000 square meters), Marshall Field's set a new standard for marketing and selling to the American consumer. Burnham's role as the maestro of the 1893 Columbian Exposition added to his luster. Typifying the bigness and brassiness for which Chicago was famous, the iconic "great clock" on the corner of the Marshall Field's store became a familiar city symbol. The presence of the great building declared a scale of architecture to which Wright aspired, but for now he was a designer of houses.

On October 13, 1902, he mounted the stage of the lecture room in the Scoville Institute to address the Nineteenth Century Club. His subject was "Art as Related to Life." Typical of the expansive topics he chose (a few months later, he would address the River Forest Women's Club on "The Nature of Things"), it enabled him to range widely on matters of aesthetics. The local newspaper reporter's effusive reaction, if he was not being sarcastic, may have exceeded even Wright's expectations:

> Mr. Wright dwelt on the necessity of a love for "the true and the beautiful." He spoke of the lack of taste displayed alike in the homes of Chicago's most wealthy men and of her middle classes. He made a strong plea for originality in American architecture and deprecated the use of architectural ideas originated by and for other nations. Mr. Wright's ideas are brilliant and positive, and he most ruthlessly demolished the cherished idols of many of his hearers, leaving them weeping and wandering among the ruins, but hoping that at some future time he may speak as delightfully again and give them new and true idols to replace the old and false idols that they may worship unblushingly, correctly and understandingly.[11]

The audience would have included Wright's mother, Anna, and his wife, Catherine, but not Borthwick. As noted in chapter 1, she had yet to join the club for reasons that are not entirely clear. She was from a long-established Oak Park family and the wife of a successful businessman, so she would have been a prime candidate for membership in the Nineteenth Century Club. Founded in 1891 by tony local women, it had come to embody what was essentially the Oak Park female establishment. And yet Mamah Borthwick, whose Kappa Alpha Theta membership practically shouted her establishment credentials, did not become a member of the club until October 1907.[12]

Women's clubs in America had multiplied dramatically since the Civil War, bringing unprecedented benefits to their communities. The Ladies Library Association in Port Huron, to which Borthwick and Chadbourne had belonged, was an example. Women's clubs offered their members opportunities for self-improvement. Meetings were seen as opportunities for continuing education as well as advancing charitable causes. Thus, as a teacher in Cedar Rapids, Mattie Chadbourne was asked by her club to provide lessons in vocabulary and syntax, while in Oak Park Mamah Borthwick could be counted on to supply comments and translations for readings of plays chosen by the French Club. Anna and Catherine Wright were especially active in the Nineteenth Century Club's "departments" of special interest. Catherine Wright's specialties were education, child-rearing, and social services.

Catherine and Frank first met at a costume party held at his uncle's All Souls Church in 1887 when, dressed as a buccaneer, he tripped over his sword and bumped into her. She was just sixteen. Instantly smitten, he resisted his mother's efforts to slow the courtship, and, in his usual hurry, he married "Kitty" in 1889. Their first child, Frank Jr., was born a year later, followed by a total of five more over the next fourteen years. Catherine became ever more absorbed in the children and in managing the household while Wright was consumed by his work. The strains in their relationship were showing by the time Mamah Borthwick married Edwin Cheney.

The Cheneys rented a house at 628 North East Avenue in the fall of 1902.[13] Lizzie Borthwick, Mamah's sister, continued to live with them and to help raise little Jessie, their niece (daughter of their deceased sister, also named Jessie). When soon afterward Mamah became pregnant, she and Edwin began to consider building a house of their own. If the proximity of Wright's new projects in their neighborhood encouraged them to choose him as their architect, it is also likely that she promoted him as the best choice. Unaware that her purpose was to see more of him, Edwin agreed.

CHAPTER 10

CHENEY HOUSE

The timing was perfect. The Cheneys preferred to build in the neighborhood where they were renting: Fair Oaks, where several lots were still available. In a few years, a developer would build dozens of two-story "colonial-type" houses at the south end of the suburb, but in 1903 the more expensive, custom houses were being built on lots with quality improvements. A forty-acre tract with graded streets and stone sidewalks, Fair Oaks began as an association in 1890. One joined the association by buying one of the lots.

Their rented house was not far from the house Wright had designed for William E. Martin, the brother of Wright's client Darwin Martin in Buffalo. Larger and more ostentatious than what the Cheneys had in mind, it rivaled another Wright house in Fair Oaks designed for William G. Fricke. The latter's soaring, three-story central tower surrounded by cascading rooflines dwarfed what Wright would eventually design for the Cheneys. Theirs was to be one of the smallest Wright homes in Oak Park. Its outsized reputation comes not from its design but from its role as the epicenter of a scandal.

Borthwick gave birth to her first child, John, on May 10, 1903.[1] Two weeks later, on May 25, Edwin Cheney purchased the lot on which they would build.[2] Wright's son John would later write in a book on his father that Borthwick was "a cultured, respected and sensitive woman—a bright spot in Oak Park" whose close involvement in the design of the house cemented her relationship with his father: "Her laugh had the same quality as had Dad's, so did her love and her interest in his work. The many contacts in the designing and building of the Cheney house brought about an understanding between their hearts that made them one."[3]

The three major area newspapers of this period were the *Chicago Tribune*, the *Chicago Examiner*, and the *Inter Ocean*. The *Inter Ocean* had a more upscale readership and would become Borthwick's nemesis. The *Tribune*, the largest and oldest, was considered the newspaper of record. It would eventually break the story about Wright and Borthwick. The *Examiner*, the most inclined to mix editorializing and gossip with news stories, seized upon the house's role in the affair. Its reporter, Magda Frances West, admitted that she came to this conclusion based on rumors: "So the arbiters declare, the shadows began to fall. A little shadow at first, and then it grew to a large one and though they tried to keep it out of sight of the rest of the town everybody nearly knew that it was the beautiful Mrs. Cheney that they saw out with Mr. Wright in his automobile so frequently. Others declared they had noticed them in Chicago at the theater together, dining in the cafes and at the various parks."[4]

Wright had no car at the time. He was not squiring Borthwick around or taking her to the theater, but it can be assumed that they regularly met at his studio to discuss plans for the house while Edwin Cheney was at work. According to Wright's testimony, he was in love with Borthwick by the time he began designing Cheney House, if not well before. Even so, contrary to the account provided by West, their interaction was initially constrained by their family obligations and Wright's busy work schedule. They had to be careful in public. Not until their final year in Oak Park do they appear to have let their guard down, causing rumors to proliferate. After the revelation of the affair in 1909, neighbors told the press that they had long suspected the relationship. This may well be something we can write off as Daniel Kahneman's "frequency illusion" (in which, upon learning about an event, one imagines it has been going on for a long time).[5] A Wright employee, Robert Hardin, is said to have quit because of the affair, but the timing is unclear.[6]

Wright's initial proposal for Cheney House envisioned two stories based on an H floor plan. Edwin and Mamah found it too large and ambitious, so he followed up with a single-story design with an entrance on the side that opened into a reception area and a large living room. That, too, was rejected in favor of a proposal based on a square floor plan with four bedrooms in the rear separated by a hallway and fireplace from the living spaces in front.[7] With this last design, Wright proposed a nine-foot-high privacy wall that would stretch across the property in front, turn at the border with the neighbors, and then return to the house halfway along. Although much of the wall was not built, his intention was clear. As he worked to unify and simplify the design, he sought to protect the inhabitants from scrutiny.

The overall design is smaller and simpler than most houses Wright designed at the time. Architectural historian Gwendolyn Wright describes middle-class

Edwin H. Cheney House. Bird's-eye view drawn by Wright's employee Marion
Mahony. Wright, *Ausgeführte Bauten und Entwürfe von Frank Lloyd Wright*, plate
XXX(a). Special Collections, J. Willard Marriott Library, University of Utah.

taste as trending toward smaller sizes and less ostentation, and away from
sentimental styles.[8] Borthwick may have rejected the upper-class pretentions
exhibited by some of the largest Oak Park houses in favor of building something smaller and more efficient.

Like other women who were Wright clients, Borthwick wanted her house
to express her lifestyle. Cheney House suited her intention to entertain informally in the way it removed walls and integrated living spaces. The relaxed,
more informal design of the house's interior spaces was appropriate for Borthwick, who similarly dissolved boundaries in her social life. Disregarding previous constraints on the domestic world of the housewife as the corresponding
secretary for Kappa Alpha Theta, she was spending time away from the house,
socializing in Chicago and across the Midwest as far as St. Louis and Ann Arbor.[9]

And yet from the outside, as if in counterpoint to these facts, the house
appears closeted, its occupants ingeniously sheltered from view. One had only
to look up and down the street at other houses to see what a departure this
was from traditional architecture. A wall in the center of the house projects
forward as if in defense. Its immediate purpose is to support and enclose a
terrace off the living room, but it also massively blocks observation from the
street. Just to visit the house, one must follow a walkway far around to the
right, past a brick pillar and through a side garden. There, one turns left along
a low wall and, after reaching the house again, turns left along a short passage
to a wall with an art glass window. Only then does a "front door" become

Cheney House, street view. Short perimeter walls once extended from each side of the terrace. Photograph by Richard Guy Wilson.

visible, several steps to the right.[10] This convoluted path to entry, typical of a Wright house, was meant to be like a rite of discovery. It suited his clients, but not always first-time visitors.

Inside, a dynamic space unfolds, revealing a capacious interior stretching the length of the house. A low, vaulted ceiling joins three areas: library, living room, and dining room. Wright insisted on using casement windows, which swung out instead of moving up and down. He despised sash windows, even though he allowed a few of them to be placed at ground level in the rear. The Cheney House casement windows designed by Wright use vertical strips of leaded glass and accents of art glass. Grouped in series, they allow plenty of light to enter while again preventing easy scrutiny of the interior from outside. If, as Wright said, he designed houses from the inside out, there is an interior aspect of Wright himself in Cheney House, a desire to protect its special occupant from scrutiny. To be sure, the same trait appears elsewhere in his work, but Cheney House exemplifies Wright's ability to create a tension between the seen and the unseen, the included and the excluded. Years later, in the so-called Wasmuth portfolio of his early works, Wright would publish a floor plan of Cheney House alongside that of another house intended for "an artist," perhaps

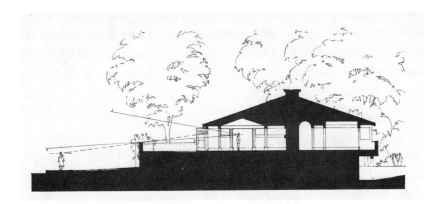

Lines of sight, Cheney House. From inside Cheney House, one's view across the street is relatively clear. As shown here, however, the elevation and perimeter walls cleverly block observation from the sidewalk in front. Drawing by Grant Hildebrand and William Hook (in Hildebrand, *The Wright Space*).

himself. It is the only place in the portfolio where two floor plans appear on a single page—as if to declare that his house and Cheney House were meant to be together.[11]

Although Mamah and Edwin Cheney welcomed the sense of seclusion the house afforded, they were among the more socially active couples of Oak Park. They enjoyed hosting parties. One of the many design achievements of Edwin H. Cheney House was its ability, despite its modest size, to host a fairly large party. Wright accomplished this by integrating the interior spaces of dining room, living room, and library, preserving their functions while keeping each space open to the other. In warm weather, still more space can be added by opening the trio of living room doors onto the terrace.

The effect is a segmented but large living space. Bold stripes of fir wood cross the vaulted ceilings. Broad, continuous bands above the windows integrate the rooms visually. In 1904, the result was unequivocally modern, all the more so to those who were accustomed to Victorian-style houses. Not least, the fireplace, always symbolically important to a Wright house, is centralized within this space, yet made intimate by a kind of alcove with a lowered ceiling.

Edwin Cheney's influence on the house's design is difficult to discern. A car enthusiast like Wright, he first asked for a full basement garage, but the city of Oak Park would not hear of it; no gas tanks were allowed in basements. In response, Wright slightly raised the basement and turned the space into storage and a live-in suite for Lizzie Borthwick, with bright windows facing the rear at ground level. This made the house slightly higher, effectively a two-story house, while giving the appearance of a one-story dwelling from the front. The terrace off the living room became higher, with the result that its supporting wall is even more of a visual barrier. Two young trees were allowed to grow through openings in the terrace floor. One is evident in a photo of Albert Pitkin seated there with his daughter and nephew. It reflected Wright's preference for yielding to nature.

Cheney House is an early example of Wright's Prairie Style of architecture, upon which he expounded over the next five years in a body of work that most architects would consider a lifetime achievement. In this sense, Cheney House enjoys distinguished company, even if its fame comes more from its owner than its lineage. Although its design probably helped catalyze their relationship, it is unlikely to have been a venue for their trysts. It was, after all, a bit crowded. Its occupants from the start were Edwin Cheney, Mamah Borthwick, her sister Lizzie, a nanny, a servant, and two children.

This all makes Margaret Belknap Allen's published memories deeply suspect. As mentioned in chapter 1, she lived next door. Five years old when the house

Albert Pitkin at Cheney House, ca. 1905. Soon after Cheney House was finished in 1904, Albert Pitkin posed with his daughter, Jessie, and Borthwick's son, John. Higgins family photograph.

was built, she was no older than nine when she claimed to have regularly spied on Borthwick and Wright in broad daylight. In a house that she wrongly locates to the east of Cheney House, she writes that she and her sisters, "giggling and laughing," stood tiptoe on a trunk in an upper floor closet in order to peer "down into the Cheney living room below to watch the two of them making love."[12] The living room where the alleged lovemaking took place is in the center of the house, out of sight of any such vantage point. The Cheney House windows through which the young voyeur says she peered are those of the library just off the entrance, an unlikely location for covert lovemaking. Wright made clear as early as 1901 that he believed the suburban house should be private from neighbors. The house itself should not crowd the boundaries of the lot, he felt. In this spirit, he created the subdivided, reflective glass surfaces of the windows as a screen to curious neighbors. Architectural historian Grant Hildebrand has noted that "plain un-ornamented glass, when seen from the exterior in typical daylight conditions, is opaque; therefore the occupant within the building cannot be seen from outside." From within Cheney House, he observes, the "screening characteristic" of its windows gives the sense "that one is hidden in the dark recesses behind the foliage and the branches of a grove."[13]

Cheney House windows. Photograph by Richard Guy Wilson.

Belknap Allen added an anecdote about Wright that casts further doubt on her testimony. She states that he appeared on her family's doorstep one Sunday morning to ask for a cup of cream and was accosted by her mother, who shouted, "I would not tarnish the Sabbath day by giving you cream. You who are breaking the Ten Commandments every day of the week." No explanation is offered for why Wright, who lived a half mile away and claimed to know very few of his neighbors, "came over" to the Belknaps on a Sunday morning to ask for a cup of cream. Such stories have the effect of also leaving Belknap Allen's flattering description of Mamah Borthwick in doubt: "Mrs. Cheney was a very beautiful lady, sleek, always moving with grace and charm. We would watch her play hide-and-seek with her two children, Martha and John, hiding behind the trees in their yard. The baby would watch from her buggy. To me she was like a Greek goddess."[14]

Practical limitations constrained Borthwick and Wright's interaction with one another while the house was being designed and built. She lived in a crowded, rented house. His household consisted of his wife, their newborn, and five older children. His hectic schedule required juggling the Cheney House project with completing the ambitious Darwin Martin House and the huge Larkin Building in Buffalo. Nevertheless, the Cheney construction progressed rapidly. By early November 1904, the house was finished.

Within days, Borthwick found an opportunity to show it off to her Kappa Alpha Theta sisters, who had arrived in Chicago for the big Minnesota–Northwestern football game. Since nearly all of them were staying downtown, they agreed to get together for lunch at the Marshall Field's Tea Room. Access from Oak Park was relatively easy. Borthwick could ride the L to the Loop, disembark at Lake Street, and step onto a cable car as it headed south toward the giant department store. A fast-disappearing relic of the previous century, the cable car provided an open-air view of the street where, according to the *Kappa Alpha Theta Journal*, the Minnesota football fans had made their presence known. The school's gold and maroon colors adorned street signs all the way to the clock jutting out from the Marshall Field's building. Upon entering the Tea Room, Borthwick found it filled with no fewer than fifty of her Theta friends at tables. Undaunted, she invited all of them to her new house for tea the following Saturday. Those who accepted tested the house's capacity. According to the *Journal*, it passed with flying colors.[15]

Another gathering is likely to have mattered more to her: on New Year's Eve, Mamah and Edwin hosted thirty people at a housewarming party with music and dancing. The evening almost certainly included the Wrights. The local newspaper reported afterward: "One of the most enjoyable parties given on New Year's Eve was that in the beautiful new home of Mr. and Mrs. Edwin H. Cheney, 624 [*sic*] East Avenue, where they entertained thirty of their friends at a dancing party. Just before twelve, the guests were seated around a glowing grate fire and refreshments were served. At the stroke of twelve many good wishes for the New Year were expressed and the orchestra commenced to play 'America,' when everyone stood and joined in the song."[16]

As Americans often did at the time, they welcomed the New Year patriotically by singing what for many is a more melodic tune than the official national anthem. The atmosphere of cheery optimism and goodwill may have served to mask a subtle level of communication between two of the participants. We cannot know how far their relationship had progressed at this point from their initial "electrical" encounter, but at the stroke of midnight on January 1, 1905, amid the party's celebratory embraces and congratulations, who can say what passed between them?

CHAPTER II

MODERN DRAMA

Borthwick began 1905 in her new house, newly pregnant with her second child, and preoccupied with projects like the Oak Park French Club and its study of French drama. On March 11, she hosted a regular meeting of the club for a reading of *Le Verre D'eau*, the 1840 play by Eugène Scribe, in preparation for seeing it performed in Chicago's Steinway Hall. Typical of Scribe's well-paced, superficial plays, it was not a work to be taken seriously. Borthwick loved the theater but seems to have limited herself to its lighter side, as exemplified by Scribe, master of the opéra comique, a forerunner of vaudeville. In the words of one critic, "His best play, whatever it may be, was a plot and nothing more, a story in action, so artfully articulated that it kept the spectators guessing until the final fall of the curtain—and never caused them to think after they had left the theater."[1]

Borthwick's tastes seem to have changed in 1905: she abandoned the frivolity of Scribe and immersed herself in reading and translating modern European drama. Her new interest in plays with complex characters may indicate that her relationship with Wright was growing and, with it, her disillusionment with marriage. The change also happens to coincide with a landmark event in American theater history. At Powers' Theatre in Chicago on April 27, 1905, Ethel Barrymore debuted in Henrik Ibsen's *A Doll's House*. The twenty-five-year-old Barrymore had already achieved international acclaim. In London she had even received a sincere wedding proposal from a besotted Winston Churchill. It is difficult to imagine that the theater-loving Mamah Borthwick would have passed up the chance to see Barrymore in *A Doll's House*.

The play affected nearly everyone who saw it.[2] Its final scene, in which the heroine Nora leaves her husband and children, was a dramatic departure from the norms of respectable Western society, and one can imagine its complicated effect on a woman unhappy in her own marriage and in love with another man. One wonders if Borthwick could hear herself in Nora's blunt remark to her husband, Torvald: "You do not understand me and I have never understood you."

The play challenged the traditional notion that a woman's self-fulfillment should come only from her roles as wife and mother. The final argument between Nora and Torvald presaged Borthwick's coming conundrum.

TORVALD: It's exasperating! Can you forsake your holiest duties in this way?
NORA: What do you call my holiest duties?
TORVALD: Do you ask me that? Your duties to your husband and your children!
NORA: I have other duties equally sacred.
TORVALD: Impossible! What duties do you mean?
NORA: My duties toward myself.
TORVALD: Before all else you are a wife and a mother.
NORA: That I no longer believe. I think that before all else I am a human being, just as much as you are—or, at least, I will try to become one.

A Doll's House launched a new era in theater history with a bang when it premiered in Norway in 1879. Nora slams the door in the final scene when she walks out on Torvald, having come to realize that he and her father have always treated her as a possession. Despite his entreaties, she tells him that to repair their marriage would take "the greatest miracle of them all." The play had an international cultural impact: a heroine leaving her husband and children was an unthinkable ending. The door slam was—eventually—heard around the world.

And yet the play got off to a slow start in Europe. Theaters in Berlin refused to even stage it as long as it involved a mother leaving her children. In order for his play to be performed in Germany, Ibsen agreed to a drastic alteration of its final scene, a "happy ending" in which Nora surrenders and stays home. He called the change "a barbaric act of violence." Eventually the original was restored, but not before the altered play had reached American shores. In the late nineteenth century, the watered-down version was what many Americans saw. The veteran actor Minnie Maddern Fiske performed the original a few times on the American stage, but she was too old to have much impact. Having performed the original "unhappy" ending in Chicago, Ethel Barrymore is credited with drawing attention to A Doll's House in America, especially the attention of American feminists.[3]

Chicago's professional critics were modestly approving, but to the audiences, Barrymore was a sensation, with curtain calls after every act, at least seven at the end. Perhaps the play's impact explains the fact that within a year the Chicago area saw a burst of interest in the study of modern drama by women's groups. Many of them read and discussed the works of the European playwrights who had followed Ibsen's lead in their portrayals of modern women. In line with this new fashion, and perhaps for her own private reasons, Borthwick too began reading modern drama.

In March 1905, Wright left for Japan with his clients Mr. and Mrs. Ward Willits. It did not take much for them to persuade him to accompany them. He was exhausted and in need of a reprieve from his workload as well as keen to see Japan. Mr. and Mrs. Willits also invited Catherine Wright. It has been suggested that they did so to help Wright's troubled marriage, but if that is the case, it was too early for Borthwick to have been the source of the problem. Wright was, however, growing distant from his wife, whose willingness to leave her six children for three months (the youngest was aged barely a year and a half) is indicative of how desperate she must have become to salvage their marriage.

It was the first of many trips Wright would make to Japan. His early interest in Japanese prints and aesthetics appears to have been inspired by the Japanese exhibits in the 1893 World's Fair and the St. Louis Exposition in 1904. The prints' bold flat planes, subtle color combinations, and unusual perspectives appealed to his instincts. Like other artists drawn to the Japanese aesthetic, Wright acknowledged that Japan's art and design had long been more "modern" than their Western counterparts.

While there, he put his time to good use. Ukiyo-e prints could still be purchased at a reasonable cost, allowing him to make major strides in building what became a formidable collection. Equally important was his wide-ranging exploration of Japanese landscape and architecture, recorded in his photographs. The trip appears to have also benefited his marriage. Although Catherine missed her children, she gained an admiration for Japanese culture. Her presentation to the Nineteenth Century Club after their return in April featured a model of a Japanese house. But in the view of many who heard her, the real theme was her husband, whom she openly admired. For his part, Wright felt refreshed and energized, ready to tackle the projects that awaited him when a new commission unexpectedly presented itself in Oak Park.

On the night of June 6, a fierce storm broke over the area. Lightning struck the wooden spire of the Unitarian church, setting it on fire. By daylight it was gone. When word of the disaster reached Wright, he hurried the half mile down Kenilworth Avenue to where the church once stood. There, Rodney Johonnot, the pastor, was gazing dumbstruck at the smoking ruins. Wright promptly offered to design a new church. Providence smiled regularly on him in those years. The new church, Unity Temple, is widely acknowledged as one of his masterpieces.

Things were not going as well for Edwin Cheney. No sooner had he begun to enjoy his new home than a proposal surfaced for a new hospital to be built very near the Fair Oaks neighborhood. He joined his prosperous neighbors in opposing it, attending meetings and signing a petition in opposition to what many saw as a public good. Stating that he had paid a great deal for his new home and did not intend to see it depreciate, he agreed with the petition's objections to the prospect of the "sights and sounds and smells" of a hospital next to his neighborhood, which it described as being "principally for residents of the better class." (Suburbs that had grown up around prisons or hospitals were considered lower class.) As the controversy over the planned hospital heated up, Cheney learned that his father had become seriously ill. He rushed out to Los Angeles, where his parents were living, and arrived just in time to see his father die.

His wife remained in Oak Park and despite her pregnancy kept her membership in the Westward Ho Golf Club. Her pregnancy may eventually have prevented her from actively playing golf, but the clubhouse would have been a place to relax and meet people, including Wright. She and Cheney were also members of the tennis club in River Forest, as were the Wrights. The two couples were often seen together at its parties. They socialized in other settings as well long after Cheney House was completed.

Contrasting worlds competed for Borthwick's time and attention. While the needs of the two children and her family filled her life, Wright's world of ideas, designs, and creativity drew her in. Unity Temple alone provided a spectacular demonstration of his gifts. As its massive, concrete walls were poured into forms, it resembled a dark fortress rising. Upon completion, the intimacy and ethereal quality of the interior space defied all expectations. Compared with Wright's massive Larkin Building in Buffalo, the church has an atmosphere of sanctity, a quality that Wright and Borthwick both took seriously. Their shared interest in the sacred and its manifestations would become evident in 1910 with their pilgrimage to the Passion play at Oberammergau in Bavaria, Germany.

Unity Temple was plagued by repeated cost overruns and unconscionable delays, mostly owing to Wright's poor planning and management. He juggled too many commitments and allowed himself to be distracted. Not until fall 1909 would Unity Temple finally be dedicated.

In September 1905, Borthwick gave birth to her daughter, Martha, named after Martha (Mattie) Chadbourne, now Brown, who by then lived in Boulder with her husband and two children. The women missed one another and made plans to spend the following summer together at a Chadbourne family property on the coast of Maine. It's unknown whether she expected or wanted Edwin to join her. Always busy and rising in the realms of business, however, he would remain in Chicago through the summer of 1906 without Borthwick.

The specific nature of her unhappiness with Edwin Cheney remains unclear. The few testimonies we have are complimentary; even Wright praised his gentlemanly behavior. In his formal divorce filing in 1911, Cheney sued only for desertion, not for the more devastating charge of infidelity. But the contrast he presented to a dynamo like Wright must have worked against him, underscoring for Borthwick the reasons she had put off marrying him in the first place.

"Marriage Basis of Trouble. William Norman Guthrie Says Its Purpose Is to Bring Trials and Tribulations." In early 1905, the headline in the *Chicago Tribune* summed up the message of the guest lecturer at Chicago's All Souls' Church, overseen by Wright's uncle, Jenkin Lloyd Jones. One of the best-known ministers in Chicago, "Uncle Jenck," as Wright knew him, had invited his friend William Norman Guthrie to give a series of lectures while they both served on the faculty of the University of Chicago Extension. Like Uncle Jenck, Guthrie had a talent for spoken performance, a formidable intellect, and abundant energy. Both were popular public lecturers for the university in the early 1900s. Their topics sometimes overlapped, as in the case of the subject of modern drama, but Guthrie had standing both in the academy and as a minister. A professor of comparative literature, he did not patronize his audiences when delivering his university-caliber lectures on modern drama.

His speaking style, however, typical of the oratory of the times, was more in keeping with the stage than the classroom. Chicago poet and critic Alice

Monroe called it "the old school, orotund, gesticulatory style." In an era when linguistic flourishes and erudite digressions were all part of the entertainment, ministers like Guthrie and Jenkin Lloyd Jones rose to the top ranks of their profession through a combination of charisma and spellbinding sermons. Lloyd Jones's sermon lauding Ibsen's *A Doll's House* became well known beyond Chicago. He delivered it multiple times, all across the Midwest. Several women went on record to say it changed their lives. Further, his commentary on Ibsen's *An Enemy of the People*, delivered downtown at the Fine Arts Building in November 1901, burnished his reputation for opposing conventional wisdom and speaking "truth against the world."[4]

Guthrie's 1905 lecture on marriage was deliberately provocative. He contended that marriage was a necessary sacrifice made for the higher purpose of having children. It was not intended to make men and women happy, he said, but to bring them an abundance of trials and tribulations as they suffer for their children.

In declaring that marriage was a cross to be borne on behalf of children, Guthrie gave voice to a cultural shift taking place concerning the importance of childhood. The idealization of a sheltered, nurtured childhood was growing and with it, an elevation of the importance of parenthood.[5] In this light, deserting one's spouse and children seemed a heinous crime.

Although Guthrie would eventually become an important influence for Wright and Borthwick, they are not likely to have welcomed his ideas about marriage. Decrying the "doctrine of the flesh," he declared: "Through trouble and sacrifice for the offspring are man's courage, intelligence, strength, and beauty developed." Women, he insisted, should "pretend" to be subservient to their husbands: "Men and women are equal, but women should not flaunt their equality before the man. . . . Men always recognize the superiority of the woman who goes about her duties pretending obedience to her husband as to a master. Men must be allowed to believe that they are the masters, and those women are wise who know it."[6]

The well-educated, multilingual Guthrie could sound like a progressive in one lecture and like a thundering fundamentalist in another, but overall, his reputation was of someone who blended traditional values with a modern outlook.[7] His anachronistic lectures on marriage stood in contrast to his sophisticated talks on modern drama. It was this latter topic that attracted Borthwick, particularly when Guthrie agreed to deliver a series of lectures in Oak Park in the coming year. She prepared by reading and translating the works of the

German playwright Gerhart Hauptmann, who had become her favorite. Virtually unknown to Americans at the time, Hauptmann would win the Nobel Prize for Literature in 1912.

On November 21, 1905, a group of reporters spilled out of an elevator on the top floor of Chicago's Congress Plaza Hotel and milled about until they saw a man at the end of the hall guarding the door of actress Sarah Bernhardt's apartment. Eager for their scheduled interview, they rushed down the hall, knowing she would be good for a story. With a genius for publicity and self-promotion that set a high bar for everyone in her profession, the sixty-one-year-old Bernhardt was a global superstar. Her announcement in 1905 that she would make a "farewell tour" of America, stopping early in Chicago, had set the city abuzz in anticipation. Even her arrival at the LaSalle Street station on a train christened the Bernhardt Special had been a theatrical production. Walking forward along the train to thank the engineer, she caused near pandemonium while the police and the entire French consulate pressed back against the reporters. Then, taking the hand of the engineer, she blew kisses to the crowd, looked aloft, and exclaimed, "Ah, zees is ze great Chicago!"

Famous for her use of body language on stage, Bernhardt often performed as the eponymous star of *Camille*, the stage adaptation of the novel by Alexandre Dumas *fils* that became derided as a stereotype of melodrama. "Camille's frailness, her weakness, was so great that the slightest exertion brought perspiration to hands and brow, her struggle for breath," wrote one breathless Chicago critic. "It was the triumph of art—of an art the like of which comes rarely to inspire and benefit mankind."[8] In the Congress Plaza Hotel, the reporters entered her apartment to find themselves in a hallway crowded with steamer trunks and crates. Finally entering a bright living room with a view of the lake, they found her seated at a small table before the windows. She was having lunch.

"Come, come close," she cried, and motioned to her attendants to arrange seats. "Non . . . Non. Non, nonnn!" she exclaimed as the waiter tried to take away a saucer of ice cream. Facing about and resting her chin upon her arms on the back of the chair, she gazed inquiringly at the reporters, one of whom asked her to name her favorite American playwright.

"I think that you have made tremendous progress in the last twenty years, both in writing and producing the drama, but France is still superior to the

United States in these things. Of your American playwrights, I should think Hauptmann is good."

The reporter gently suggested that Hauptmann was German. Madame Bernhardt laughed at her mistake. "Why do you not play more problem plays?" he asked, referring to modern drama.

"Because their parts are generally too small for what the public expects of Bernhardt," she replied. "I do play some of them though."[9]

This exchange appeared in Chicago newspapers the next day with unflattering hints at Bernhardt's age. Bernhardt's mention of Gerhart Hauptmann, mistaken nationality aside, may have been the first time many of the article's readers would have seen the name—but it would have already been familiar to Borthwick. It is likely that, years earlier, as a girl with a passion for the theater and acting, she knew of and probably admired the famous Bernhardt too. But in 1905 the aging actress's ignorance of modern drama testified to how theatrical styles were changing. It would fall to the next generation of actresses, the Ethel Barrymores, to depict contemporary women on the stage.

Reverend William Norman Guthrie appreciated modern drama as a source of commentary, but he used it primarily to dispense moral instruction. He especially valued the plays that supported his message: "It is the human soul, not the circumstances of life, that makes our dignity."[10] It may have been through his Uncle Jenck that Wright first met Guthrie, thereby leading to Guthrie's invitation to deliver lectures on modern drama in Oak Park. Guthrie had become better known for his lectures on the subject following Ethel Barrymore's performance at Powers' Theatre. The Oak Park community was eager to hear him speak, but his busy schedule and involvement in his own parish out in Berkeley, California, kept him from appearing in Oak Park until early 1907. In announcing the delay, the local newspaper opined that the Oak Park female audience would require more time to prepare anyway.

Feeling that Mr. Guthrie would find a somewhat barren field unless special efforts were made to cultivate ideas on this rather difficult subject, these ladies have arranged to hold meetings in the fall in preparation for his course. The dramatists upon whom he will lecture are Ibsen, Hauptmann, Sudermann, Maeterlinck, Rostand, d'Annunzio, Echegaray, Hovey, Phillips and Yeats, ten in all. Each of these subjects has been assigned to some member of the class, who will make a thorough study of it and ask whatever friends she chooses to assist her.[11]

The study groups began to form in early 1906. Borthwick volunteered to cochair one on Gerhart Hauptmann with Edith Winslow, who, as noted in chapter 2, lived in a house designed by Wright. Borthwick threw herself into the project by translating Hauptmann's plays. Her study group was such a success that by November seventy-five women crowded into the lecture room at the Scoville Institute to hear her discuss and read from her translation of Hauptmann's *Der arme Heinrich* (*Poor Henry*).

It is a curious play for her to have chosen, a dark, fable-like story drawn from German medieval literature about a man who can only be saved from a fatal illness by the sacrifice of a young virgin. A great success when it debuted in Vienna in 1902, it ends happily, an unusual outcome for a play by Hauptmann. Her choice suggests that Borthwick was closely following cultural trends in modern Germany even though the play itself reflected the society's fascination with its medieval past. She may also have been aware that Hauptmann wrote it amid a family crisis that caused him to leave his wife and remarry.

Soon after her presentation on *Der arme Heinrich*, Kappa Alpha Theta asked her to write a report for its national journal on the induction of a new chapter at Washington University in St. Louis. It was undoubtedly a welcome distraction for her. Alumnae from chapters around the country converged on St. Louis for three days of celebration. Her report to the sorority extolled the merits of the new initiates, especially their patience and determination. Having learned that the new chapter had waited seven years for their application to be approved by the national sorority, she concluded her article with the observation that "a house that could withstand the winds and rains of seven years is certainly not built on sands."[12] The irony was surely not lost on her, now in her seventh year of marriage. She lived with a man she didn't love in a house designed by one she did.

She left St. Louis for Chicago on December 3, 1906. As her train bore northeast away from a lowering afternoon sun, Wright would probably have been engaging in his late afternoon routine of riding his black stallion, Kano, in the chilly air north of Oak Park.[13] At the age of thirty-nine, the prospect of reaching forty appalled him. What better way to respond to the nagging intimations of aging than to gallop across the remaining open stretches of prairie? He also apparently wanted to get away from home. He felt trapped in his marriage to Catherine. His architectural practice was taking off, with more than a dozen commissions each year. The pace was becoming exhausting and exhilarating, leaving him with little time or patience for the day-to-day domestic concerns that absorbed Catherine.

If his wife seemed to live in another world, so did his rival, Edwin Cheney. The managing director of three companies, Cheney had the abilities of a manager, not a creator. Still, he treated his wife well, and it is likely that when she arrived at Chicago's Dearborn Station, he was there to greet her in his Cadillac touring car. Cheney and Wright had something in common in their love of cars. Cheney was one of the early adopters of cars in Oak Park, a suburb that rapidly outpaced all others in car ownership. Nothing would have pleased him more than to drive his wife home from the station on the thoroughfare of Michigan Avenue along the tall buildings facing the lake, a vista that, in the words of historian Thomas Schlereth, represented "Chicago bravado in the era when it became the most American of American cities. The robust and outgoing character . . . a panoply of color, texture, and scale . . . solid yet boisterous, confident yet brassy."[14]

Where Michigan Avenue narrowed toward Randolph Street, horse-drawn wagons became more numerous. Turning west along the line of the Lake Street Elevated Railway Company, the L, the straight streets made for an easy drive all the way to Oak Park. Whatever discomfort she may have felt with Edwin would have been dispelled by the reunion with her children, Martha and John; her five-year-old niece, Jessie; and her sister Lizzie. Neighbors may have viewed her as a self-indulgent "New Woman" who used her role in her sorority as an excuse to escape her family responsibilities, but she had made sure her children were well cared-for in her absence. Their aunt Lizzie was with them, along with a forty-year-old Canadian nanny, Hanna Swain, and a twenty-two-year-old Swedish servant, Elnor Allard. The standard story, that she was indifferent to her children and too interested in intellectual pursuits and Wright to attend to them, finds no support in the record.[15] She had spent that summer on the coast of Maine with Mattie Chadbourne and her children. It had been a chance for them to introduce their three-year-old sons to one another, the boys having been born only a month apart.

That Borthwick loved her children and felt her familial obligations keenly seems clear, but equally clear is that by the end of 1906 she was helplessly drawn to the charismatic Wright, just as unhappy in his own marriage. We cannot know for certain what Borthwick saw in Wright. She had yet to develop her own sense of high purpose and may have been captivated by his optimism about the ability of art and architecture to reshape modern society. Their relationship seems to have drawn special strength from their idealism and sense of a spiritual connection, fueled in part by their love of poetry (Tennyson, Browning, and later Blake). To all appearances, however, their relationship had not yet been consummated in 1906. Both were frustrated in their marriages, but they would have found little opportunity to be alone. Given his frenetic work schedule, encounters between them were unlikely to have gone beyond secret conversations, embraces, and telephone calls.

The whirl of holiday planning and shopping had begun, and the downtown streets became crowded with shoppers. The *Inter Ocean* proclaimed, "Chicago has never seen such a Christmas bedlam."[16] Even so, New Year's Eve ranked equally with Christmas as an important holiday in the first decade of the 1900s. An aura of optimism about the dawn of a new century led many to usher in the New Year with enthusiasm matching that of their ebullient president, Theodore Roosevelt.

On the night of January 8, 1907, Mamah Borthwick made the cold, fifteen-minute walk from her home to the Scoville Institute, its brightly lit windows trimmed with the remaining holiday decorations to greet the night's guest speaker, William Norman Guthrie. In anticipation of his lecture series on what Guthrie called "The Contemporary Poetic Drama," she and others in the women's study group had been discussing his recommended readings. In the vestibule, hallway, and wide stairwell, people were making their way to the lecture room on the second floor to find good seats.

As a member of the University Extension Lecture Committee, Borthwick was given the role of greeting the speaker in a room adjoining the lecture hall. Until then, she had not encountered his strong personality. The tall, dark, thirty-eight-year-old Guthrie was renowned as an orator who fixed his listeners with piercing brown eyes. This was his first appearance in Oak Park, a community that would come to know and admire him. His lectures on modern drama had been heavily promoted with the assistance of his employer, the University of Chicago. He had a flair for the dramatic and the instincts of an actor. With the committee chair, Minna Ferrell Johnson, he entered the lecture hall and sat with her on the platform. After she stood and introduced him, he strode to the podium, elaborately thanked the committee, and took command.

"Realistic drama is architectural, not filigree," he began. "But there is at the same time tremendous poetic power in plays where ugly stuff—crude, unspoiled, naked human stuff—is used, since divine things do not come from above but grow up out of the ground, and we must look today for the ideal in the real."[17]

It was his standard beginning, allowing him to prepare the audience for the potentially offensive content of modern drama. His subject that evening was simply titled "Ibsen." The audience, made up almost entirely of women, reflected the observation by a contemporary observer that "it has been left to the drama of our own day to depict woman in a new aspect."[18] Whatever influence the feminist literature of the time may have exerted on her, Borthwick appears to have begun to question the obligations of marriage at a time when she was exposed to the controversial depictions of marital dilemmas in the new, modern dramas.

Her interest in modern drama, specifically Hauptmann, provides a hint about Borthwick's frame of mind at this stage in her relationship with Wright. She appears to have been more drawn to the psychological tension and symbolism in Hauptmann's plays than to his sociological and politically oriented work, and Hauptmann's *Einsame Menschen* (*Lonely Lives*) echoed her own predicament. It is about an idealistic married man and unmarried woman whose love is doomed by family and marital obligations. On his recommended reading list of Hauptmann plays, Guthrie placed *Lonely Lives* at the top. The anarchist-feminist activist, writer, and lecturer Emma Goldman wrote about *Lonely Lives* in a 1914 treatise on the modern drama: "What significance in the bitter truth that those who struggle for an ideal, those who attempt to cut themselves loose from the old, from the thousand fetters that hold them down, are doomed to lonely lives!"[19]

Borthwick's presentation on Hauptmann in November had been a success, so she followed up with another in February. *Oak Leaves* described it as "her own translation of certain plays [by Hauptmann] which have not previously been given in English."[20] It can be assumed she was reading other literature as well, but she appears to have missed a distinctive voice from Europe. As described in the *Chicago Tribune* just three days after Ethel Barrymore performed in *A Doll's House*, the feminist Ellen Key, widely published in Germany, had become a sensation there:

[Key is] talked about, written about, and gossiped about more than any other woman in years. Her photographs have sprung up magically in the magazines, illustrated papers, and shop window and postcard likenesses of her are hawked about the streets as if she were a royal personage. Miss Key is 55 years old. Her "newer ethics," as far as concern the married state, are founded upon two main ideas. She advocates first of all easier divorce for men and women, who, after vowing to love, cherish, and obey, find that they drew a blank in the matrimonial lottery. She would make it not only possible but absolutely legal for married couples to divorce themselves by mere mutual agreement or by this or desire of either husband or wife. She considers it criminal for human law to compel people to live together as man and wife who do not in their hearts cherish the fullest affection and trust for each other. "Facilitate divorce" is her remedy for much of the world's marital unhappiness.[21]

It was a revolutionary argument for the time. Ellen Key was to become a force in Borthwick's life whose influence was second only to Frank Lloyd Wright. Yet if the *Tribune* article made her aware of Key, it did not lead her directly to her writings. That would come later at a pivotal moment.

CHAPTER 12

⟳

LUNCH AT
MARSHALL FIELD'S

Every third Thursday of the month, Borthwick lunched with Kappa Alpha
Theta alumnae at the Marshall Field's Tea Room. Few venues in Chicago
could match it for elegance and style. Featuring a bright, two-story atrium
with a marble fountain, it demonstrated the marketing genius of Harry
Gordon Selfridge before he immigrated to London. Women who preferred to
shop under Marshall Field's Tiffany favrile glass ceiling considered its Tea
Room (christened the Walnut Room in 1937) to be the premier lunch spot
in Chicago. Its atmosphere rivaled that of Selfridge's Palm Court restaurant
in London.

One of the women Borthwick regularly met there was Alice Wadsworth.[1]
She and Alice had joined Kappa Alpha Theta together and became closer
when their fathers, both of whom had come to Chicago from Iowa, died
within months of one another. Wadsworth had been secretary of Theta's
national Grand Council. She was to be one of several speakers on the program
at the closing banquet of the national convention in July. Borthwick was to be
the toastmistress of the banquet, a sign of the esteem in which the sorority
held her. Wadsworth is likely to have used one of their lunches to consult with
Borthwick about the banquet and her planned remarks, on the subject of
"The New Woman and the Old." The program listed each speaker along with
a quotation of her choosing. Wadsworth had chosen a line from the Jacobean
farce *The Noble Gentleman*.

> Nothing is thought rare
> Which is not new and follow'd, yet we know
> That what was worn some twenty years ago,
> Comes into grace again.[2]

Marshall Field's Tea Room, ca. 1908. Chicago History Museum, DN-0007502.

Her remarks were not recorded, but she may well have been speaking more or less directly about the sorority's growing generational divide. The "first generation" of women in Theta were concerned with expanding opportunities for women in education, developing a strong national organization, and maintaining high standards for membership. The "second generation" was interested in social events and recreation, with less focus on the founding purposes. Having entered the sorority together in 1893, Borthwick and Wadsworth may have felt that they represented a transition between the two generations. While the intergenerational tensions had not yet caused an open rift in the sorority, they had become apparent by 1907.[3]

Wadsworth hailed from one of the oldest families of Chicago, a fact that might have served as her entry point for remarks about old versus new. And yet the quote she selected, essentially a put-down of passing fashion, suggests she may have felt on the defensive with her younger peers. While not necessarily an object of criticism, the New Woman was for Wadsworth a cause for concern. Her generation felt that Theta was in danger of compromising its standards and losing its higher purpose.

Their lunch, while not heavy, had been selected from a menu that included the famous "Mrs. Hering's Chicken Pot Pie." Hering, who may even have dropped by their table to say hello, had been the key to the success of the Tea Room from the beginning. She was still its manager; her talent having been spotted by Selfridge years earlier. With the aim of attracting upper-middle-class women to have lunch at the Tea Room, she included selections of wine and sherry on the menu. This drew stern disapproval from bastions of male authority who found it unsettling that middle-class women, having already achieved greater liberty and independence, should presume to drink alcohol in public without a man present.

Establishments like the Tea Room were considered the chief offenders. They allowed a woman to order a glass of wine or sherry as casually as a man might order liquor in a saloon. This simply would not do, according to Reverend Frederick E. Hopkins of Chicago's Pilgrim Congregational Church, who equated this behavior with that of a "public woman" whose body was for sale. After conducting a month-long public campaign against the practice, he launched raids on establishments like Marshall Field's, trying to catch female tipplers in the act. His intrusions reflected the fact that the freedoms enjoyed by women like Borthwick had become disconcerting for members of the conservative religious establishment who warned against the decay of home life and the spread of drunken hedonism. Cultural historian Emily Remus summarized the attitude: "Allegedly, by indulging in improper public pleasures, the tippling lady revealed herself as unwomanly, selfish, and reckless with her purse and her body."[4]

Mamah and her friends did not see themselves as tippling ladies and might have reacted with anything ranging from amusement to outrage if Reverend Hopkins had burst in on one of their Marshall Field's luncheons. Still, more moderate churchgoers shared some of the views of extremists like Hopkins and were uneasy with the "moral implications" of the freedoms that were now bestowed on married women. To be absent from their families on a casual, daily basis just to go shopping struck many as selfish and self-indulgent.

Borthwick's double life left her increasingly out of phase with her friends in Kappa Alpha Theta. While she dined with them in post-Victorian respectability at Marshall Field's, she craved time alone with a man who was not her husband. She knew that they would reject her out of hand if they discovered her secret. Her best hope lay in obtaining a divorce from Edwin and in Frank obtaining one from Catherine, a course that would prove difficult under the best of circumstances.

Rev. Frederick E.
Hopkins. Redpath
Chautauqua Collection,
University of Iowa
Special Collections.

That year, the Census Bureau conducted a major research project on divorce in America. Commissioned by Congress with the aim of making divorce law more uniform, it produced a richly detailed report with quotable statistics that provoked hand-wringing sermons across the nation about the rising divorce rate. Newspaper articles made much of the census report and President Roosevelt's expression of concern about "the divorce question."

Women filed most of the suits for divorce and yet were also the ones most often viewed as the source of the problem. Stories about the divorces of prominent people featured photographs of wives but rarely of husbands. The reasons given by a woman for divorce were the butt of jokes or otherwise made to seem strange, freakish, or illegitimate.[5]

Notwithstanding the *Chicago Tribune's* complaint that the city was the "divorce center of the nation,"[6] divorces were not easy to obtain. Court judges

would deny a divorce application if in any way it appeared to be the result
of cooperation by the divorcing couple. The catch-22 argument: if a couple
could cooperate enough to file for divorce, they could go right on cooperating
in marriage. As Wright would discover, to his regret, a woman could exercise
power in the question of divorce by simply refusing to grant one, no matter
how much her husband wanted it, as long as she gave him no legal basis for
ending the marriage.

Society offered no practical solution to Borthwick's predicament. The silver chain of Theta womanhood in which she had pledged to be a link now
loomed large. She would have dreaded the prospect of social disapproval from
the sisterhood of Kappa Alpha Theta, especially that of the older women who
had helped build the sorority. That summer it held its national convention at
the Chicago Beach Hotel. Located on the edge of South Side Chicago's beach-
front parkland, landscaped with flowers down to the water's edge, the hotel
was not far from the neighborhood where they had convened in 1893. At that
time, she had been a new face in the crowd. Now, she stood in the welcoming committee with the Thetas from Northwestern University. As the toastmistress of the closing banquet, she introduced each speaker and kept the
proceedings going with lively precision. At the end, she encouraged different
chapters to shout out their school yells. The Theta magazine observed, "The
banquet was well served and the toast program, which followed, was one of
the best that we have ever listened to. Mrs. Cheney of the Chicago alumnae
chapter was a charming toastmistress and carried her honors well."

Prominent in the national sorority, charming as an Oak Park hostess, lively
in intellectual conversation, Borthwick must have made Catherine Wright feel
at a disadvantage. The latter remarked of her rival years later, "I never felt I
breathed the same air as she did." Borthwick does not seem, however, like
the kind of person who tried to make others feel inferior. She is likely to have
treated Catherine Wright with respect, and their joint presentation on Goethe
at the Scoville Institute suggests the women were on friendly terms, before the
storm broke. It is interesting to note that this is one of the few times Wright
participated in the Study Group, even though her mother-in-law, Anna Lloyd
Jones Wright, was much involved.

They titled their presentation "The Life and Short Poems of Goethe." Catherine's part probably involved giving an account of Goethe's life, followed by
Mamah's reading and discussion of his poetry. They encouraged attendees to
purchase a twenty-five-cent copy of Guthrie's "Modern Poet Prophets" even
though there was relatively little about Goethe in the pamphlet. Why Catherine

Wright agreed to this rare involvement in the Study Group is a mystery. Borthwick's motives in making the effort were clearly mixed, since this gesture of friendship also created an excuse to see Frank Lloyd Wright whenever she visited his wife. During the previous month, Borthwick had finally become a member of the Nineteenth Century Club, electing to join the club's Literature and Home Economics Departments. Frank Lloyd Wright's wife and mother were already members of both.[7] When she joined the club, it is unlikely that she had immediate plans to leave Oak Park, but in less than a year everything would change.

On November 6, 1907, the day before Mamah and Catherine gave their presentation, Frank Lloyd Wright and ninety other men crowded into an artist's studio in the Fine Arts Building. It was a large loft with high walls and bright windows belonging to the artist Ralph Clarkson. Unframed canvases and art works had been shoved up against the walls, as was often done when Clarkson hosted meetings. Many in the group were the artists and writers known collectively as the "Little Room," so named for the space where they often met. The members included the writer Hamlin Garland, who had taken it upon himself to issue the invitations for the meeting. Garland quieted everyone and asked them to recognize Harry Pratt Judson, president of the University of Chicago. By unanimous consent, they made Judson the chairman of the meeting. The men's purpose was to organize a new arts club for Chicago.

Near the back of the room, a dark-haired, bearded man moved further to the rear. He was Henry Blake Fuller, author of the novel *The Cliff Dwellers*, which many considered to be a good name for the new club. The irony was not lost on Fuller, whose novel depicted an elite group in Chicago in an unflattering way. He had been a leading member of the Little Room arts club until Garland took it over and essentially hijacked it for his own purposes. A sulky Fuller could only look on helplessly as several prominent businessmen joined the meeting. He believed Garland was betraying the whole idea of the Little Room club by including businessmen and other non-arts professionals. In his view, the inclusion of crass commercial interests would inevitably compromise the arts. He refused to join what became the Cliff Dwellers Club. Out of respect, they named him a charter member anyway.[8]

Wright, a close friend of Garland's, embraced the idea of including businessmen. To that end, he had persuaded Garland to invite William H. Winslow, whose house Wright had designed in River Forest. The two had also collaborated on the design of a custom printed art book, *The House Beautiful*. Businessmen like Winslow, Wright said, had "unspoiled instincts and untainted minds."

Wright had not joined an organization since 1897, when he had become a charter member of the Chicago Arts and Crafts Society with Jane Addams and others at Hull House. Since then, he had not deigned to join even the Chicago Architectural Club. But joining the Cliff Dwellers was different. It confirmed him as one of Chicago's creative elite and enabled him to rub shoulders with them regularly.

Hamlin Garland once explained that he created the Cliff Dwellers because so many members of the Little Room network had moved away from Chicago. But his ecumenical ambitions, which prompted the inclusion of businessmen, only extended so far: he excluded one of Chicago's most formidable talents, the writer-intellectual Harriet Monroe, because of her sex. She would go on to found *Poetry* magazine and be remembered as a national treasure. Wright, for his part, did not dismiss her. He took her seriously and valued her judgment. When she published a critique of his work in 1907, bluntly finding some of it wanting, he sparred with her in a spirited, respectful exchange of letters.[9]

The prospect of rubbing shoulders with the other Cliff Dwellers appealed to Wright, but it would take more than that to keep him in Chicago. His deteriorating marriage and relationship with Borthwick seem to have made him restless. It was becoming a question of when, not if, he would abandon the city. Beyond the complications of his private life, he craved more than what Chicago offered. The 1893 World's Fair had been invigorating, but since then the arts community, at least parts of it, had become involuted and conservative. The Little Room arts network shriveled as it rejected new member applications from promising avant-garde artists. Louis Sullivan saw his architecture practice decline in the wake of the fair's conservative celebration of Beaux Arts design. The tradition-minded Cliff Dwellers would one day openly reject the modernist Armory Show when it came to the Art Institute.[10] In short, Chicago was atrophying in areas of culture that mattered to Wright. Among the multiple causes of his restlessness in this period, one may have been the antimodern undercurrent.[11] As if to make the point even more sharply, a year later the magnate Harold McCormick briefly considered Wright's proposal for his grand residence on Lake Michigan until his wife, a Rockefeller, expressed a preference for a conventional Italian villa design by Charles Platt. If that was not the last straw for Wright, it must have contributed to his impatience.

Borthwick may have also felt an impulse to leave, but for different reasons. Her joint presentation on Goethe with Catherine Wright had served to underscore her dishonesty. Whatever purpose she may have had in involving herself closely with Catherine, the presentation seems to have added to her resolve to depart. If it had any benefit, it was to draw attention to William Norman Guthrie's forthcoming lecture on Goethe. This proved to be such a success that he had been invited to begin a new lecture series in the fall.

Frank Lloyd Wright and Mamah Borthwick were among Guthrie's most enthusiastic boosters in Oak Park. In February 1908, they placed an advertisement in *Oak Leaves* for his lantern slide lecture on the poet William Blake. Tickets could be obtained from, among others, "Mrs. E. H. Cheney, or reserved by telephone to Mr. Frank Lloyd Wright, Oak Park 53."[12] Obviously they did not fear that the appearance of their names together in a public announcement would start tongues wagging. It was at this time that Borthwick would have begun writing *Woman of the Hour*, expressing her discontent with Edwin Cheney. If she felt her hour was indeed approaching, it would account for her poem's declaration:

> I am going to leave you,
> But do not despair,
> I shall never forget
> That you're here,
> And I'm there.

CHAPTER 13

~~~

WISCONSIN ROAD TRIP

The rising whine of a car engine awakened residents of Oak Park at dawn on February 28, 1908, as Buffalo mechanic George Schuster pulled the throttle wide open on his racecar. The Thomas Flyer soon reached its top speed of sixty miles per hour as he sped down a straight, nearly deserted street. He held first place in the early stage of a sensational auto race around the world, the great New York to Paris Race of 1908. His immediate destination was Rochelle, Illinois, ninety miles away. Eventually, he would reach San Francisco, Alaska, Siberia, and, finally, Paris. Twelve hours later, two more cars roared through Oak Park, a De Dion-Bouton representing France and a forty-five-horsepower Zust representing Italy. The German Protos was not far behind.[1] Sponsored by the *New York Times* and the Paris newspaper *Le Matin*, the race garnered worldwide attention even though some of its major segments were of necessity traversed aboard ships.

Given how undeveloped automobiles were in 1908, not to mention the quality of roads, part of the fascination with the race lay in the outlandishness of the idea that a journey of such length and duration could be made in a car. Nevertheless, the famous racing models that dashed through Oak Park may have sparked envy in Frank Lloyd Wright and may have given urgency to his decision to rent a flashy, yellow Stoddard-Dayton roadster early the following year. During the few months before he returned it to its owner, a Chicagoan named Charley Vail, Wright was caught more than once violating Oak Park speed limits. The image of him cruising around in the "Yellow Devil" during good weather in the spring of 1909 with Mamah Borthwick seated beside him took its place in Oak Park legend.

Car ownership in Oak Park exceeded that of any other Chicago suburb; at least one hundred of its residents owned the coveted machines by 1906.[2]

The president of the Chicago Automobile Club, John Farson, hailed from
Oak Park. He and Wright became the butt of a joke in a burlesque performed
in the community that year. It depicted Farson desperately calling up "Mr.
Frank Lloyd Wright Elsom" to supply a new car to replace the one he had just
wrecked.

Edwin Cheney's Cadillac touring car must have been the envy of the neighborhood in 1906, but car technology was evolving rapidly, with significant
improvements every year. His advertisement for his old Cadillac confirms that
he bought a new car in 1908. The make of the new one is unknown, but it
must have been a touring car capable of carrying four people and their luggage
comfortably. At least that would help explain his willingness to make a road
trip that August with his mother, his wife, and Frank Lloyd Wright.

The trip is unlikely to have been his idea. In all probability it was Borthwick who persuaded him and her mother-in-law that it would be an adventure to drive with Wright to see his projects in Wisconsin, the first being one
known as Rocky Roost. Located in Madison on an islet of Lake Mendota,
the vacation home was owned by Wright's closest childhood friend, Robert
Lamp—"Robie," or "Ruby," as he was known. Wright had unified Lamp's three
previous cabins into one cottage with a second story and wraparound porch.
The four travelers would stay there overnight and then continue to Milwaukee, where they would spend another night before heading home. Altogether,
it would be a round trip of 350 miles.

The journey has been overlooked in the Wright historical literature in terms
of both its significance and the trip's roster. The evidence lies buried in a small
announcement in the *Wisconsin State Journal* of August 18: "A motor party
consisting of Mr. Frank Lloyd Wright, Mr. and Mrs. Edwin Cheney and Mr.
Cheney's mother of Chicago were over Sunday guests at 'Rocky Roost.' They
returned home yesterday by way of Milwaukee."[3]

At last Frank and Mamah could look forward to spending days together
away from Catherine. The latter may have been miffed at being left behind,
but if she had been suspicious, she would not have allowed it to proceed. Only
nine months earlier, she and Mamah had made their joint presentation on
Goethe. Similarly, Edwin Cheney suspected nothing when the party set out.
He was probably too busy driving the car and looking after his mother to
pay much attention to Wright and Borthwick, but putting the two of them
together for three days in vacation-like circumstances was asking for trouble.

Wright's friendship with Robie Lamp had been one of the closest of his life.
In his autobiography, he described their relationship from the age of fourteen

as having been very special. He used "comrade" for especially close friends like Robie Lamp. The only woman he referred to in this way was Borthwick. In introducing her to Robie, he was, in effect, asking for his friend's blessing.

A cross-country trip in a car in 1908 presented a challenge even for an experienced driver. The car race around the world may have made it seem simple by comparison, but the three-day trip was no small feat. The quality of the carmaker and road conditions were critical factors. Since Wright did not have a car, they must have used Cheney's upgraded vehicle, which may have been a Cadillac or similar model, such as a Pearce Arrow or a Packard 30.[4] Manufactured in Detroit, the Packard 30 had more than enough room for four people and their luggage. The Pearce Arrow, manufactured in Buffalo, would have been closer to Wright's heart, but Cheney was a Detroit man.

A comfortable car with upholstered leather, the four-cylinder, sixty-horsepower Packard 30, or its equivalent, cost $4,500 in 1908, a considerable sum at the time. Like all cars, it had to be cranked to start; this posed a slight

1908 Packard 30 Touring Car. Like most cars manufactured in the United States before 1910, the car had right-hand drive with ready access to three gear handles and a squeeze bulb for honking. The canopy had roll-down curtains in case of rain. Courtesy of the National Automotive History Collection, Detroit Public Library.

risk for the unwary if the engine kicked back and caused the crank to strike the person's arm. In 1911, Wright's arm was broken in precisely that way. When cruising on the open road, the Packard ran with a slight clatter. Loud, but not excessively so, it could easily reach thirty miles per hour and had a top speed of forty-five.

The travelers faced the usual risks and annoyances of a flat tire or an overheated engine, but the prevailing worries for any such trip were weather and road conditions. Although the car had a canopy that could be put up in case of rain, mud and dust were the real problems. Most roads beyond city limits were unpaved and best suited for horse-drawn vehicles. Thus, the choice of route was critical. Since he was familiar with the roads as far north as Madison, Wright knew they should take the Elgin Road west to Elgin and Rockford, then north through Janesville. He is likely to have chafed at not being the driver, but Cheney would naturally have taken the wheel of his own vehicle.

If he was not driving, Wright would surely have preferred to sit in the back with Borthwick, however unconventional that might have seemed. Women often sat in the back seat, but Cheney's mother was intrepid enough to have agreed to make the journey and to sit in front beside her son. At the age of sixty-three, Armilla Amanda Cheney was the national treasurer of the Women's Relief Corps. Descended from Puritan ancestors, she had lived in Long Beach, California, since the death of her husband and spent a month every summer in Oak Park with her son and his family.

Perhaps such a seating arrangement was what Borthwick and Wright had in mind all along. No cars in 1908 had a rearview mirror; the driver was blind to passengers in the rear. If Cheney's mother sat in front beside him, the engine and wind noise would have discouraged her from turning around often. All four of them wore "motoring clothes," bulky over-garments that remained a status symbol as long as cars remained scarce and expensive. A woman's light-colored summer driving coat had become a fashion statement that implied car ownership (even if some of its wearers didn't own a car). The coats served a real purpose, however. With goggles and hats, they provided protection on dusty streets and roads. The tall front windscreen on an open car made travel breezy but protected, while the suspension provided a relatively smooth ride on unpaved roads. On their route to Madison, they would have purchased gas from hardware stores and blacksmith shops, making impromptu stops to admire the country and refreshing themselves in the towns.

In Catherine's absence and with Cheney distracted by driving, Borthwick and Wright may have become incautious in how they interacted. It appears that an incident of some kind gave them away. Cheney later indicated that he had become suspicious of their intrigue about a year before Borthwick left him. That would place it around the time of the trip to Rocky Roost, when he could observe them together for three days. What he saw must have concerned him.

Arriving in Madison in the late afternoon on August 15, they drove around to the north side of Lake Mendota and crossed a short causeway to Governor's Island. It was there that Robie Lamp usually met his guests and rowed them in a small skiff to the cottage on Rocky Roost a few hundred yards away. He had a walking disability and used crutches, but it had not prevented him from drilling a well on the little plot of land, even erecting a windmill to provide running water. Before the cottage burned in 1934, it had been a charming, comfortable retreat.

A photograph of Rocky Roost shows the long balcony decorated for a party with Japanese lanterns. From there they could see the sunset reflecting on the water. Perhaps it was at such a moment that Wright confided to Borthwick about how he had come to know Robie in their childhood. When he discovered schoolboys bullying the disabled boy, "unmercifully . . . they were burying

Rocky Roost, ca. 1905. Wisconsin Historical Society, WHS 39339.

him in the fallen leaves until he was all but smothered, wherefrom he would finally emerge, raging, sputtering, and crying," he drove them off. Ever since, they had been fast friends.[5]

The next day, they set out for Milwaukee, a journey of about eighty miles. Starting the car was no simple matter. It involved a sequence of steps that often failed on the first try if, for example, Cheney forgot to adjust the air/gas mixture when he shut off the engine the night before. The main road from Madison to Milwaukee was well maintained. Women rarely drove in those days, but one can imagine the vivacious Borthwick insisting, and the ensuing gleeful shouts punctuated by the clownish honk of the squeezable, rubber bulb horn. As they entered downtown Milwaukee, they would have had to navigate through its dense network of streetcars as they headed for a hotel, most likely the Hotel Pfister, a belle epoch grande dame, or the Plankington House, an old classic. Wright always insisted on a luxury hotel whenever he couldn't mooch an overnight stay with a client.

While the road trip was said to be for the purpose of seeing Wright's project at Rocky Roost, their return route indicates that he had more than that in mind. The fact that they drove east to Milwaukee before heading south is evidence that he wanted to stop and show off one of his finest houses to date. He was known to drop by unexpectedly to look at his houses, which he once referred to as his "children." He had reason to be proud of the Thomas P. Hardy House (built in 1905) in Racine, just south of Milwaukee.[6] Situated on a bluff overlooking Lake Michigan, the house has Prairie Style characteristics when viewed from the street. Viewed from the lake side, its two stories tower symmetrically under a single roof with a wall and forward-thrusting terrace that remind one of Cheney House. Here on full display is the assertive confidence with which America began the century. A photograph from summer 1908—just when the Cheney family and Wright would have seen it—shows its street-facing side proudly bearing a large American flag.

They returned to Oak Park the next day, and everyone began to privately digest the trip. Cheney must have seen enough. It is possible that the trip sealed Wright's determination to leave Oak Park. If, as it appears, he and Borthwick had aroused Cheney's suspicion, the architect's hand may have been forced at a time when, according to his autobiography, he had been hesitant and full of uncertainty. Referring to this critical time in his life, he added enigmatically, "The motor car brought a disturbance of all values and it brought disturbance to me."[7] While it may be asked when his relationship with Borthwick began, the more important question is when it ceased to be a secret. In all likelihood,

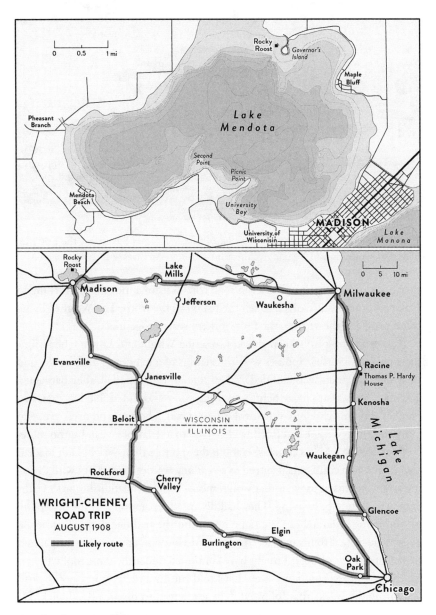

Wright-Cheney Road Trip, August 1908.

Thomas P. Hardy House, Racine, Wisconsin, in 1908. Photograph courtesy the Eric M. O'Malley Collection / Organic Architecture + Design Archives. All rights reserved.

the answer is during the Wisconsin road trip. Within a month of returning to Oak Park, they had resolved to tell their spouses the truth. The Wrights' living room provided the setting, the four of them seated together.

After recovering from their shock, Catherine Wright and Edwin Cheney initially replied that their spouses were the victims of a temporary infatuation and that their judgment was clouded. When that argument failed, they bargained and asked for a year's delay before anything else was decided. No less than two families and nine children were involved, they said. There was no need to upend everyone's life. Wright and Borthwick agreed to a delay of a year, but no more.

The meeting was less conclusive about the specifics than Wright later made it sound. The two couples had agreed to a yearlong waiting period but with differing arrangements as to what that would mean. Wright's relationship with Catherine was already past saving. They had discussed separation and the possibility of him living separately in the same house, but he had decided against it. As he later described to his mother in a letter, "I would in any case have separated from Catherine—though I might have continued under the same roof with her for the sake of the children—even that I told you I was determined not to do."[8]

During the weeks that followed, Cheney agreed to divorce Borthwick. He demanded custody of the children and asked that she and Wright marry before going away together. Catherine Wright would not commit herself to a divorce but seems to have left open the possibility.[9]

In practical terms, little had changed. The stalemate lasted a year and made everyone miserable. Obligated to pretend in public to be happily married, Wright confessed to his mother and a few confidants how unhappy he was. He described himself and Borthwick as living "separate from" their spouses: "The established order and claims of daily companionship with little children were pitted against the integrity of life that is the only real life. All was wretched, all false, all wasted."

Amid competing feelings of discontent and success, ambition and ennui, he tried to understand his own mind. At some time during this critical year, he received a letter of invitation from the distinguished Berlin publishing house Ernst Wasmuth Verlag, requesting his cooperation in the publication of a book of photographs of his works.[10] It was a singular honor that allowed him to seriously contemplate going to Berlin. A small constellation of people in Germany and America who knew him or his work had encouraged the publisher to take the initiative.[11] Wright recognized it as an opportunity to become better recognized in his own country through a quality publication of his work. Borthwick, interested in German culture and fluent in the language, undoubtedly provided encouragement.

By late 1908, he and Borthwick appear to have had made their decision, informing their spouses they would leave for Germany the following year. In his youth, Wright had turned down an all-expenses-paid opportunity offered by Daniel Burnham to live in Europe and study at the École des Beaux Arts. He knew what he wanted well enough to realize it would be of no value, perhaps even a hindrance. This time, he was willing to live in Europe even if it meant abandoning his thriving practice in Oak Park.

Like Wright, Borthwick sought to leave an unhappy marriage and pursue a new love, but her age was a factor as well. If the prospect of turning thirty had pushed her to marry Edwin Cheney in 1899, turning forty in June 1909 brought her to a crossroads again. It was not that she felt life was passing her by. Rather, she had met someone who elevated life itself. She would have answered like Nora in *A Doll's House* when Torvald asked what could be more sacred than her duties to her husband and children: "My duties toward myself."

Having resolved to leave their marriages, they seem to have lowered their guard. After Wright rented a Stoddard-Dayton roadster, they began to ride openly together in it. If they became reckless, even insensitive to their spouses' feelings at this time, within a year their attitudes would change. Borthwick would be devastated by an event beyond her imagining. Wright would become defensive and defiant in the face of public approbation. The modernist outlook they thought they stood for provided no refuge. In September, the *Chicago Tribune*, mindful of its vast Catholic readership, reported on the pope's visit to his hometown of Venice: "With tears streaming down his face and choked with emotion, the Holy Father spoke lovingly of Venice, the happy days he passed there, and his affection for the people. Recollection of these things, he said, afforded him consolation amidst his sorrows. He concluded by warning the Venetians against modernism."[12]

The pope's fear of modernism concerned its threat to church doctrine but also reflected larger currents of antimodernism that fed nationalism and militarism, the two major threats to European stability. With similar heedlessness, Wright and Borthwick pressed on toward a storm of their own making. Wright sensed the danger and yet was unwilling to turn back. As he wrote to his Buffalo client Darwin Martin, "It is difficult for me to square my life with myself, and I cannot rest until it is done or I am dead."[13]

CHAPTER 14

❧

HYDE PARK HIDEAWAY

Their lives with their spouses in Oak Park having become too difficult, Wright and Borthwick decided to spend much of their time in Hyde Park, the neighborhood of the University of Chicago. She enrolled in the university's graduate school and began attending classes. He took up residence nearby at the Chicago Beach Hotel to be near her and his new project, Frederick C. Robie House.[1]

Borthwick had decided to become a writer. Exactly what kind is unclear, but she knew that the novelist Robert Herrick, who enjoyed a stellar reputation as a writing teacher, was on the faculty of the University of Chicago, and had recently returned to the city to teach full time. He would be her teacher in composition and in a class titled Techniques of the Modern Novel.[2] Known on campus as "that professor who writes about sex,"[3] his latest novel, *Together*, had already gone through eight printings and topped the national best-seller list. To his surprise and alarm, it had made him a controversial figure. Under fire from critics who viewed his treatment of sex as downright scandalous, he had unwittingly written the *Lolita* of his day. The book was banned in Canada, and American libraries refused to purchase it.

As fellow members of the Cliff Dwellers, Herrick and Wright were well acquainted. Whether or not Borthwick knew Herrick, she must have been attracted to his portrayals of upper-middle-class marriages, described by one of his characters as "the great experiment of converting illusion into reality." His themes, according to his biographer Blake Nevius, were "concerned not so much with the development of the illusion as with the process by which the characters are made aware of the illusion and then have to find a way back to reality."[4] In short, his fiction had captured Borthwick's experience in marriage. His strength as a teacher lay in his ability to show how to structure a novel and use problems in marital relationships to illustrate social problems. The 1908–9 academic year ran from October to mid-June, and Borthwick may have relished the echo of her beloved University of Michigan days.

How much time Wright spent living at the Chicago Beach Hotel is unclear, but when asked his reason for living there, he no doubt cited his local project, Robie House.[5] Designed for the manufacturing executive Frederick C. Robie, the Prairie Style masterpiece still stands in Hyde Park as one of Wright's supreme residential achievements. His design enabled its great rectangular spaces to magically fit within a confining, narrow lot. In Robie House he gave full expression to the impulses of the Prairie Style. "The house leaps out beyond its confines," observes historian Robert Twombly, "and, with its incredible cantilevers, soars off into space, yet its insistent horizontal lines keep it securely earthbound. With these contradictory tendencies, the Robie House remains in a state of perpetual tension. Its almost unbounded energy, and the aggressive individuality of its several members, threatens to tear the building asunder, yet its parts are subtly and resourcefully woven together."[6] Construction began in early 1909 and was completed while Wright was in Europe. The fact that he could leave Chicago and allow something as grand as Robie House to be built mostly in his absence testifies to the restlessness he felt.

Chicago Beach Hotel. Library of Congress, LC-D4-13262.

His part-time residence at the Chicago Beach Hotel, arguably the finest of the grand apartment hotels of Chicago, went undiscovered by his biographers because it was as improbable as it was unnecessary. Robie House was only starting and did not require frequent on-site attention. His main reason for keeping an apartment at the hotel was probably to spend time there with Borthwick. Conveniently located at East Fifty-First Street on the lake, not far from the campus, the Chicago Beach would have been their refuge from Oak Park. She knew it well: her sorority had used the hotel for its convention in 1907 and would do so again in 1909.

If proximity to Robie House and the University of Chicago had been the only consideration, a better choice of hotel would have been the Del Prado, but the Chicago Beach suited Wright's taste. An uninterrupted system of beautifully landscaped parks designed by Frederick Law Olmsted and Clavert Vaux

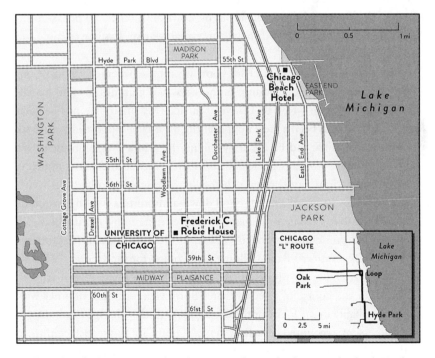

Hyde Park and Chicago, 1909. The Chicago Beach Hotel, where Frank Lloyd Wright kept an apartment in 1908, was close to his Robie House project. It was also conveniently located near the University of Chicago, where Mamah Borthwick attended graduate school. She commuted from Oak Park on what is now the "Green Line" of the L.

enhanced its view of a pristine lakefront. Begun in the 1870s, the parks had helped make the village of Hyde Park a resort destination well before it was chosen as an area for the 1893 World's Columbian Exposition. Located at East Fifty-First Street and South Chicago Beach Drive, the Chicago Beach Hotel was among the more lavish of the many hotels constructed to accommodate the Exposition, offering vistas of the lake from a sweeping, covered veranda.[7] With exclusive beach access and a host of amenities and services, the hotel suited Wright's taste for luxury and, as a bonus, also housed wealthy residents who might become his clients.

Catherine Wright was no fool and objected to her husband occupying an apartment in a hotel near the university where Borthwick was attending classes. This was not what she had understood the yearlong waiting period to entail. It was one thing for them to have fleeting moments together in Oak Park, but their use of a hotel bordered on cohabitation. Accompanied by her mother, she accosted Edwin Cheney in his downtown office. To her astonishment, he said he could do nothing about it, that Mamah was free to come and go as she pleased.

After that, the Wright's Oak Park home must have become even more unhappy and uncomfortable, adding to the stress and glumness he said he felt. On December 2, he wrote to Darwin Martin, "My affairs are not in good order. This year has been a great disappointment so far as opportunity to work is concerned." What did he mean by calling the year a disappointment? He was beginning to work on the Robie House masterpiece and was completing several commissions. Some projects had fallen through, but others were starting up. Perhaps he was trying to sound down-and-out to a wealthy patron he expected to ask for a loan, or perhaps he was referring to his marital limbo.

Two important commissions for Wright at this time were in Mason City, Iowa: the City National Bank building and a house for Dr. George C. Stockman. The latter was so impressed by Wright that he made several trips to Chicago, in the course of which he met Borthwick, encountering her with Wright probably in the lobby or the dining room of the Chicago Beach Hotel. His impression, recounted years later in the Mason City newspaper, confirmed that he, like many, found her to be intellectually impressive and genuinely charming: "Mrs. Wright [sic], whom the doctor met while calling on Wright to make the final arrangements on the plans, was a very lovable and noble woman. She was a graduate of an eastern college and a member of the Kappa Alpha Theta society and a very brilliant woman."[8]

The Nineteenth Century Club Literary Department had declared November to be Shakespeare Month, and Borthwick had volunteered to lead a program.[9] The topic could be any Shakespeare play of her choosing. Pointedly enough, she picked *The Taming of the Shrew*, a comedy about a woman who, having resisted marriage, is trapped and forced to submit to one.

Her presentation on November 18 in the familiar conference room of the Scoville Institute began with reading excerpts from the play, after which she turned to her main subject, titled "Three Famous Kates." With no record of who the three Kates were, it can be assumed that one was the Kate of *Taming of the Shrew*. For consistency, she would have chosen the other two from the theater. One natural inclusion would have been the Kate from Shakespeare's *Henry V*, a Frenchwoman who is about to be made a queen—but she is only a pawn between the rival French and English kings. Borthwick the linguist would have enjoyed the chance to explain the clever scene in which King Henry tries to teach the French Kate how to speak English using words that sound dangerously like French obscenities.

With no other famous Kate available in Shakespeare, the third may have been the Kate of *She Stoops to Conquer*, by Oliver Goldsmith. An especially popular play in America in the early 1900s, it features the smart, upper-class Kate Hardcastle, who must "stoop" or humble herself, pretending to be lower class in order to attract a certain man. All three Kates, in short, must demean themselves and navigate the hazards of being chosen in marriage with no real freedom to choose for themselves. Considering her audience, she must have discussed the Kate of *The Taming of the Shrew* in a lighthearted manner even if it is generally viewed as the Bard's most misogynistic play. A source of laughs as well as laments, lines such as Kate's retort to Petruchio, "Asses are made to bear, and so are you," would have drawn laughter. On the other hand, Kate's acquiescent closing words, "Thy husband is thy lord, thy life, thy keeper; thy head, thy sovereign," may have met with a more muted response. The whole program, as reconstructed, effectively serves as a kind of Rorschach test of Borthwick's frame of mind at the time.

As Christmas approached, Wright had to linger at home in Oak Park to entertain his newly arrived houseguests, Robert Ashbee and his wife, Janet. If Wright tried to pretend that his marriage was happy, he didn't fool the Ashbees. They had last visited in 1900 when the Wrights' marriage was in far better shape. Now they saw it plagued by a palpable tension. The fact that the Ashbees' marriage, too, was in crisis has escaped the notice of Wright's biographers in describing this episode. For five years, Janet Ashbee had been in an emotional affair with Gerald Bishop, an associate of her husband's. The stress had brought her to the point of a nervous breakdown while in London. She had broken off the relationship with Bishop just two weeks before she and Ashbee embarked for America.[10] Always brutally honest with herself in such matters, Janet was at that point exquisitely tuned to Catherine Wright's emotional state. She described the thirty-nine-year-old Catherine in her journal:

> There is something wonderfully tender and lovable about Mrs. Wright. With so many other of the best and finest American women she has an abiding youngness—a suppleness of gait, gesture, & smile—combined with that maternal gathering-in elderliness which always brings tears to my eyes. I feel in the background somewhere difficult places gone through—knocks against many stone walls—& brave pickings up from sloughs of despair. . . . And I am certain too I hear beginnings of a different kind of sadness—a battle with what will be an increasing gloom & nervousness (spite of success) in her husband. If her children do not comfort her she will be hard-pressed. And yet, she is almost the girl still—slender and lovely—but strongly built—& when she laughs, you forget the tragic lines about her mouth. But people do not kiss one in that way unless they are lonely in the midst of plenty.[11]

Robert Ashbee urged Wright to come visit them in London and tour Europe with them, not realizing how much it would add to Wright's desire to leave both Oak Park and Catherine. After returning to England, Janet wrote a thank-you note to which Catherine responded, telling Janet that her note had been more helpful than she could have imagined. She added that someday she might tell Janet more about "that year" (1908) and why her coming at Christmas had meant so much.[12]

"That year" was the penultimate phase in the disintegration of Frank Lloyd Wright's marriage. Upon learning the truth, Catherine Wright had decided to blame her long-standing marital problems on a hidden rival rather than confront the fact that her husband had changed. William Norman Guthrie bore witness to this drama when he lectured in Oak Park in 1908/9. Visiting Wright often, he became the architect's good friend and seems to have become close to his family. In his 1915 play *Beyond Disillusion*, the barely disguised characters of Frank, Catherine, Mamah, and others appear in scenes of the 1909 crisis (named in the play Richard Walter, Laura, and Edith Dwight). Even Wright's assistants Marion Mahoney and Walter Burley Griffin make a brief appearance.

Subtitled "A Dramatic Study of Modern Marriage," the play portrays Wright's family life, along with his inner turmoil and depression, with some accuracy. The play's plot falls apart near the end and descends into farce. Laura Walter (Catherine) runs away to New York to become an interpretive dancer and then reunites with Frank. Edith Dwight (Mamah Borthwick) winds up in the arms of an alternative, wealthy suitor. The play was performed once in Guthrie's church in New York and deservedly forgotten.[13]

In his autobiography, Wright remained silent about what transpired between him and Borthwick in Oak Park, but he did refer to the inner turmoil he felt at the time. "Everything, personal or otherwise, bore down heavily on me. Domesticity most of all. . . . What I wanted I did not know. I loved my children. I loved my home. A true home is the finest ideal of man. And yet . . . to gain 'freedom.'"[14]

His unhappiness in this period of his life is poorly understood partly because he did not understand it himself. Wright biographer Ada Huxtable believes that in 1909 his sense of what he had yet to achieve was part of what pushed him toward Europe: "Underlying his personal unhappiness was something deeply, disturbingly important to him—the conviction that he had reached the end of the line, that he had done all he could with domestic architecture, that he needed to find a way to move on. This sense of an impending professional dead end overshadowed everything else; it was the final, overwhelming spur to action."[15]

And yet, artistic turmoil aside, it seems doubtful that Wright would have gone to Europe if Borthwick had not been with him. Throughout his adult life, he seems to have needed a woman at his side—wife, mother, or true love. Borthwick in particular seems to have given him direction and support as he contemplated a new start. He would write to his grandson nearly half a century later, "Love is the spark plug of it all."[16] It is true, however, that he did not even address the destabilizing effect of his affair in his autobiography, possibly because of his jealous third wife's scrutiny of every word as he wrote it. Even if he failed to mention it, though, he surely knew it to be true: Mamah Borthwick played a central role in his decision to pursue "freedom" in 1909.

CHAPTER 15

FLIGHT

It was January 6, 1909, at 8:00 p.m., and Wright was surrounded by men he knew. In small groups and individually, they had all been whisked up the fast elevators of Chicago's Orchestra Hall to their new clubhouse on the top two floors. Wright and his Cliff Dweller compatriots, nearly two hundred in all, had come to explore what they called their "khiva," the Pueblo word for a special-purpose building used by the ancestral Puebloans.

In the main room, walnut paneled, cavernous, and ninety feet long, they strolled to the great windows facing the lake and gazed into the darkness, as if the spectacular view were available to them so late on a January day. Then, as instructed, they gathered on one side to begin the inaugural ceremony. The lights dimmed until only two glowing blue globes were visible. The room quieted, and the stentorian voice of the actor Donald Robertson, Master of the Pageant, rang out:

> We call to the dwellers of the ancient dusk
> Call to the finders of the golden way,
> And to the stern spirits, furrowing wintry deeps,
> Who hither fled from alien tyrannies!
> Behold the dwellers of the Nether Cliffs
> Up from their dreary, rock-bound citadels,
> Threading the ledges worn by patient feet
> Of generations that had died ere Troy
> Went down in thunder echoing into song.
>   Ghosts from the dim gray morn of time, we greet you.

Beneath a spotlight, two men appeared dressed as Anasazi cliff dwellers followed by four more, bearing a stereotyped Native American peace pipe. As they began a procession, a group of Spanish explorers fell in behind, then French missionaries, Cavaliers of Virginia, Puritans, Lewis and Clark, and mountain men until the pageant's costumed representatives reached modern times. Robertson lit the great fireplace with appropriate ceremony, using driftwood from the Atlantic and Pacific coasts contributed, respectively, by the Tavern Club of Boston and Bohemian Club of San Francisco. The pageant was followed by a grand dinner during which greetings were read aloud from dignitaries around the country, including President Theodore Roosevelt, Edward Everett Hale, William Dean Howells, and Joaquin Miller. A few club members rose to give short speeches laced with appropriate good humor and appreciation for their president, Hamlin Garland, addressed as "the Czar, Hamlin the First."

Borthwick's teacher Robert Herrick delivered the keynote. While acknowledging that his roots were eastern, he went on to deplore the influence of New York ("the predatory giant of America"). Chicago, he said, and the country as a whole would provide alternative sources of creativity. "New York is and will

Cliff Dwellers Club, Chicago, ca. 1909. Harper's Weekly, May 15, 1909.

forever remain the Great Barbarian, the creature of spoil and pelf, rather than the Creator. . . . Our country differs from every other nation in the fact that here we have many centers of national vitality instead of one great cosmopolis."[1]

It was Hamlin Garland's genius, if one wants to call it that, to know that an arts group could manage to host such an expensive affair at such a spectacular Chicago venue simply by including the right business leaders. Of the nearly two hundred members, seventy-five did not really belong to the artistic and literary community.[2] If this annoyed some of the artists and writers, it suited the architects just fine. They outnumbered the other professions among the initial Cliff Dwellers and used its meetings to cultivate potential clients. On that occasion, however, Wright had little incentive to find clients. He was keeping his plans to himself, heedless of the cost they would exact on his social standing. By the end of the year, because of his adulterous relationship, he would be expelled from the Cliff Dwellers.[3]

A week later, just two blocks away, Edwin Cheney entered the lobby of the Marquette Building and may have paused to admire its Tiffany frieze depicting the life of the French missionary and explorer Jacques Marquette. He was taking yet another step up the corporate ladder, this time as the Chicago General Manager of the Wagner Electric Company. His new office suite on the sixteenth floor was the latest sign of success in his well-calculated climb through ever more senior positions in four different companies. Never had his career seemed so full of promise.

And yet, regardless of how his professional life seemed to be soaring, his personal life was falling apart. He enjoyed all the appurtenances of success. A member of Chicago's Columbian Yacht Club and Sports Club, he owned a strikingly modern house designed by a leading architect and, to outward appearances, enjoyed a lovely family. And yet his wife was about to leave him, and his house would always remind him why.

Frank Lloyd Wright and Edwin H. Cheney, rising in their careers, braced for what lay ahead. The yearlong waiting period with their spouses would expire in September, but it was merely a formality at this point. Wright had informed his wife of his intention to leave for Europe. Borthwick had told her husband that she would accompany Wright.[4]

A few days after the Cliff Dwellers ceremony, Wright addressed the Nineteenth Century Club on the topic of the "Ethics of Ornament." If anyone asked him to explain the meaning of "ethics" in his title, there is no record of his reply, but he is known to have attacked frivolous, superfluous ornamentation as a kind of sacrilege. Using language about moral purity, "the soul of the thing" and a "spiritual reckoning," he might easily have been expressing his feelings about his marriage. After all, his wife was sitting in the audience. "We are living today encrusted with dead things, forms from which the soul is gone, and we are devoted to them, trying to get joy out of them, trying to believe them still potent."[5]

It was the beginning of a fateful year when, as Wright famously declared in his autobiography, "What I wanted I did not know."[6] To all appearances, this was untrue. He may have been undergoing a crisis at the time, but he was clearly seeking a new life with Borthwick and spiritual renewal of some kind. As he told Darwin Martin, "I am leaving the office to its own devices, deserting my wife and the children for one year, in search of a spiritual adventure, hoping it will be no worse."[7] What he meant by "spiritual adventure" is unclear, but it was more than just a break with the past. In his speech on ornament, he referred to "an expression of the quality of the soul . . . a real expression of ourselves."

He remained available for public appearances. On March 26, he lectured at the Chicago School of Applied and Normal Art on the topic "The Machine

Frank Lloyd Wright, ca. 1909. The Frank Lloyd Wright Foundation Archives (The Museum of Modern Art | Avery Architectural & Fine Arts Library, Columbia University, New York).

and Modern Architecture." The newspaper described his purpose as "a distinctive movement to combine beauty with the environment and the needs that a
home suggests . . . creating a demand for home architecture that is beautiful."[8]

But "home architecture" would no longer suffice for the scope of his ambition. He wanted to achieve something of a different order and wished to
finally see architecture in Europe. As he searched for someone to take over his
practice in Oak Park, he began raising funds to cover a year of travel abroad.

For her part, Borthwick planned to go to Boulder, Colorado, to spend the
summer with Mattie Chadbourne Brown. She would remain there until after
her friend had given birth in late September, after which she would join Wright,
and together they would leave for Europe. It meant she would leave Oak Park
nearly three months before he did. She planned it carefully, informing Edwin
Cheney several days in advance that she would leave him on June 28, which
not coincidentally was the opening day of the national convention of Kappa
Alpha Theta. She would stop at the convention at the Chicago Beach Hotel to
see her old friends, possibly Wright too in his apartment, before heading on to
Boulder.

She took all three children with her.[9] Her niece, Jessie, was eight. John was six
and Martha was almost four, but when she left Oak Park on June 28, 1909, they
must have remained temporarily with Lizzie Borthwick, since women attended
Theta conventions without their children. Upon arriving at the Chicago Beach
Hotel, she did not register as a delegate. Her purpose was simply to greet old
friends, who were unaware that they would never see her again. The visit was
undoubtedly difficult for her. However much she may have grown apart from
the world of Kappa Alpha Theta, she would not have timed her departure to
coincide so perfectly with the convention if the sorority did not mean a great
deal to her. The sorority's records are unclear, but they suggest that within a
year she submitted her resignation. More than just saying goodbye to friends,
she was saying goodbye to virtually everything and everyone she had known.
In 1909, for a woman to do what she was doing was almost unthinkable.

But the die had been cast; there was no turning back. The transcontinental train schedule dictated the next steps. She said a more temporary farewell
to Wright and left for the station to meet Lizzie Borthwick and the children.
After embracing her reluctantly cooperative sister, she gathered the children
and boarded the train.[10]

Train travel across the Midwest in summer was uncomfortably hot. Ice-
chilled air had yet to become a standard Pullman car luxury. Still, the novelty
and adventure of riding the train must have distracted the children, who were

Lizzie V. L. Borthwick.
Lizzie was a surrogate
mother to the children
of the Cheney
household in Mamah's
absence. Higgins family
photograph.

further entertained, as one exasperated traveler wrote, "by the incessant visitation of the train-boy, with his books, candy, and other articles for sale."[11]

It took half a day on the Union Pacific to reach Omaha, where they turned toward the southwest, tracing the old Overland Trail blazed by the Pony Express. That night Borthwick settled the children into a sleeper car as the train crossed the Great Plains toward Denver. At sunrise after a slow, steady climb through the foothills and mountains to the mile-high city, they wearily disembarked at Union Station and transferred to the new, electric interurban train to Boulder. The large car of the train was surprisingly posh and provided a smooth, quiet ride. Amid frequent stops, they could enjoy the views of distant mountains and cattle grazing in fields between scattered urban settings.

This was Borthwick's first experience of the West. Her teenage Dakota adventure had been through the north-central frontier on a relatively flat prairie. Here, rugged mountains punctured the horizon and the clean, cool air provided a refreshing contrast to Chicago's humidity. As the train passed by the mining town of Marshall, she may have inwardly braced herself at the sight of its bleak, gritty buildings, imagining that they foretold what Boulder would be like. Instead, the landscape began to assume a more settled, finished look as the train entered and briefly stopped at the University of Colorado campus.

The city of Boulder usually surpassed a newcomer's expectations. More than a mining town, it boasted a sanatorium for well-heeled patrons who came for relief in the mountain air. The city's electric streetcar system was as up-to-date as any, and the new luxury Hotel Boulderado had just opened to the public. It took only a few minutes in a carriage to reach Mattie Brown's modest house at 404 Mapleton Avenue. Visibly pregnant, she was there to greet them with her children, Alex (age six) and Mary (age four). The children knew one another and must have been as excited as their mothers to be together again. Notably absent from the scene, Mattie's husband, Alden Brown, was still en route to Boulder from the east, returning from a business trip to New York.

Once they were settled, Borthwick's first task would have been to confess that she had left Cheney (if she had not already informed her friend of this in a letter). It would have been no secret to Chadbourne Brown—who had known them both since college—that Borthwick was unhappy in her marriage, but the drastic action she was now taking may have come as a shock. In any case, it is likely that they kept all of this from Alden Brown during Borthwick's stay in Boulder. The uncertainty over her future would have hung over them during their summer together as much as Mattie Brown's approaching childbirth. Brown was by then thirty-eight, and her history of frail health had to be of concern.

The accepted story has been that Borthwick took the children to Boulder and dumped them there, telling Cheney to come get them as she rushed off to join Wright. This canard first appeared in the *Chicago Tribune* in November 1909, with no named source, and was picked up by other newspapers to be repeated by Wright biographers thereafter. Paul Hendrickson, for example, imagines this scene of desertion: "Having placed—perhaps on a dresser in Mattie's guest room—a letter of so-called explanation to her spouse. We don't have such a letter. But this part is fact: Decent Edwin Cheney rode out on the train in early October to collect John and Martha and bring them home."[12] While "Decent Edwin Cheney" did indeed go to Colorado to collect his children, it was in late August, while Borthwick was still there. The apocryphal story of his going to Boulder to rescue them after Borthwick had abandoned them defies all evidence.

Two key events of the summer of 1909 governed the actions of everyone concerned: the beginning of the school year in Oak Park and the birth of Mattie Chadbourne Brown's child. School would start on September 6, while the infant was due in late September. Cheney, Borthwick, and her sister Lizzie, an elementary school teacher, were all committed to the children's education. There was no question that the two children who were of school age, Jessie and John, must be back in Oak Park by the time school started.[13] The only acceptable arrangement was for Cheney to collect the children in Boulder in late August while Borthwick remained with Brown until she gave birth. Their nanny, Hanna Swain, undoubtedly accompanied him to help manage the children on the long train ride back to Chicago. Weeks later in Oak Park, amid rumor and speculation, the children's return with their father was presumed to have coincided with Borthwick fleeing the country. The truth was that when the children began school, she was still with her best friend in Boulder. A few years later, a more sympathetic newspaper would report that Borthwick told friends she hoped one day to have some kind of joint custody of the children.[14] She made clear in a letter that she would never have left them had Lizzie Borthwick not been present to provide the continuity of motherly care.[15]

Having communicated with Cheney about when he should come collect the children, Borthwick must have struggled to disguise her emotion when the time came to hand them off to their father. How would she have explained to them her forthcoming absence? Cheney had told friends she might be gone until Christmas but had declared she would return. Within a few months of her departure, however, his mother joined the household—although Lizzie Borthwick is likely to have remained the critical maternal figure.

Desperate to cut himself free, Wright struggled to arrange for someone to take over his practice. The difficulty was that his colleagues knew how much the practice depended on him. When an associate finally agreed, the negotiations foundered over how Wright should be compensated for the projects he had begun. He had many other arrangements to make as well, not least those involved in marshaling the funds for travel and an extended stay abroad. To that end, in September he sold a particularly valuable set of Japanese prints, thirty single-sheet images of Hokusai's *The Thirty-Six Views of Mt. Fuji*, to Kansas City's doyen of Asian art, Sallie Casey Thayer.[16]

Borthwick yearned to join Wright and leave for Europe, but she could not leave until Brown's child was born. Above all, Wright needed to depart before September 26, when Unity Temple would be dedicated. He knew what a shock he was about to deliver to everyone who would be present at the ceremony.[17] Just in time, he received a telegram from Borthwick on September 23 informing him that Mattie Brown had successfully given birth. He left that very day, but it is likely he went no further than the Loop. He probably checked in at his favorite downtown hotel, the Congress Plaza, and waited for her to arrive.

He is reputed to have left behind a grocery bill for $900, often presented as Exhibit A in the case made against him about his selfishness. But while his reluctance to pay bills was legend, the apocryphal story of the unpaid grocery bill is questionable for several reasons. First, the amount, at least $25,000 in early twenty-first-century dollars, is hardly to be believed. That level of credit is unlikely to have been extended by any local Oak Park merchant to a notorious deadbeat like Frank Lloyd Wright. Second, the source of the story, his son David (1895–1997), was not objective: on September 26, 1909, David turned fourteen. Wright had left Oak Park three days earlier. It was a sensitive age to have his father either forget or intentionally miss his birthday and, in the bargain, leave his mother. Even seventy years later, he was still livid when he told the tale to Wright biographer Meryle Secrest.[18]

Third, the unpaid grocery bill bears a suspicious resemblance to an unpaid grocery bill of $850 mentioned in Wright's *Autobiography*, which David would have read. The bill was allegedly owed in the 1890s, not 1909. Wright is likely to have expressed its approximate value in dollars at the time he was writing in the late 1920s, the buying power of which had dropped by at least half from the 1890s. David probably did not recall that the date of his birthday coincided with the dedication ceremony for Unity Temple. Wright, desperate to be gone before then, was in a double bind. He later sent David a birthday gift, a flute, to which David responded with the complaint that he needed money for lessons. Wright's only defense was to claim (in a letter to his mother) that he sent Catherine Wright a total of $4,500 to cover her bills and ongoing expenses.[19]

The birthday that mattered even more than David's in Wright and Borthwick's plans was that of Mattie Brown's child. Martha Holway Brown was born on September 23, 1909.[20] Borthwick had only to remain a few days longer to assure herself that mother and child were in good health before taking a fast train to Chicago. She would have arrived in Chicago to join Wright by September 29, whereupon they boarded a train to New York. Notice of his departure for Germany appeared in the *Tribune* on October 3. By then, they had established themselves in New York's Plaza Hotel.[21]

Their arrival in New York coincided with the grand Hudson-Fulton Celebration, the combined three hundredth anniversary of Hudson's discovery of the eponymous river and the one hundredth anniversary of Robert Fulton's paddle steamer. The month-long event had concluded with a major street parade and a procession of ships on the Hudson. Despite the entertaining distractions of celebratory events, their immediate need was to confirm a berth on a ship bound for Germany. No steamers were leaving on Sunday, October 4, so they booked for the fifth on the SS *Kaiser Wilhelm*. It turned out to be the very ship and itinerary that the Cheneys had taken in 1901.[22]

That evening they returned to the hotel to find it wearing a high crown of lights in keeping with celebratory lighting all over the city. The next day, with time to kill, they probably found themselves in the midst of the ongoing celebrations featuring a public flight by Wilbur Wright, then renowned for his demonstration flights in Europe. Using Governor's Island as an airfield on October 4, he made a half-hour flight over the Hudson River to Grant's Tomb and back, enabling perhaps a million New Yorkers to see their first airplane in flight. Glen Curtiss, the famous aviator and motorcycler, also appeared but made only very brief forays into the air, preferring not to challenge the windy conditions.

The risks being taken by the airborne Wright that day symbolized those being taken by the Wright on the ground. A year earlier, Wilbur's brother Orville had crashed, killing his passenger, a military officer. It made national headlines. Extraordinary progress in aviation had been made over the five years up to that point, but it was incremental. The press, unaware of the implications of the many innovations occurring in the field of manned flight, had taken little notice until the tragic setback. Only then did the importance of the airplane and how far and fast its progress had advanced come to the attention of a mass audience.

A disaster or major setback in a field often draws attention to the progress being made in it. Now, another Wright who also had been metaphorically flying high was about to crash in front of the whole world. He was throwing away his practice and reputation, apparently to be with the woman he loved. If the setback and scandal drew national attention, it also caused people to take another look at what modern architects were up to. Like aviation, architecture would be driven by its own imperatives, but the sensational events of 1909, outwardly disastrous for Wright, put a national audience on notice that something "modern" was happening in domestic architecture, led by a visionary in the Midwest. Thus, Wright was seen nationally as a pioneer in his field, whether one liked the man or not. Owing in part to the publicity surrounding the scandal, his work began to be recognized more widely as an American style associated with his name.[23]

As he prepared to board a ship bound for Europe and begin his self-imposed exile, Frank Lloyd Wright knew only that he had abandoned virtually everything and everyone but Mamah Borthwick. Like his counterpart in the air that day, he was constantly taking chances, and now he was taking the biggest one of his life. In Berlin, he published his first portfolio, *Ausgeführte Bauten und Entwürfe von Frank Lloyd Wright*, known as the Wasmuth portfolio. His instinct and timing in publishing it were correct insofar as it was to become one of the most famous architectural treatises of the twentieth century. But it did not place his career in any less jeopardy.

The uncertainty may have affected Borthwick more than it did him, although she encouraged him in his sense of mission. Her doubts may have grown amid the events that swept her along. Indeed, unknown to her, a catastrophe was unfolding. In Vinton, Iowa, Dr. T. L. Chadbourne, Mattie Brown's brother, had just received an urgent telegram from Boulder summoning him to his sister's bedside. It informed him that she was not expected to live.

PART III

CHAPTER 16

BERLIN SETUP

Ocean travel was an ordeal for Wright. Prone to seasickness, he must have welcomed the excuse to leave the ship at the port of Southampton. But he had not thought through this side visit. His main reason for disembarking in England was to visit Robert and Janet Ashbee in London. Robert had extended a written invitation to Frank and Catherine the previous January, but Wright had accepted only for himself, saying that he hoped to see Ashbee "within a year." It is hard to fathom how he could have interpreted the invitation to include Borthwick. He may not have given her a full picture of the situation; nevertheless, they disembarked and boarded a train to London.

Ashbee's house in Chelsea was located on a street named Cheyne Walk; coincidentally, the pronunciation for Cheyne sounded uncomfortably like Borthwick's married name. Wright registered himself and Borthwick in a hotel, probably as a married couple, and with Ashbee's address in hand, they set out to find the house. Ashbee had designed several of the row houses on Cheyne Walk. He used number 37 as a studio, and number 74 still served sometimes as his residence.

An eccentric hodgepodge of Arts and Crafts and Queen Anne styles, 74 Cheyne Walk had once been rented to the painter James McNeil Whistler, who died there in 1903. Whistler had found the house not entirely to his liking, but he considered its location so desirable he would not live anywhere else. Located along the Thames Embankment with a fine view of the river, the Cheyne Walk neighborhood was known for its writers and artists, such as George Eliot, Henry James, J. M. W. Turner, and Dante Gabriel Rossetti. Even Jack London, who had met Ashbee in America in 1900, had once briefly rented number 74. The street had relatively little traffic, making it an ideal place for a stroll along the Thames. A row of plane trees along the embankment leaned toward the water as if beckoning the passerby to take in the view. Nearby, the spectacular Albert Bridge crossed to the south, its ray-like supporting rods streaming from pylons.

The notoriously confusing street signage in the area probably required the new arrivals to ask directions. When asked for the location of 74 Cheyne Walk, anyone who knew the neighborhood would have told them to look for "the house with the copper door." Ashbee had installed a door on his house with a copper flashing over the wooden frame and two small windows at the top. Eventually they spied the house on the opposite side of the street. Its first story of soft-toned pinkish brick was surmounted by a rough, gray plaster, then a brick third story. Casement windows revealed small, dotted Swiss curtains tied back at an angle.[1]

Borthwick must have been puzzled when, perhaps after a brief hesitation, Wright led her on past. They may have missed them in any case; the house on Cheyne Walk was only one of the Ashbee's residences. They spent much of their time at their home in the Cotswolds. Yet that probably is not why Wright

Cheyne Walk, Chelsea, 1903. Robert Ashbee's residence at 74 Cheyne Walk is center left, darkened. Walter William Burgess, *Whistler's House in Chelsea*, etching, late nineteenth to early twentieth century. Open Access Image from the Davison Art Center, Wesleyan University. Photograph by M. Cook.

did not try to call on his friend. He had failed to come to terms with the reality of their situation. The Ashbees knew Catherine Wright well and would have expected to see her, not Borthwick, with their American friend. Accustomed to brazening his way out of awkward moments, in London Wright found himself at a loss. The social challenges they would face as a couple had begun to sink in. The following year, he apologized to Ashbee in a letter: "I passed your little home in Chelsea with a longing and disappointment hard to bear."[2] It was an inauspicious beginning. They retreated from London, crossed the Channel, and arrived in Berlin sometime in late October.

Relatively new to its status as a world-class city, Berlin stood in favorable comparison to Chicago. Wright had first encountered Chicago in 1887 as a naive young man applying for work. But if he expected Berlin to be like his home city, he was in for a surprise. During its early growth, it had been dirty and polluted like Chicago, but by 1909, major parts of Berlin were noticeably clean, decorated with parks and tree-lined streets. From a modest provincial city, it had transformed itself into a powerful industrial metropolis, an imperial capital in every sense of the word. Its wide boulevards, museums, grand municipal buildings, and equestrian statues were intended to impress and inspire German pride. Yet it lacked a distinctive history and tradition, making it all the more ready to be modern.

Their arrival point was undoubtedly the gigantic Schlesischer Station in central Berlin. (Today, the station—badly damaged in World War II and rebuilt after the war—is called Ostbahnhof.) The colossal 207-meter roof of the original Schlesischer Station, described at the time by awe-struck Berlin architect August Endell, was "supported by countless slender iron columns, so slender, that you can hardly make out where they join up, and they appear almost painfully sharp to the eye. As architecture it is hideous, but when a fine haze fills the wide hall and turns the iron rods into an endless, glittering spider's web— the effect is unparalleled."[3]

Inside the station, a policeman might have asked them their destination, handed them a metal ticket for the kind of taxi they needed, and directed them to a second policeman who could show them which one to take. Soon they were headed for the Hotel Adlon, Berlin's new luxury hotel. They joined a mix of buses, horses, private cars, trucks, and electric trams on the grand boulevard Unter den Linden until they reached the Adlon and stepped out of the cab, where "outdoor servants" in French gray livery would take care of their luggage while looking them over in case they were celebrities. The

Hotel Adlon, Berlin, 1910. Library of Congress, LC-B2-404-2.

Adlon had a reputation for attracting famous people, including even the Kaiser himself.

Located on Pariser Platz with an unobstructed view of the Brandenburg Gate, the Adlon boasted hot and cold running water, an on-site laundry, and a power plant for electricity. What it did not always provide was privacy, as Borthwick and Wright would soon discover to their regret. Nevertheless, a well-heeled British guest at the time described the benefits of its extravagant furnishings:

> The great hall of the hotel looks like the museum of a millionaire; so many beautiful things have been collected there. There are some beautiful works of art from Japan, a wonderful clock, a wonderful staircase, cream marble pillars with bronze capitals, magnificent carpets, Venetian mosaics, fine furniture, a large bust of the Kaiser in coloured marble, a magnificent fountain, but if there were fewer beautiful things and less magnificence it would be in better taste. The view of the little garden seen through the back entrance is, however, charming. It is the latest expression of the Teutonic desire to possess the most gorgeous hotels on the Continent, and it is just a little overdone.[4]

To reach the offices of Wright's new publishing house, Ernst Wasmuth Verlag, the next day required only a walk down Unter den Linden. Crossing the river Spree on the ancient Schloss Bridge, where statues of Athena and Nike instruct youths on the art of war, they soon reached the address: Markgrafenstraße 35. Wright introduced Borthwick to everyone as his wife. The clerks promptly handed him a pile of telegrams and letters that had arrived addressed to him. He had given the Wasmuth address not only to colleagues but also to Edwin and Catherine, unaware of how his wife might use the information against him.

The venerable Ernst Wasmuth Verlag had a reputation for quality production of books on art and architecture. Its executive director, Otto Dorn, was eager to impress Wright by showing him their large-format publications on architecture. One would have been a folio of the recent work by Joseph M. Olbrich. Perhaps for variety, he included a recent folio of the architecture of Constantinople. Such impressive portfolios inspired Wright to commit himself to producing more than a book of photographs of his work. He decided to be more ambitious, with a full portfolio of drawings, even if it would require him to subsidize its production. A less welcome development arose in early November as they neared agreement on the contract. Apparently, Wright was warned that a part-time reporter for the *Chicago Tribune* was aware of his presence in Berlin. The details that emerged suggest that this disclosure came via the Wasmuth office.

Wright and Borthwick checked out of the Adlon on November 3. Arriving at the hotel too late to catch them, the reporter nevertheless managed to persuade the front desk clerk to allow him to see the register. He found what he wanted, the entry "Frank Lloyd Wright and wife, Chicago," written in Wright's own hand. It served as key evidence in the lead story that appeared in the *Tribune* on November 7.

Wright biographer Meryle Secrest speculates that Wright's mother or Edwin Cheney may have disclosed their whereabouts to the newspaper, but neither of them wanted a public scandal. Catherine Wright, on the other hand, although she was humiliated, may have tipped off the *Tribune* in a desperate gamble that her husband might succumb to public pressure and return to her.[5] This would account for why the postcard she mailed to him on October 20, care of the Wasmuth office, was read and duly recorded by the *Tribune* reporter before Wright ever laid eyes on it. Featuring a photograph of Unity Temple, the card declared Catherine's long-suffering forbearance in stilted, guilt-inducing phrases.

My Dear,

   We think of you often and hope you are well and are enjoying life as you
have so longed to. From the children and your wife, Catherine L. Wright.

The use of "Catherine L. Wright" instead of "Catherine" or "Kitty" and the
arch-sounding phrase "from the children and your wife" suggest that the card
was not intended for her husband's eyes only. The story created a sensation in
Chicago, where the quote and the postcard's precise description appeared as
the pièce de résistance of the story.[6]

   The possibility that Catherine Wright cooperated in advance with the *Tribune*, alerting the newspaper to approximately when Wright would arrive in
Berlin, is supported not only by the postcard but by the lengthy, articulate
interview she gave the *Tribune* as part of the breaking story on November 7.
She seemed to admit as much in declaring that she was now in "the publicity
part of a struggle that has been going on for a long time." When challenged
with the fact that her husband had lied in signing the Adlon Hotel guest register, she was ready. It was a demonstration of his honesty, she said.

   Why, do you know the fact that he signs his name on the hotel register "Frank
   Lloyd Wright and wife" is a tribute to his sincerity and honesty. If he was an
   ordinary rake, if there could be anything low or common about him, do you
   think he would do that? He is honest in everything he does. A moment's insin-
   cerity tortures him more than anything else in the world. Though I have not
   been able to accept all the things he has done, I never for a moment have ques-
   tioned the honesty and truthfulness of his relations with me.[7]

At the end of the interview, she interjected, apropos of nothing, that she admired how "fairly" the *Tribune* was handling the story.

   Meanwhile, the reporter returned to the Wasmuth office hoping for a last
tipoff on Wright and Borthwick's whereabouts. He was told that more mail had
arrived for her addressed to "M. B. Cheney" and that she had recently picked
it up. He was shown a final, plaintive telegram from Edwin Cheney that was
too irresistible for the *Tribune* not to quote: "Have letters and cablegrams sent
in your care been delivered to M. B. Cheney?" The Wasmuth reply had been
"Partially, holding the remainder." Wright attempted to misdirect the press
pursuit by leaving word that he and Borthwick were traveling next to Japan.

   The timing could not have been worse for Mamah. One of the messages from
Cheney would have brought the devastating news of Mattie Brown's death.

A blow like no other, it would have left her struggling to comprehend what had happened. Details of the death were scant. No explanation appeared in the record apart from a medical assessment indicating that it had been caused by "heart disease with involvement of the lungs." The collapse of Brown's health had taken place just after Borthwick had left Boulder after having assured herself that all was well. The Boulder newspaper, the *Daily Camera*, confirmed, "Her death has caused a shock to the entire community, her apparently excellent health giving no warning."[8] The cause may have been delayed postpartum preeclampsia, which can appear with little warning weeks after childbirth. The mysterious illness that forced Mattie Brown (then Chadbourne) to leave Port Huron in 1896 may have been involved as well.

The story in the *Tribune* described Wright as having declared himself to be on "a spiritual hegira," a reference to Mohammed's flight from Mecca to Medina in 622 to escape persecution. As a result, the word "hegira" appeared as a running joke in the *Tribune* for several days, its usage implying that a man was running away from his wife with a mistress. For years afterward, newspapers used it to stigmatize Wright. One would refer to him scornfully as "Hegira Wright." When and where he originally used the word "hegira" is unknown, but the underlying sentiment was genuine. He had told Darwin Martin he intended to go on a spiritual journey.

He planned to travel to Italy after Berlin to establish a temporary studio in Florence. There, with the help of assistants, he would assemble drawings for reproduction by Wasmuth. In addition to a book of photographs, a large-format portfolio of one hundred drawings was planned. This meant that drawings would have to be shipped from the United States and traced and reworked.

The project had become more ambitious than originally envisioned, requiring him to call upon additional help. Through a friend, he summoned his nineteen-year-old son Lloyd to leave the University of Wisconsin and come join him in Florence to work as a draftsman. If, as seems likely, he did this without consulting Borthwick, the decision probably did not please her in the least.[9] Having planned to live with him in Italy, she was no more prepared to face Lloyd alongside his father in Florence than Wright had been prepared to face the Ashbees with her in London. Upon news of Lloyd coming to join them, she decided that she would live temporarily in Leipzig, hoping to involve herself with its ancient university until Lloyd returned to America.

Thus, after they hurriedly left Berlin, it is likely that they made a first stop in Leipzig to enable Borthwick to make inquiries about future lodgings. Their exact itinerary from there is uncertain, but Wright is known to have written a letter from Nuremberg on November 4. They proceeded to Darmstadt, where he was eager to see buildings designed by the brilliant Secessionist architect Joseph M. Olbrich and to meet Olbrich in person. His hopes were apparently dashed, however, when he learned that Olbrich had recently died at the age of forty.[10]

They appear to have traveled next to the French city of Nancy, where the 1909 Nancy International Exposition had just ended. The stopover has not been previously considered part of their flight from Berlin, but Borthwick's description of it in a letter years later is unmistakable.[11] The Nancy Exposition was a popular success in Europe. While not comparable to the massive 1893 Chicago Exposition, it highlighted the resources and achievements of the Alsace region. Large pavilions had been commissioned to house the exhibits. They appeared in the drawings and photos of architectural publications that Wright would have seen in the Wasmuth office. No fan of Nancy's Art Nouveau style, he may have dismissed all the buildings out of hand—that is, all except one, the Pavilion of Metallurgical Industries by Eugène Vallin and Louis Lanternier. Modern and industrial in scale and character, with ranks of tall windows marching between great pylons at each end, the pavilion was nearly a hundred meters long. The reddish illumination of its interior at night was meant to give the impression of blast furnaces at work inside. Murals evoking the new century's industrialism had been commissioned for the building. Instead of appearing in the interior, they were built into its exterior base.[12] He may have wanted to stop in Nancy and have a look.

We do not know Wright's reaction to Vallin's structure, but we do know Borthwick's state of mind at the time. She was in crisis. The news of Mattie's death must have added grief and guilt to her already overburdened conscience, especially once she became aware that she had left Boulder at such a key moment. The weight of her isolation undoubtedly bore down on her like a punishment. She had given up her family, even her country, to become a pariah with Wright. Later, she described the feeling of having entered darkness. The justification she had felt when she left America had not prepared her for this. On leaving Oak Park, she had figuratively slammed the door behind her, like Ibsen's Nora. It had given her a sense of an ending but not of what would come next. Everything seemed to have gone wrong.

They checked into a small hotel, the antithesis of the great Adlon, to escape reporters who might be in pursuit. While Borthwick sometimes accompanied Wright on his explorations, she mostly holed up in their room, depressed and anxious. It was there, while reading a book she had purchased, that she began

Pavilion of Metallurgical Industries, 1909 Nancy Exhibition. Municipal Archives of Nancy, dimension 106 Fi 1509.

to recover her equilibrium. Written by the Swedish intellectual Ellen Key, it was probably *Love and Marriage*, which had been translated from Swedish in French and German. Borthwick had never encountered a message like Key's. It spoke directly to her situation. With its forceful argument for individual rights in marriage, it resembled nothing she had encountered before in world literature. Its longest and most significant chapter, "Divorce," presents detailed reasoning for why either partner should be free to legally leave a marriage without the consent of the other. Key provided a rationale for pursuing one's personal truth in defiance of societal strictures. Much of what she wrote resonated with Borthwick, but Key also had advice for Wright:

A poet or an artist, for example, has a wife, as to whose insufficiency for him all are agreed—so long as he still has her. Suddenly he finds the space, that was empty and waste, filled by a new creation; the air becomes alive with songs and visions. He not only feels his slumbering powers awake, he knows that great love has called up in him powers he had never suspected; he sees that now he will be able to accomplish what he could never have done before. He follows the life-will of his love, and he does right. Marriages kept inviolable have doubtless produced many great advantages to culture. But it is not to them that art and poetry owe their greatest debt of gratitude. Without "unhappy" or "criminal" love, the world's creations of beauty would at this moment be not only infinitely fewer, but above all, infinitely poorer.[13]

Key argued for "free divorce" in the case of a marriage in which one or both individuals had developed in ways that were unforeseen at the start. If a partner became conscious of emotional needs that may not have existed at the time of their union, that person should not be prevented from finding his or her "highest happiness" in another love. Equally important, she argued, individuals who fail to break away from a dead marriage out of a sense of duty imposed by society have committed a crime against themselves.

These were revolutionary ideas for the time. Conservatives considered them an invitation to anarchy, but Key was held in high regard in Europe as a thinker and writer. In Nancy in 1909, Borthwick became one of her disciples, after what historian Alice T. Friedman describes as a conversion experience.[14] Later, in one of her letters to Key, Borthwick would write, "You cannot know what you have been and are in my life—the embodiment of so many ideals, scarcely formulated until your light burst upon me in the little hotel in Nancy, where I was struggling so hard, against such frightful odds to live the truth that you alone gave me strength and encouragement to cling to."[15]

Key's book was restorative for Borthwick, but it cannot have entirely lightened her load. Tension between her and Wright may have risen in Nancy when, feeling besieged and bereft of friends, they needed one another's support. Instead, they decided to go in different directions. Wright's sudden decision to summon Lloyd to Florence may have been a key reason for that. It is hard to imagine that amid their passion in America they had planned to separate so soon after their arrival in Europe. And yet that is what they did.

The days were unremittingly cloudy and rainy. Frequent storms had been saturating France all year, foreshadowing the historic flood that inundated much of central Paris in January. The weather is likely to have deepened their depression over the unplanned turn of events. Wright needed to proceed on to Florence to establish his studio. Borthwick, contemplating living alone in Leipzig, must have struggled to imagine what was in store. Evidence suggests they went as far as Paris together before finally saying goodbye. From there, Wright would go to Florence and Borthwick would turn back toward Leipzig.

Germany held great appeal for Americans at the start of the twentieth century, before its roles in the world wars would forever mar its history. That appeal was embodied in the ancient market town of Leipzig, where in 1909, with pomp and ceremony, the university celebrated its five hundredth anniversary. Greats like Leibniz, Schiller, and Goethe (Borthwick's idol) had lived and worked in the city center of closely built seventeenth- and eighteenth-century houses. Even J. S. Bach had made his living as the organist for the St. Thomas Church, where he wrote cantatas and conducted the boys' choir.

Smaller and older than Berlin, Leipzig had a settled, human scale that drew American students. The university was known for accepting female students from abroad. Two American women novelists, Josephine Bontecou and Elfrieda Hochbaum, had been students in Leipzig and had incorporated their Leipzig experience in their fiction. Many of the graduates of the University of Michigan who aspired to further education in Europe eventually attended school in Leipzig. Borthwick's professor at Michigan Edward L. Walter, who wrote her a glowing letter of recommendation, had received his doctorate there and may have been the source of her interest in Leipzig.

But this was Imperial Germany, the Germany of Kaiser Wilhelm, and the nation's self-destructive politics would not be slowed by the better angels of its nature. Goethe, his statue nobly presiding over the Leipzig market, could not help. Just as Borthwick arrived, the regional government instituted a new policy closing off formal university registration to foreign female students. A product of the country's growing nationalism and its hypermasculine university traditions, the policy allowed only women who were German nationals to register as "guest students."[16] Perhaps the lack of an association with the much-revered university was a great disappointment to her, but Borthwick would have had no difficulty in supporting herself as a language tutor.

She had left Wright alone and forlorn in Paris. He had no business to attend to and had never been enthusiastic about the city. In his autobiography, he described staying there overnight in early November, depressed and walking the streets.[17] It seems to have been at that point that his doubts about his course of action reached their depths. But there was no turning back. The next day, he boarded a train to Florence.

CHAPTER 17

HOME FRONTS

On the evening of November 5, 1909, the *Chicago Tribune* reporter had trouble finding the front door of Cheney House in the dark. His assignment was to get a quotable reaction from Edwin Cheney before the newspaper broke the story of the scandal. Upon answering the door and learning the man's purpose, Cheney slammed it in his face, ordered everyone to bed, and turned out the lights.

The next morning, he and Lizzie Borthwick left for work early. He did not return at the end of the day but remained downtown. As prearranged, he met her in the lobby of Orchestra Hall shortly before 8:00 p.m., when a musical performance was about to start. They assumed no one would notice them among the concert crowd, but they were mistaken. The *Tribune* reporter watched as they conversed. After Lizzie Borthwick departed, he approached Cheney and asked for a statement about his relationship with his wife.

"I have no comment to make," Edwin said.

"Will you seek a divorce or take any other court action?" the reporter asked.

"I have nothing to say."

"Did you suspect that she was with Wright when you sent messages and letters to the Wasmuth Company?"

"I don't care to talk about the matter at all," said Edwin as he turned away, but he turned back and asked, "Did Mrs. Wright know that her husband and Mrs. Cheney were together?"[1]

The reporter took note of the question. It meant that Cheney had not been in touch with Catherine Wright for some time, perhaps months. In their respective press interviews, he and Catherine would express their continued loyalty to their spouses but in different ways that would shape the events to come. Catherine Wright would continue to cling to her marital rights and her faith in her husband. Edwin Cheney would eventually give up on Mamah.

As he took leave of the reporter and entered the concert hall, he added, "If I can do anything for you subsequently in the matter you can find me at my offices." As he should have expected, the reporter appeared in his office the next day. Consenting to an interview, he began with a vague defense.

"Mrs. Cheney has been getting the worst end of this deal right along, and it is not fair," he said. "Those of her friends who understand the situation know that she should not be blamed in the way she has been. It is because of the faith friends have in her that I have refrained from discussing the matter more fully, and they have been reticent for the same reason."[2]

This oblique, carefully worded statement would serve for the time being as a counter to Catherine Wright's statement, which included an attack on his wife. It was obvious to everyone that Borthwick had left him, and yet his lack of bitterness suggests there was some kind of understanding between them. Per his request, she had made a best effort to avoid scandal, hoping that Catherine would relent and give Wright a divorce. But he would only go so far. Instead of declaring his continued faith in her, he invoked that of their friends. "Our friends know that she is not deserving of this censure. It seems to me that all has been printed about the affair that should be. Many friends would be grateful if the matter were allowed to drop now."[3]

Here, Cheney's statement displayed a key aspect of his character. Reticent, self-controlled, and capable of a forbearance that bordered on masochism, he endured this heartbreak and humiliation without publicly uttering a reproach. He seems to have clung to the hope that she would return, but that hope would not last long. He was prepared to take the children and start a new life without her.

Catherine Wright, on the other hand, was still in denial. She thought she could hold out until her husband came to his senses. If anyone bought into the idea of Frank Lloyd Wright as a hero, it was Catherine, whose self-image was wrapped up in his. After their return from Japan in 1905, she made presentations about the trip in which she would interrupt herself with paeans of praise for his genius. Ever the astute observer, Janet Ashbee noted how desperately alone Catherine would be if Frank were to completely withdraw from her.

Unlike the fortress-like Cheney House, where reporters had difficulty finding the front door, the Wright home, thanks to Catherine, was always open to the press. Flanked by her mother and mother-in-law, Catherine had so much to say to the reporter from the *Chicago Tribune* that he must have had trouble keeping up. A man such as Wright, she declared, was above what was being said of him. He could not be sullied by "the trappings of what is low and vulgar. . . . There is nothing of that sort about Frank Wright. He is honest and sincere. I know him. I tell you I know him. I have fought side-by-side with him. My heart is with him now. I feel certain that he will come back. When, I don't know. It will be when he has reached a certain decision with himself."

In more than one press interview, she sought to evoke admiration and sympathy while appealing to her husband's conscience: "Most of all I have fought beside him and the struggle has made me. Whatever I am as a woman, aside from my good birth, I owe to the example of my husband. I owe myself to him and I do not hesitate to confess it."

By elevating Wright's artistic struggle against "obstacles," she portrayed Borthwick as just one of the obstacles, the latest of the people who had tried to drag him down to their level. "When he came here as a young architect, he had to fight against every existing idea in architecture. He did fight, year after year, against obstacles that would have downed an ordinary man. The determination of character that he possessed to fight these obstacles until he reached

Catherine Tobin Wright, 1909. Wisconsin Historical Society, WHS 87746.

the summit of success is the power that either makes or breaks a man. He has fought the most tremendous battles. He is fighting one now, and I know he will win. This is a struggle that he has fought out before."

When asked what she thought about Borthwick, she replied, "With regard to Mrs. Cheney, I have nothing to say. I have striven to put her out of my thoughts in connection with the situation. It is simply a force against which we have had to contend. I have never felt that I breathe the same air with her. It was simply a case of a vampire. You have heard of such things."[4]

At the time, "vampire" did not carry the connotation of horror so much as the power of seduction. Bram Stoker's 1897 novel had not yet become a best seller, and *Dracula* would not be a sensation until the vampire starred in a motion picture. Comparing Borthwick to a vampire was Catherine Wright's way of attributing the failure of her marriage to Borthwick's control over Wright.

It was left to Reverend Frederick E. Hopkins, the minister who had crusaded against the "tippling ladies" of the Tea Room at Marshall Field's, to accuse the fugitive couple of depravity. Upon reading about the scandal in the *Tribune* on Sunday morning, November 7, he extemporized from his pulpit at Pilgrim Congregational Church with such vehemence that it earned its own small headline the next day. He placed the blame on both Wright and Borthwick but singled her out as typical of the kind of woman

who becomes weary of the husband who is working hard and doing his best to provide for her comfort. She tires of her home life. She tries to make herself think she understands a lot of gab from the platform of her club about the larger, the fuller life and her sphere. Along happens a knave. Together they begin to think and talk about how they understand each other. They look a long time at each other in silence and breathe deep, like an old sitting hen. What wonderful things they discovered together and how different the world looks to each other's eyes. Thus they proceed through weeks and months of slush, until one day there is a splash, and both have tumbled into the same old hog pen where thousands have tumbled before them.

Hopkins went on to idealize Catherine Wright as

the wife who can make biscuits that melt in your mouth, whose children are clean minded, who loves her husband, and can make hat, and dress, and shoes, and everything else last wonderfully to help him in his business. He gets rich,

but she made the wealth as much as anybody. But now listen to him as he begins
to talk about his wife's looks and for a woman made by milliners, dressmakers,
dancing academies, hairdressers, and the devil, he wants to exchange his wife,
his helper, the architect of his fortune, whose hands were taught their skill by
a heaven-sent love. He wants to exchange for what he calls an affinity a glorious
woman made in the image of God. If you have gone down into the refrigerating
rooms of a big packing house and looked at that row of pigs faces hanging on
their hooks you have seen a perfect picture of affinity fools unmasked.[5]

As if this was not enough to stoke the fires of public outrage, Catherine
Wright still had some ammunition left. She invoked the innocence of their
children and her willingness to sacrifice everything for them. "Any indignity
can be pressed upon me. I can bear everything. It does not count so much,
because you see, our lives practically have been lived. But I would do anything
in this wide, wide world for the protection of our children. Why must they
suffer for they worship their father and love their mother. If I only could protect them now I would care for nothing else. I am living for them now."
    When asked about the possibility of a divorce, unlike Cheney, she held
nothing back. In the name of saving her marriage and family she took the high
road: "I shall make no appeal whatever to the courts. . . . I stand by my husband right at this moment I am his wife. He loves his children tenderly now
and has the greatest anxiety for their welfare. He will come back to them. . . .
I do not say a word against my husband."[6] She was determined there should
be no grounds for divorce and that above all Mamah Borthwick should not
become Mrs. Frank Lloyd Wright.
    The events of 1909 turned the world upside down for another woman left
behind in Oak Park. Lizzie Borthwick, Mamah's dependable middle sister, had
always been there for her. Willing to stay behind and hold down the fort, she
had remained at home when Mamah and Jessie went off to the Dakota Territory. They, not she, had been the ones to marry and bear children. Like her
namesake, Lizzie Borthwick Felton (see chapter 1), she had no children but
was a loving surrogate mother for her niece Jessie. The Cheneys' growing, busy
household had been her joy for nine years. Now that was about to end unless
she could change Mamah's mind. As will be seen, she would try her best to
do so and must have exchanged many letters with her sister. None have survived, nor have any of Mamah's letters to her children, but it can be assumed
she wrote often, perhaps promising to take them on a long summer vacation
just like in old times.

A sense of loss and uncertainty gripped both the Cheney and Wright households. In a scene in William Guthrie's play *Beyond Disillusion*, Laura (the Catherine character) presides over a family dinner on her wedding anniversary, June 1, with a vacant chair for her husband, his framed picture sitting next to her. Nearby in Cheney House, Edwin Cheney and Lizzie Borthwick must have held similar vigils as they wondered how the drama would play out.

Despite the blow to his personal reputation, Wright felt he would be able to revive his career by promoting the Wasmuth portfolio. Borthwick did not have a plan for herself beyond living with Wright, but now she found herself alone in Germany. Nothing had prepared her for the bleakness of her situation at the onset of winter in Leipzig.

CHAPTER 18

MISSION TO STOCKHOLM

Leipzig was the center of Europe's fur trade, a seasonal business that thrived during an especially cold winter like that of 1909/10. Buyers and sellers of fine furs like ermine, sable, marmot, and mink crowded the city, where languages other than German, especially Russian, were heard on the street. Borthwick had left America when the weather was warm; she probably needed a fur coat. Since it was almost Christmas, Wright may have bought her one.

They rendezvoused in Paris at Christmas after she had gone to Berlin to retrieve their mail.[1] Except for a time in late November, when he stopped to see her on his way to Berlin, she had been living on her own, poring over Ellen Key's works in French and German. She seems to have realized that as much as she was devoted to Wright, he could not provide her with direction or financial security. She resolved to try to become Ellen Key's translator.

Only one of Key's books, *Century of the Child*, had been published in English, translated from German and published by G. P. Putnam's Sons in 1909. The long-overdue ideas it contained about education and more relaxed rules of child-rearing were eventually picked up and expanded by pioneer educators like Maria Montessori. The book had sold well on both sides of the Atlantic, with sales seven times higher in the United States than in the UK. Clearly there was a strong market in America for translations of Key's books. The British author Havelock Ellis had urged Key to authorize more translations in English. A skilled translator in French and a pioneer in the new field of "sexual science," Ellis was eager to find someone in England with a command of Swedish to translate Key's works. In effect, he competed with Borthwick in a race to publish such translations. She would have to act quickly if she was to become Key's designated English translator. Ellis won the first heat of the race, managing to arrange an English translation of *Love and Marriage* in

160

1911, but much more of Key's work remained stubbornly in Swedish, German, and French.

Borthwick knew that only through a face-to-face encounter with Key could she gain the author's confidence in her dedication and ability. Happily, there was an opportunity to connect through an organization in Leipzig. Five years earlier, Key had helped found the Bund für Mutterschutz und Sexualreform in the city. Known also as the Mutterschutzbund, the organization was dedicated to equalizing the legal rights of women in marriage and bringing state support to unmarried mothers, an unthinkable proposition in much of the world at the time. It is likely that Borthwick reached out to Key through the Mutterschutzbund. She must have been relieved to receive an answer. Their initial correspondence is lost, but it is clear that they arranged to meet in Sweden.[2]

Having spent several years speaking and traveling across Europe, Key had been mostly absent from Sweden. Returning to her homeland in late 1909, she began looking for a place to build a home and decided on a location on the shore of Lake Vättern in the central southern part of the country. The name of the house would be Strand ("beach" in Swedish), and she would live there for the rest of her life. But this was the winter of 1909/10, the ground was frozen, and construction could not begin until March.

On the occasion of her sixtieth birthday on December 11, 1909, Key had received unremitting attention from her admirers. This proved to be an exhausting experience, after which she sought solitude in a rural location, probably with her sister Ada in Värmland, followed by a stay in Stockholm with the wealthy publisher Karl Otto Bonnier and his wife, Lisen.[3]

In early 1910, Borthwick boarded a train in Leipzig to begin the journey to Stockholm. No one was there to see her off (Wright having left for Italy in November) as she departed on what would prove to be for her the most consequential part of her European journey. In Berlin, she boarded a special overnight train to Stockholm called "the King's Route" because it had been inaugurated by King Gustaf of Sweden. Her sleeper car, unhooked upon arrival in the port of Sassnitz, was rolled onto a ferry for the seventy-mile trip across the Baltic. Upon reaching the Swedish port of Trelleborg, it was reattached to a train that continued to Stockholm.

Nestled in its island-strewn passage off the Baltic, Stockholm displayed its winter snow like a dowager countess who takes her jewelry for granted. There was no ostentation, just a splendid vista from the Grand Hotel, where Borthwick probably stayed, facing the Royal Palace across a wide canal. From there the view of the city extended to include the opera, the banks, and the great business houses, creating a facade that, like that of every European capital, disguised the poverty in which much of its population lived. As one visitor observed of the winter there, "Behind the Palace, tucked away beneath its skirts, are the dark and ugly streets of the poor. The tenements are close together and the alleys narrow. Light rarely penetrates to the lower floors. In winter it is dark at three in the afternoon. From then on, through the long night, the poor remain in utter darkness. The fuel has to be used for heat, not light."[4]

Soon after arriving, Borthwick would have called on Key, who was living with the Bonniers on one of the city's central islands, Djurgården, where the family owned two houses: a smaller one, Villa Mullberget, built in the Swedish folk romantic style, and a larger one that had been the home of the Spanish ambassador. Ellen Key may have received Borthwick in one of the houses.

Years later, an American woman, Madeleine Doty, would meet Key in the winter of 1917/18 and describe her as a warm, receptive host. On assignment

Villa Mullberget, Stockholm. Designed in the national romantic style, the villa belonged to members of the wealthy Bonnier family with whom Ellen Key sometimes stayed. It may have been where she received Mamah Borthwick in the winter of 1910. Villa Mullberget at Djurgården in Stockholm by Holger, Ellgaard, CC BY-SA 3.0 AT.

for *Good Housekeeping* magazine to write a special on the women's movement in Europe, Doty had exited Russia through Finland, transited through Stockholm, and from there found her way to Key's doorstep. Key's warm greeting upon her wintry arrival was probably like the one Borthwick received.

> Ellen Key greeted me at her front door. By daylight the youth in her eyes was even more apparent. Her body might grow old, but her spirit never would. She led me to the open fire in the big living-room. She felt my stockings to make sure they were dry. . . . There is so much mother love in Ellen Key. She ought to have had a dozen children. Soon we were deep in talk, and I was telling of my trip around the world, and presently I felt Ellen Key's hand on mine, and tears were in her eyes and welled over as she said: "Oh, I am so glad you're a woman who understands. I was afraid you might be the other kind of American, and then I should have had to say things that would hurt you." I had come to Ellen Key out of the unknown; She had never heard of me, but in a few minutes it was as though we had known each other all our lives. Our hearts beat for the same purposes and the same end. We recognized each other as part of the great woman's movement which we loved. It was a day of sheer gladness.[5]

A historical figure like Key with a lifetime that straddles two centuries tends to lack a clear association with either one. In 1910, she was arguably one of the best-known women in Europe, and yet, partly because of her birth in 1849, her reputation faded in the twentieth century. A gifted orator, she was not bombastic but held her audience by quieting her voice rather than raising it. Her willingness to question society's cherished cultural assumptions earned her a reputation for sincerity and honesty, but it also attracted powerful enemies. In Sweden she became so controversial that by 1900 she had decided to spend more time in other parts of Europe.

Key's intellectual interests spanned many aspects of human development. As a young woman, she wrote about and spoke effectively on behalf of women's rights, and more generally individual human rights (although the concept of human rights would not be thoroughly developed until later in the twentieth century). Despite having been raised amid the conventions of nineteenth-century Sweden, she challenged public policies affecting women. This led to ever-increasing criticism from social conservatives until she left Sweden to lecture and travel in Europe.

Key established her international reputation initially by writing on the education and the upbringing of children. With the publication of *Kärlaken och*

Ellen Key. Ellen Key Society.

äktenskapet in 1903 (*Love and Marriage*, 1911), she became the leading voice for
women's rights and sexual freedom as well. Never married, she had an intense
love affair with a married man until she was forty. It ended bitterly. Childless,
she found herself serving as a surrogate mother to her brother's children when
their mother's mental health collapsed. She became very close to them. By integrating these experiences with her philosophical perspective, Key engaged
audiences with conviction and authority. Schooled by private tutors in an aristocratic family, she was heavily influenced by her father, a liberal politician.

    Wherever she happened to live, Key surrounded herself with intellectuals
and artists, many of whom idolized her. In Sweden, her group of friends called
themselves Sällskapet Junta (the Junta Society). They advocated a kind of "life
reform" that drew inspiration from the Arts and Crafts movement as well as
other artistic and literary reform movements. Committed to folk traditions and
progressive social ideas, they sought to establish a new national identity based
on the kind of "everyday beauty" that Key espoused. If Borthwick remained

for a few extra days in Stockholm, she may have been introduced to Key's friends, especially those in the women's movement. Key and her friend Amalia Fahlstedt had started a network for women in Stockholm called Tolfterna, with members from all classes and walks of life.

Women in Sweden had begun to express their point of view more forcefully in literature, as in Elin Wägner's novel *Pennskaftet* (*Penwoman*), published in 1910. It was an instant best seller and a flagship statement for the Swedish women's movement. An exchange in the novel, in which an annoying man in the boardinghouse where the young journalist Penwoman lives tries to goad her, illustrates the new cultural atmosphere:

> "No, it can't be easy for someone with such a pugnacious spirit to be a woman," he teased. "Tell me, Miss Penwoman," he said, squinting up at her, as she stood by the door, "Wouldn't you love to be a man?" Penwoman screwed up her left eye and pondered for a moment.
>
> "No, but wouldn't you?" she asked in turn.[6]

Elin Wägner eventually became Key's critic after effectively succeeding her as the leader of the Swedish feminist movement. As was so often the case with Key, the disagreement was over the limitations that motherhood should impose on a woman's role in society. The irony cannot have been lost on Borthwick. She had chosen as her mentor a conservative who believed that a woman's obligation was to prioritize her role as a mother. It must have been a delicate moment when she tried to explain why she, a married woman with children, was living abroad. She may not have explained her whole story, but Key herself had had an affair with a married man and believed in a woman's right to leave her husband. Eventually, it would seem, Key accepted Borthwick's circumstances while being gently reproving of her decision to leave her children.

The two generally agreed on the issues facing women and appear to have seen modern theater as an effective means of expressing these issues. One of the projects Borthwick and Key initially agreed upon was a translation of Key's essay on Ibsen, *The Torpedo under the Ark*, which later became subtitled "Ibsen and Women." No longer a new subject in Scandinavia, Ibsen's critique of bourgeois culture in the context of how women were treated was by then relatively familiar, and Key sought to inject fresh insights.

She must have been impressed from the outset by Borthwick, who somehow managed to convince the author of her linguistic abilities and gain her

Caricature of Ellen Key by Anders Forsström. By 1900 when this political cartoon appeared in the Swedish humor magazine *Söndags-Nisse*, conservative opposition to Ellen Key had so intensified that she decided to leave Sweden to deliver her feminist views in other countries. Universitetsbiblioteket, Lund University.

trust as a translator. Key is likely to have been pleased by Borthwick's admiration for Gerhart Hauptmann and the fact that Borthwick had translated some of his work, since Key was a family friend of the Hauptmanns and was a frequent guest at their residence in Paraggi, Italy. A further connection might have been the fact that both women had Scottish ancestry and took pride in it.

The two agreed that once Borthwick had acquired a reading knowledge of Swedish, she would translate *The Torpedo under the Ark*. If that went well, she would translate three Swedish essays for a book titled (in English) *The Morality of Woman*. Initially, however, she would translate the book *Liebe und Ethik* (*Love and Ethics*) from German. It was a reasonable, low-risk way to allow Borthwick to demonstrate her skills. They adopted a filial relationship from the outset; Borthwick later told Wright's assistant Taylor Woolley that Key had treated her like a daughter. Still, her attitude to Key was more like that of a disciple. Key became her mentor, her guiding philosophical light, and a trusted friend.

Aboard the train on her return, we have to assume that Borthwick was in a buoyant mood: she had achieved her purpose in going to Stockholm and would now potentially become a mouthpiece for a leader of Europe's "Woman Movement." Key's philosophical guidance about love and personal freedom had come at a pivotal moment, enabling Borthwick to rationalize the sacrifices she had made at great cost to herself and her family. Upon returning to Leipzig, she began to learn Swedish and apparently made connections with several German women's organizations, some with religious affiliations. It is likely that through one of them, she arranged in advance to stay in a residence for single women in Berlin called Amalienhaus, where she lived temporarily in September.

Key sought to educate Borthwick on the societal problems of European working-class women and about issues of peace and human rights. In a letter from the fall of 1910, Borthwick thanked Key for a copy of her article on the "peace question," presumably Key's widely praised address to the Stockholm Peace Conference in August 1910.[7]

They continued to correspond with one another despite uncertain postal service. Given Key's voluminous international correspondence, the fact that she gave this much attention to Borthwick suggests that she saw something special in her new acolyte. After their first meeting, they had one or perhaps two more meetings from which they forged a partnership based purely on trust rather than a contract. In later years, their relationship was strained by Havelock Ellis's insinuations behind Borthwick's back that she had fallen short as Key's translator, but her devotion to her mentor was unshakable. What is harder to assess in light of Key's complex personality is her trust in Borthwick as a translator. Her contradictions were summarized by someone who knew her well, the Swedish essayist and translator Hellen Lindgren:

> In Ellen Key there are two people, one personal, the other quite impersonal; one extremely sensitive, the other dryly sensible, almost matter of fact; one hot and passionate, the other absolutely self-controlled. This characteristic contradiction may also be observed in her gently modulated voice, and her very energetic mode of expression. The smooth, nunlike hair, and the generally dark, plain dress give the impression of one who wishes to efface herself, while, on the other hand, there is something almost despotic in her unwillingness to yield in a discussion.[8]

As Europe's most prominent female intellectual, Key attracted a following through her intellect and force of personality. It was all the more remarkable, then, that upon their very first meeting she had agreed to make Borthwick her

translator. It was not for lack of options; in addition to Ellis's sustained interest, another American translator named Mary Bright had offered her services
to Key in a letter—and had been turned down.[9] Something about Borthwick,
despite her incomplete knowledge of Swedish, had made Key decide to take a
chance on her. She only required that Borthwick perfect her reading knowledge of the language.

CHAPTER 19

~~❦~~

LOVE AND ETHICS

Entrance into the city was largely effected through the vast late medieval gates
on whose walls painted saints watched over the inhabitants' welfare and
spiritual well-being. . . . And yet by the end of the nineteenth century
conditions were changing fundamentally. . . . Modernism was already beating
at the gates in the guise of the clearcut lines of the railway that swept into the
town to the west of the Fortezza da Basso.

—BERND ROECK, *Florence 1900*

It was an unusually cold winter. Snow rarely falls in Florence, but that January frost was plentiful; it lingered daily on the statue of David in the Piazzale
Michelangelo, where Wright often strolled to take in its fine view of the city.
He lived nearby, along the steep Erta Canina Street, where he rented an apartment from a Scottish woman, Alice Mary Henderson.[1] Joined there by his two
assistants, Taylor Woolley and his son Lloyd, he began the task of redrawing
his works for publication by Wasmuth.

The work was slow and uncomfortable, requiring them to warm hands
numb from the cold next to braziers. Lloyd later wrote of the long hours spent
working at drawing tables and the constant difficulty of heating the rooms
where they traced the drawings that had been done by Marion Mahoney,
Wright, and others in America, keeping their original size and scale. Periodi-
cally, Wright would leave to take these drawings to Berlin, with train itineraries that conveniently stopped in Leipzig. Wasmuth photographically reduced
or enlarged the drawings to a uniform size, then transferred the images to
lithographic stones for printing. Various editions were to appear in the coming
years, some magnificently presented.

Meanwhile, an assertive modernist movement, Futurism, had surfaced to
fan the flames of Italy's culture wars. While the pope pursued his antimodern-
ist campaign in Rome, in Milan the poet Filippo Tommaso Marinetti issued
his Manifesto of Futurism, an anarchistic rejection of the past in all art and

politics. Distributed in fliers across Italy, it even appeared on the front page of *Le Figaro* in Paris. In the Café Giubbe Rosse near the Duomo in Florence, writers and artists debated the Futurist's call to "spit on the altar of art." The manifesto's underlying spirit became obvious when its adherents, including Marinetti himself, became enthusiastic Fascists in the 1920s. In any case, neither the pope's remonstrations nor Futurism had any discernible effect on Wright or on the distinguished Italian artist Giorgio Morandi, who overlapped with him in Florence at this time. A pioneering modern of the twentieth century, Morandi instead found much of his inspiration in late medieval and early Renaissance artists such as Giotto, Masaccio, and Piero della Francesca. The city had a similar effect on Wright. Like Morandi, he took inspiration from his venerable surroundings in ways that would one day be reflected in his work.

In February, he took the opportunity to move to nearby Fiesole, an ancient Etruscan town high in the hills overlooking Florence. Known for having attracted visionaries over the centuries, Fiesole had in fact summoned giants. It was where Dante had owned land, Leonardo had tested his ideas for manned flight, and Galileo had gone to die. With opportunities for fine walks along old roads and a panoramic view of Florence from the "cream white villa" Wright rented, Fiesole would provide the perfect home for him to share with Borthwick.

By late February, much of the work on his portfolio had been completed and Wright took a break, traveling to Leipzig and Berlin. He had been paying his two assistants what were called "tracer's wages," so he gave them a bonus that would allow them to go off together and tour beyond Italy. When the time came for Lloyd to return to America in early March, he and his father met in Paris while Woolley returned to Fiesole to help finish the work. After saying goodbye to Lloyd, Wright returned to Leipzig to meet Borthwick. It is possible that he met her in Coblenz (Koblenz); a letter he wrote to Woolley in July hinted that by then he had traveled down the Rhine from Coblenz to Cologne, a romantic journey he is likely to have taken with Borthwick.[2] From there, they traveled to Fiesole, arriving in mid-March.

At last, they could live together and savor life. Despite the initially chilly weather, they would have occasionally taken the tram line into Florence, one of Italy's most historic and artistically rich cities. Wright described their house in Fiesole, Villino Belvedere, in a letter to Ashbee as "a charming little place with its tiny enclosed garden hanging out over the valley." Their depression and dissatisfactions of the previous fall were forgotten. Wright wrote happily to Ashbee of their situation: "I have been very busy here in this little eyrie on

Garden, Villino Belvedere, Fiesole. The small garden of the villino where Borthwick and Wright lived had expansive views of the countryside. Photograph by Taylor Woolley. Special Collections, J. Willard Marriott Library, the University of Utah.

the brow of the mountain above Fiesole—overlooking the pink and white, Florence spreading in the valley of the Arno below—the whole fertile bosom of the earth seemingly lying in the drifting mists or shining clear and marvelous in this Italian sunshine—opalescent—iridescent."[3]

Their Chicago contemporary Theodore Dreiser visited Fiesole shortly after Wright and Borthwick left. He was similarly enchanted with what he described as "the wind singing in the cypresses, a faint mist blowing down the valley of the Arno, all Florence lying below and the lights of evening beginning to appear."[4]

They dreamed of one day returning to Fiesole. Wright even worked on a design for a house he imagined for them there, to be located on the hillside near the Villa Medici, not far from where they were staying. Like Cheney House and the nearby Italian villas, it would have been protected by a wall, its residential area unobservable from the street. But it could not have matched the charm of where they were staying, the Villino Belvedere, with its small, open garden and a breathtaking view of the countryside. The villino came with a cook and was well furnished. It even contained a cello and piano.

As the days grew warmer, the two men and Borthwick set about their respective tasks. Her first attempts at translating from Swedish were complicated by Key's convoluted writing style and her own inexperience as a translator. For example, she used the word "erotic" in its old-fashioned Webster's dictionary sense to mean the "passion of love," despite its sexual connotation in common usage. Nevertheless, the translations further exposed her to Key's wide-ranging humanist vision. In the words of Key's biographer Ronny Ambjörnsson, "She was in the best meaning of the word a European intellectual, and one of the last people in Swedish cultural history for whom the whole European tradition of ideas was real."[5] While Key occasionally employed naive ideas of Darwinian evolution and the inherent natures of the sexes, she synthesized the views of philosophers like Friedrich Nietzsche, Auguste Comte, John Stuart Mill, and Herbert Spencer into a unique vision.

In translating *The Torpedo under the Ark: Ibsen and Women*, Borthwick encountered for the first time the full force of Key's feminist argument. It seemed to speak specifically to her. "It is the woman who has wholly desired, wholly loved, yes, often wholly sinned. Almost invariably it is the woman who breaks out of the cage, or the ark, or the doll house. And he believes that she, without the barriers, will find her right road, led by a surer instinct than man. She, less than he, needs to submit to the social moral code; for her greater power of devoting herself wholly endows her with a nobler instinct and therewith the right to a greater ethical freedom of choice."[6]

Key's small book *Love and Ethics* was especially relevant to the circumstances that confronted Wright and Borthwick. Less challenging for Borthwick to translate because it was written in German, its style of expression was nevertheless ornate. But because of a strange misunderstanding, someone else had begun translating *Love and Ethics* as well. Apparently with Key's blessing, a woman in America named Amalie K. Boguslawsky, an authority on Tolstoy's writing on women, was working on it for the publisher B. W. Huebsch. Boguslawsky's version would be published the following year, well ahead of Borthwick's translation, even though Borthwick had received Key's promise that she would be the exclusive translator in English. It was perhaps fortunate that Borthwick remained unaware of this debacle while she was in Europe and so avoided a confrontation with Key about it until later.

Wright helped with the translation of *Love and Ethics*, even though he did not speak German. Named as her cotranslator on the book's title page, he may have contributed more than style and expression—in particular the use of the word "soul" (*die Seele*). In addressing the justification for leaving one's spouse, Key argued against "the irrational doctrine that it is at all times the death of the soul to sacrifice others, and the life of the soul to sacrifice oneself for others." Influenced by Darwin's theory of evolution, she had asserted elsewhere that the soul is an object of evolution in a process enabled by love. She was far more specific about the soul's development than Ralph Waldo Emerson, Wright's prior source on the subject. The Austrian philosopher Robert Musil credited Key with having profoundly influenced his thinking about the soul. Wright was never clear about what the word meant for him, but the man being denounced as a sinner from pulpits across the nation was more concerned with the development of his soul than people realized. Raised by ministers, he took the concept of the soul seriously, even if he interpreted it differently. He had not hesitated to relate his ideas on beauty and art to the development of the soul. His influence on Borthwick's use of the word "soul" is apparent in her translation of *Love and Ethics*, where it appears twenty-three times. In the rival Huebsch publication, it is used only twelve times. As summarized by historian Alice T. Friedman, *Love and Ethics* "was one of the very first products of the spiritual and professional partnership that Wright and Borthwick embraced, and they based a great deal of their understanding of the nature of their relationship on the ideas described in the text itself."[7]

Key's views on what she called "beauty in the home" may have made an impression on Wright. She advocated that rooms should be sparse, with clean geometry and natural light, and use natural materials in architecture and furnishings. But as Wright's de facto adviser, she had a competitor in Reverend William Norman Guthrie. In late 1908, during his second set of lectures in Oak Park, Guthrie seems to have been a familiar figure in the Wright household and to have styled himself as Wright's moral compass. Long before Wright publicly admitted in his 1932 autobiography that he had been conflicted and confused as he prepared to leave the United States, Guthrie depicted him in that frame of mind in his 1915 play *Beyond Disillusion*. In one scene, Richard Walter (Wright) is preparing to run away to Europe, and his mother brings in a friendly minister to try to stop him. That minister is transparently Guthrie. In 1910, he had left his position at the University of Chicago to serve temporarily as director of extension services at the University of the South in Sewanee, Tennessee. Traveling and lecturing throughout the Upper Midwest on the topic "The Ideal Marriage," he naturally advised Wright to return to his wife and resume life in Oak Park "even if your companion in revolt is not your companion in misery and refuses to see the truth."[8]

Ellen Key was effectively arguing the opposite, that Wright had every right to stay with Borthwick and that doing so in the name of love would sustain his spiritual quest. This argument may account for his growing confidence in his course of action and his rejection of Guthrie's advice. By late August, he

had informed Robert Ashbee in a letter that his inner struggle was over and
that he would return to the United States to rebuild his practice. Left unsaid
was his resolve to build a future with Borthwick.

In contrast to Wright's growing if uncertain confidence, Borthwick's translation of *Love and Ethics* reflected her own inner turmoil. Key used the word
Nebenfrauen (concubines or mistresses) to support her view that society should
make divorce easier because "easy divorces are and were custom and law"
among ancient Hebrews and Japanese, for whom having a *Nebenfrau* was an
alternative to divorce. This may not have been acceptable to Borthwick since
it implied that in the absence of Wright receiving a divorce, her status as permanent mistress would be an acceptable alternative. Her distaste for the idea
may account for her decision to translate *Nebenfrauen* as "plural wives,"[9] even
though in the rival translation, Boguslawsky had more accurately translated it
as "concubinage."

There would be other works for Borthwick to translate from the Swedish
original rather than the German. One of the works in Swedish, *The Morality of Woman*, is built on the themes developed in *Love and Ethics*.[10] Morality
for Key was all about the integrity of a woman's love and maternity, whether
or not they were legalized by marriage. For all the criticism directed at Key
as a conservative, her positions made her a radical feminist for her time and
generation. In the case of Wright and Borthwick, she provided them with a
reasoned, moral framework for continuing to live together.

A message about love was well suited to their idyllic Italian surroundings.
In his autobiography, Wright recalled their life that summer as a high point.
They spent hours walking in the countryside,

> or out walking in the high-walled garden that lay alongside the cottage in the
> Florentine sun or in the little garden by the pool arbored under climbing masses
> of yellow roses.
>
> I see the white cloth on the small stone table near the little fountain and
> beneath the clusters of yellow roses, set for two. There were long walks along the
> waysides of those undulating hills above, toward Vallombrosa.
>
> The waterfall there finding and losing its own sound in the deep silences
> of that famous pine wood. Breathing deep the odor of great pines—tired out, to
> sleep at the cloistered little mountain inn. Back again walking hand in hand
> miles through the hot sun and deep dust of the ancient winding road: an old
> Italian road, along the stream. How old! How thoroughly a [Roman] road!

Their explorations further afield in Italy, while uncertain, are believed to have included Venice, Rome, and Milan.[11]

Together, tired out, sitting on benches in the galleries of Europe, saturated with plastic beauty. Beauty in buildings, beauty and sculpture, beauty and painting until no "chiesa," however rare, and no further beckoning work of human hands could draw or waylay us anymore.[12]

Dreiser found the area of Fiesole similarly idyllic. He recalled "white, yellow, blue, brown and sea-green houses, wooden plows, white oxen, and ambling, bare-footed friars."

Not long after Borthwick had joined Wright in Fiesole, they decided to entertain guests. They invited a young Russian couple who had lived next door to Wright when he was in Florence, Marie "Mascha" Djakoffsky von Heiroth (1871–1934), a writer, and her husband, Alexander, an artist. Mascha spoke six languages and played the piano and cello. Her diary's description of the visit is written in French.

Last Sunday [March 27] we made our pilgrimage to the Wrights in Fiesole who received us quite well. They live in the charming little Villa Belvedere near our dear old Casa Ricci, with its lovely little garden and its impressive view of Florence. Algar [Mascha's son, almost two] misbehaved without bothering anyone since I brought the maid along with us to take care of him. After lunch, which we ate in a tiny dining room, I accompanied Sasha on Wright's cello then we looked at his extremely interesting drawings of houses, palaces, and churches, after which we went to the piazza.[13]

Mascha spoke Swedish along with several other languages and as a devotee of Ellen Key is likely to have found in Borthwick a kindred spirit.[14] She was painted by several artists, including the Finnish painter Albert Edelfelt, whose portrait of her hangs in the Hermitage Museum. In the 1890s, she had been a teacher of Swedish in Helsinki, where she had been the muse and lover of the Spanish essayist, poet, and novelist Ángel Ganivet. She and Borthwick were of a similar age and had an advanced education. Much earlier, Mascha too had left her husband and children. Her reference to Borthwick and Wright as "the Wrights" suggests that they had continued to pretend to be married. The facade worked well among strangers and allowed them to postpone facing reality.

"Mascha" and Alexander von Heiroth. Exemplifying sophisticated European "moderns" of the early 1900s, the couple met Frank Lloyd Wright in Florence and later visited him and Borthwick in Fiesole. Wright bought a painting from von Heiroth. Finnish National Board of Antiquities.

But the pleasures of Fiesole had little effect on Wright's emotional turmoil. His correspondence reveals his stress over returning to America. Each letter bears a special tone and significance. Writing to Ashbee, he affirmed how important their friendship was to him in contrast to the sham he believed his marriage to be. On March 31, he tried to justify his decision to leave America with Borthwick: "I wanted to square my life with myself. I want to do this now more than anything else. I want to live true as I would build true, and in the light I have I have tried to do this thing. Advice has been of little use. The necessary light must come from within. Life is living and living only brings the light."[15]

Of his correspondence at this time, nothing expresses guilt mixed with rebellion like his letter to his mother on July 4. He had no intention of genuinely reconciling with Catherine, but he knew he must maneuver carefully with Anna Wright. Her cooperation was vital for the success of his plans. He apologized for being so long out of touch: "I have been so troubled and perplexed I have not known what to write." Anguished and defensive, he was aware of how his absence had damaged his family, but he refused to believe that their suffering had been great. In fact, he asserted that if it came to sacrificing his family for his art, he was ready to do so.

> I may be the infatuated weakling, she [Mamah] may be the child-woman inviting harm to herself and others—but nevertheless the basis of this whole struggle was the desire for a fuller measure of life and truth at any cost—and as such an act wholly sincere—and respectable—within—whatever aspect it may have worn without. This by my return I discredit because I seemingly endorse the character made for it publicly by those, whom by my returning to them I seem to endorse. This bitter draught seems to me—almost more than I can bear—the last weight of a degradation otherwise not hopeless. I turn from it in disgust, and hard as it was to throw down what I had worked hard for twenty years to build up, it is doubly hard to go to work again among the ruins—poorer in heart, in mind, in pocket—robbed even of the sustaining sense of the truth when dealing such a foul blow to the woman who trusted her all to me in the struggle as I do when I endorse the character made publicly for her by those for whom I leave her.

The realization that his actions had placed Borthwick in peril made him feel all the more outraged by his dilemma.

> I dread the aspect my return must wear, I am the prodigal—whose return is a triumph for THE INSTITUTIONS I have outraged—A weak son who infatuated sexually has had his passion drained and therewith his courage, and so abandoning the source of his infatuation to whatever fate may hold for her—probably a hard lonely struggle in the face of a world that writes her down as an outcast to be shunned,—or a craven return to another man, his prostitute for a roof and a bed and a chance to lose her life in her children, that something—some shred of self respect may clothe her nakedness—While I return to my dear wife and children who all along "knew I would" and welcomed by my friends with open rejoicing and secret contempt.[16]

He found Catherine's righteous public posture galling. Portraying herself as ready to forgive him and demonizing Mamah, she had made it clear that she planned to wait this out, aware that he was legally obligated to support her and the children. This made him increasingly bitter toward her. Whatever guilt he may have felt in leaving his family, he had resolved to see things through on his terms. He would return to Oak Park temporarily but never to ask forgiveness.

By early July, Taylor Woolley's help was no longer needed, and he prepared to leave for America. He and Borthwick had become close in Fiesole. They must have discussed word meanings often because as a parting gift she gave him a pair of dictionaries. He later described her as "one of the loveliest women I ever knew." Around the time of his departure there was only one person left who might disturb their privacy: Mamah's sister Lizzie wanted urgently to see and speak with her. In early August 1910, the sister who had always stayed home, the one who had never married or traveled east of South Bend, marshaled her courage and boarded a transatlantic steamer. It was her last-ditch effort to persuade Mamah to return to her family.

The only evidence of Lizzie Borthwick's journey appears in the record of her return on August 20 aboard the *Noordam* from Rotterdam.[17] A port so far north was inconvenient to Italy, especially for an inexperienced traveler. If Lizzie disembarked at Cherbourg, Mamah may have met her there and then for her departure escorted her to Rotterdam. Their meeting is unlikely to have been confrontational, but clearly Lizzie was desperate. She had helped Mamah and Edwin Cheney raise three children from infancy. Her role as a mothering aunt was perhaps central to her identity. But Mamah had decided to remain in Europe to complete her legal separation from Edwin, meaning she would not return for another year. The sisters are likely to have parted more in sorrow than resentment, however, since they never lost touch.

The sojourn in Fiesole served an important function in giving Wright and Borthwick greater certainty about their future course of action. Fortified by Ellen Key's philosophy, they resolved to return to America in the belief that, come what may, they had every right to remain together.

CHAPTER 20

SECESSION

When Mamah Borthwick and Frank Lloyd Wright left Fiesole, only the American consul knew their intended destination. In July, Wright had entered the American consulate in Florence and applied for an emergency joint passport for himself and his alleged wife, "Mamah Borthwick Wright." His stated reason for the application was "travel in Turkey."[1]

The Ottoman Empire had begun to modernize, but Constantinople would not be renamed Istanbul until 1923. The legendary city straddling the Bosporus held a fascination for European visitors who wished to see its architectural wonders. Wright must have known that the opportunity to see Constantinople might never come again. But he was equally keen to visit Vienna, where Secessionist architecture demonstrated the concepts he had embraced. His passport suggests that their plan was to approach Vienna not from the west but from the south on the Orient Express after having first visited Constantinople.

However, we cannot be certain of Wright and Borthwick's itinerary in the late summer of 1910. From the time they left Fiesole until Borthwick's consular appearance in Berlin in September, their whereabouts are uncertain. The passport's unambiguous purpose, "travel in Turkey," raises the tantalizing prospect that Wright used it to pursue his well-known interest in non-Western traditions of architecture and design. But the lack of further evidence and the fact that his money was running out leads to the conclusion that they did not get that far.[2]

Regardless of their travels (or not) in Turkey, they probably arrived in Vienna by early September. A city of aristocratic elegance in the nineteenth century, it was fraying at the edges in 1910. An ugly urban sprawl grew around the city center, which comprised the Imperial Palace, baroque churches, and fine residences, all encircled by the Ringstraße, the grandfather of ring roads built atop Vienna's leveled, medieval city walls. With a population of four hundred thousand in 1848, Vienna had become a city of two million by 1910. Tens of thousands of immigrants struggled to find housing. The Hapsburg image was everywhere. Paintings of Emperor Franz Joseph presided like a divinity over every public building and in nearly every home, his muttonchop whiskers replicated on many a man on the street.

In the distance stood what appeared to be a giant bicycle wheel, the Riesen-rad, erected to commemorate Franz Joseph's golden jubilee in 1898. For visi-tors from Chicago, it commemorated instead Ferris's original version from the 1893 World's Fair. The taut cables holding the wheel intact effectively symbol-ized Vienna's complex cultural tensions. Artists and architects of the so-called Vienna Secession had strained against the center's old order while the well-oiled, civic machinery kept the gears of society turning. Vienna debated new trends and ideas in fields ranging from physics to psychology, from art to architec-ture. A bold statement from the latter, known as the Secessionist Building, was only a five-minute walk from the luxury Bristol Hotel, which would assuredly have been Wright's preferred place to stay.

An outing to see the Secessionist Building might have involved passing through a street of market stalls crowded with head-scarved women from the Balkans until, in full view of the market, as incongruous as a spaceship, a great white block of a building topped by a gigantic sphere of gilt laurel leaves came into view. The words above the door, *Der Zeit ihre Kunst. Der Kunst ihre Freiheit* (To every age its art, to every art its freedom) had served, in effect, as the motto of the Secessionist art movement. Designed by the architect Joseph Olbrich, whom Wright admired, the Secessionist Building would eventually be suc-ceeded by other styles, but its interior frieze by Gustav Klimt enjoyed perma-nence. It served the concept pioneered by the Wiener Werkstätte, a group of Arts and Crafts enthusiasts who believed that a building should be a "total art experience," an idea Wright wholeheartedly endorsed.

The Vienna Secession was not new to Wright. In America, he had followed its development closely by studying pictures in a variety of publications, espe-cially *The Studio*, an illustrated fine arts and decorative arts magazine pub-lished in London.[3] There is no record of the specific buildings they visited, but the Secessionist Building is sure to have been high on Wright's list.

A short walk from the Secessionist Building were two residential buildings at Linke Wienzeile 38–40. Designed by Otto Wagner, a guiding visionary of the Secession, they display art nouveau surface decoration that is not integral to their structure—a transgression, as far as Wright was concerned. He opposed

needless decoration. So did his kindred spirit in Vienna, Adolf Loos, an architect who had just published a treatise that mockingly compared needless decoration to criminality. Loos had designed a bar not far from the Bristol Hotel
that may have intrigued Wright, if he knew about it or learned of its existence.

Located just off the Kärtnerstraße, the American Bar was not part of the
Secession, but it represented the leading edge of commercial design. Its chic
modernity was instantly popular when the bar opened in 1908. If Wright and
Borthwick entered its small space, they probably found themselves standing
among some of the more outré members of the Vienna art scene. Loos had dis-
pensed with all decoration, relying instead on sleek, unadorned surfaces and
bold quadrangles. If a bit austere, it may have been to Wright's liking. Seating
was at small tables and in nooks with upholstered bench seats, with strategically placed wall mirrors adding to the illusion of space. Still well preserved, the
bar displays clean, uncluttered linearity and no-nonsense efficiency. Its luxuri-
ous quality of finish in polished brass, black onyx, and marble adds to the
effect. If they did visit the prototypical American bar of the twentieth century,
Borthwick, the tippling lady of Marshall Field's, might even have ordered a
Manhattan.

A five-minute walk east from the American Bar was the Zacherlhaus, a six-
story commercial building that is still well preserved. Its massive cornice is
upheld by a row of sculpted atlases, their heads bowed and shoulders braced
against its apparent weight. Created by the sculptor Franz Metzner, the semi-
abstracted statues impressed Wright. Historian Anthony Alofsin correlates his
interest in this and other aspects of Secessionism with his "primitivist phase"
over the following decade: "In the work of the Secessionists, Wright saw in
simple geometry a form language that resonated with symbolic meaning."[4]

There were other buildings to see and architects to meet. At this time, Wright
is said to have met, for example, the Austrian architect Josef Hoffmann.[5] But
they could not linger in Vienna. He was already behind schedule in returning
to America, and the pair had one more stop to make before reaching Berlin:
the Passion Play at Oberammergau in Bavaria.[6] Performed once every decade
since 1634, it attracted a global audience. None other than Ellen Key may have
persuaded them to see it. She had been deeply impressed by Oberammergau
when she saw the performance in 1890. In correspondence with Borthwick,
whose travel plans she knew well enough, she may have urged her to go to the
performance. Key had just published a book, *Verk Och Manniskor* (*Man and
Works*), in which she described it at length, extolling its significance: "The Past
as well as the Present conveys to us the assurance that the highest in every age

Atlases (Atlantes) by Franz Metzner, Zacherlhaus (1903–5), Vienna. Zacherlhaus by Thomas Ledl, CC BY-SA 3.0 AT. Cropped original.

is submerged uncomprehended by the majority. The life-renewing truth is always trampled underfoot by the established order . . . It is not by the cross that men have learned to live, but by the cross they have learned to suffer—and as long as living means suffering for the majority, crosses are likely to remain on heights and in valleys."[7]

The rest of the journey took but a day, enabling them to reach Berlin by September 12.[8] After confirming the final steps in his portfolio's publication by Wasmuth, Wright prepared to return to Oak Park to recover his practice. He had never intended to be away for more than a year. Borthwick chose to remain in Berlin to fulfill the legal requirement for a two-year separation from Edwin before receiving a divorce.[9] This meant she had to register with the American consul-general and apply for a certificate of temporary residence in Germany. In the gendered manner of the time, the application referred to the applicant using third-person masculine forms. Where she was required to give the names and ages of her children and an emergency contact, she had to change "he" to "(s)he." This was easily done, but then the form asked for "name of wife," to which she responded, "Widow."[10]

It was during this period that she and Wright began collecting Secession-ist art. He had little money left, but contemporary artists were selling art prints at relatively low cost. Borthwick may have influenced the purchases. Indeed, Alofsin, who cataloged the surviving collection of prints, suggests, "It is conceivable that she alone selected them."[11] She had a deep knowledge of art history and her positive interest in modern art's incipient trend toward abstraction is confirmed, as will be seen, by her confident assessment to Ellen Key of the artist Ejnar Nielsen's effort in that area.[12]

Their venture in art collecting had begun in Italy when Wright purchased a painting from Alexander von Heiroth, a participant in the 1909 Berlin Secession Exhibition.[13] The artist with his wife, Mascha, had visited them in Fiesole. Along with Wright's purchases of Secessionist prints, von Heiroth's painting provides evidence of his and Borthwick's taste in modern art. The work's apparent title, *L'arbre "Japonais"* (*The "Japanese" Tree*), may have been part of why Wright, a Japanophile, found it appealing.

The "Japanese" Tree, *by Alexander von Heiroth*. In Italy in 1910, Frank Lloyd Wright bought this painting from the artist. Finnish National Board of Antiquities.

He worried about leaving Borthwick on her own. He told Darwin Martin he was mindful of her precarious status. But she had lived alone successfully in Leipzig and would do so again in Berlin. There was always the consulate, a social hub for Americans, although it is unlikely she ever entered its premises again. It would have been a disaster for her to meet someone from Chicago who recognized her from the *Tribune* headlines.

Her temporary residence was a hospice for single women in the Schöneberg district called Amalienhaus.[14] Supported by the Twelve Apostles Lutheran Church, Amalienhaus trained young women to become servants in private homes or to work in establishments like laundries and restaurants. Women outnumbered men in Germany by a million, and many struggled to make a living. This would have become clear to Borthwick after Wright had departed. Few if any of the women at Amalienhaus were married, but some had children, and so it also had a nursery. Here Borthwick must have witnessed first-hand the magnitude of poverty experienced by families in Berlin, so many of whom lived on the edge.

Amalienhaus was an austere, undoubtedly depressing place. Run by a team of ten deaconesses who kept strict tabs on the residents, the institution had as much the quality of a workhouse for young women as a training facility.[15] Not bound by its strictures, however, Borthwick was free to experience the typical middle-class life of Berlin. Kempinski's family restaurant, on the corner of the Friedrichstraße, offered excellent food and wine at reasonable prices with quick, polite service. But she undoubtedly led a lonely life with no one to really talk to until she transitioned to a different residence after landing a job teaching at one of Berlin's best schools.

Located in the Wilmersdorf district and founded in 1607, the Joachimsthal Gymnasium was a preparatory school for boys specializing in the classics. It probably hired her to teach English but may have utilized her knowledge of Latin and Greek as well. The Joachimsthal complex occupied nearly a city block. Built in 1876–80 in the style of the Italian High Renaissance, the main building had an arcade with niches for the statues of Plato and Aristotle by the Grunewald sculptor Max Klein. Before a major part of the complex was destroyed by bombs in World War II, it even boasted a very rare painting of Bach. Borthwick lived in the nearby pension at 23 Schaperstraße, where the school housed its teachers. The short, curved street was named for the school's first headmaster.[16]

Borthwick seems to have adapted quickly to Berlin, immersing herself in its culture and working environment. She could have lived in any major European

Amalienhaus, Berlin, ca. 1910. The training school and women's hostel was Borthwick's initial residence in Berlin in 1910. Kunstverlag J. Goldiner, Berlin.

Former building of the Joachimsthal Gymnasium. Mamah Borthwick taught at the elite school for boys from 1910 to 1911. It now houses the Berlin University of the Arts. Kunstverlag J. Goldiner, Berlin.

Teachers' residence for the Joachimsthal Gymnasium. Then called Pension Gottschalk, the building is where Mamah Borthwick lived in 1910–11. Photograph by Sanford Wintersberger.

city, but she chose the German capital. Wright's work on the Wasmuth portfolio was one reason, but another appears to have been Berlin's standing as a
world city and her fluency in German. It must have suited her to live in a
house of well-educated teachers with whom she could share communal meals
and discuss subjects ranging from the laws affecting German women to the
all-encompassing topic of Nietzsche.

On his way back to America, Wright stopped in London to visit Robert
and Janet Ashbee, spending at least a week with them at their place in the
Cotswolds. He was not an entirely congenial guest. Having asked Ashbee to
draft the introduction for the Wasmuth portfolio, he took offense at his
friend's draft, which asserted that he had been influenced by Japan. While this
was arguably true, Wright did not like the way Ashbee put it, and they had a
quarrel. Later, as he left on a ship for America, he wrote a letter of apology.

The personal problems he had left behind were waiting for him upon his
return. The newspapers pounced when they learned he was back, rehashing
the scandal and speculating about what had become of Borthwick. It was the
beginning of a year of false and exaggerated news involving her and Wright.
He tried to reclaim his architectural practice from his colleague Hermann von
Holst only to be stymied by their disagreement over how much von Holst
owed him. As alienated as ever from his wife, he nevertheless planned to turn
part of their house into a rental unit to provide her with an income. He made
it clear to her that he would fulfill the financial aspect of his marital obligation, but otherwise he did not consider himself to be her husband.

Catherine Wright did not hear it quite that way. In an anguished letter to
Janet Ashbee, she reported, "As near as I can find out he has only separated
from her because he wishes to retain the beauty and ideality of their relationship and feared by staying with her he would grow to loathe her." Wright
biographers have made much of this seemingly callous sentiment on his part
without considering what Catherine wanted to believe. She did not realize that
her husband was preparing to return to Berlin. Dissatisfied with the quality of
the Wasmuth portfolio and the delays in its production, he intended to confront the publisher. His other reason for returning to Berlin, of course, was to
see Mamah.

CHAPTER 21

BERLIN TO ALVASTRA

Having secured her lodging and employment in Berlin, Borthwick turned her attention to translating more of Ellen Key's works. A letter she wrote to Key at this time testifies to how much she yearned to see her mentor again. She asked if they could meet in Sweden. Key replied that it would not be convenient because the construction of Strand, the home she was building on the shore of Lake Vättern, was incomplete. She was staying in a pension in the village of Hästholmen nearby and could not readily accommodate visitors.[1]

Borthwick assured Key that she could wait but emphasized her reasons for wanting to go there:

> You have meant more to me than any other influence, but one, in my life. In your writings we have met close together, closer than I have been to almost anyone in the world. Trying to live, at a frightful cost, what I believed to be the only truth and light, groping in perplexity and darkness, with my poor, little dim light "close to my breast," suddenly in my darkest hour I found you, bearing a torch along the path I was trying to tread.
>
> Still however my perplexity and doubt is great that perhaps that path was not after all the one I should have taken—perhaps it is not mine. Your torch however will also light me to the true path—the path true for me—if I have mistaken it.[2]

More than a year after leaving her husband—and her children, surely of greater importance to her—Borthwick was still troubled by the consequences of her actions. By adding that "no other influence, but one" had been as great for her as Key, she acknowledged that her relationship with Wright remained paramount. But her children were never far from her thoughts. When she added,

"Of course, at any time, it is possible I may be called to America," she meant that her faithful sister, Lizzie Borthwick, would contact her if there were an emergency with one of the children.

In this, the first of ten letters Borthwick wrote that are held by the National Library of Sweden, she referred to prior correspondence with Key, none of which has been found. She began the letter reverentially with the words "Miss Ellen Key, most highly honored and beloved lady" but quickly turned to practical matters, relating errands she had done at Key's request. She mentioned having been given a reproduction of a modernist painting by the Swedish artist Einar Nielsen, which depicted Key seated in a Buddha-like pose. Borthwick took the liberty of commenting that she thought the painting's abstract, decorative drapery was poorly accomplished, confirming the familiarity she had by now come to feel with Key.

In the most telling part of the letter, she confessed that she had yet to find "the path true for me." She quoted from memory Robert Browning's "Paracelsus":

If I sink
Into a dark tremendous sea of cloud,
It is but for a time; I press God's lamp
Close to my breast—its splendor, soon or late,
Will pierce the gloom: I shall emerge one day.

Browning's poem meant a great deal to Borthwick. In all probability she also recalled the poem's preceding lines about society's ignorance and its inability to recognize the truth.

As yet men cannot do without contempt—
'Tis for their good, and therefore fit awhile
That they reject the weak, and scorn the false,
Rather than praise the strong and true, in me.
But after, they will know me!

In the spirit of the nineteenth-century romantic poet, Borthwick had embraced Wright's family motto, "Truth against the world." She sought to meet Key not only to discuss the drafts of her translations. She still needed Key's guidance in her personal life and was thus unlikely to have been willing to wait half a year to see her. Although initially rebuffed, it seems she may have succeeded in convincing Key to meet sooner; in other letters, she referred to their having met "in Alvastra," a town near where Strand was being built, and to having gone there to meet Key. Their meeting at Strand did not occur until June 1911, when the house was finally ready to receive visitors. It seems possible they met months earlier in Alvastra: Borthwick noted in her 1910 letter that from the outset she had expected to stay in Alvastra in a hotel.[3]

Another reason they had for meeting earlier arose from Borthwick's translation of *Love and Ethics*. In the fall of 1910, she had sent Key a draft of the translation for approval, but at the time neither of them was aware of an attack on Key's *Century of the Child* by American feminist Charlotte Perkins Gilman. In her magazine *The Forerunner*, Gilman took Key to task for stating that children can be adequately cared for only by mothers remaining in their homes. Contrary to what Gilman believed, Key argued that childcare services should not be provided by the state.[4]

Gilman had considerable standing in the feminist movement, and given her influence, Key had to respond. She would do so through Borthwick's translation and may have invited her to Alvastra to discuss it. The resulting change in the text of *Love and Ethics* criticizes Gilman by name. It argues that society will benefit not from state-organized childcare but from state support for mothers who remain at home to raise their children. How Borthwick viewed the argument, given her own predicament, can only be guessed at.

If she traveled to Alvastra at this time, it was probably around New Year's, during the Joachimsthal school's vacation period. Travel by train to the semi-isolated area of Sweden in winter meant arriving at a small, remote station after dark. Her experience is likely to have been similar to that of the formidable Madeleine Doty (chapter 20), who described what it was like to arrive at the station at night when she visited Key in the dead of winter.

> When I left the train, there was only a small boy on the platform. I gave him my bag, and we trudged off in the deep snow. It was a tiny village with a few wooden houses and a church. We turned in at a farmhouse, and a friendly woman with a lantern greeted us. Soon I was drinking hot coffee and eating sandwiches.
>
> In a few minutes a horse and sleigh were at the door. There was but one seat, so I climbed up beside the driver. The small boy piled my bags on behind, and we were off. The sleighing was good. We dashed along a well-traveled country road, but after a couple of miles we veered off across a field. The horse floundered in snow up to his middle. Many times we nearly upset. It was very cold; I had wrapped a blanket tight around my head and shoulders.

But it was a beautiful night. The stars shone brightly. The horse pulled us up through the deep snow, across the field, and as we mounted a great lake spread below us. It was so vast it had no beginning or end. The water sparkled in the starlight. The snow-covered fields, the whiteness and the radiance were unearthly. The lapping water, the great peace, the magic brightness thrilled me.

At the top of the hill we left the sleigh. Beyond, halfway down the hill on the other side, among evergreen trees, nestled a white house. I followed the driver. We plunged into snow over our knees. No path had been cleared. It was a hard pull to the house. When we reached the front door, there was no light, and all was still. My heart sank. But presently there was the sound of hurrying feet. A smiling, wholesome young maid greeted us. In a moment she had gone for Ellen Key. I waited in the dim hall and wondered. Then a woman, neither small nor large, with white hair and dressed in gray, came toward me. It was her eyes that held me. They were the eyes of youth, full of passionate eagerness. Ellen Key is sixty-seven, but you do not think of her age, she is so alive. Her manner is gentle and without self-consciousness. Her thought was all for me. Was I wet? Was I cold? How had I got there?[5]

Although this was at Strand in 1917, the description gives some indication of the reception Borthwick probably received from Key in Alvastra in 1911. In addition to boosting Borthwick's morale, the meeting with Key undoubtedly enabled Borthwick to discuss other translations with her and benefit from Key's extensive contacts in Berlin, which had been like a second home to Key. Her network of artists and intellectuals there was unparalleled. Early on, Borthwick met some of Key's friends in the course of doing errands for her in Berlin. Key may have provided introductions to others as well. Being Key's English translator almost certainly gave Borthwick an entrance with members of Key's network. However, no specific references to these meetings appear in the surviving letter exchange with Key.

Four women in particular were prominent members of Key's Berlin circle: Gabrielle Reuter, Ricarda Huch, Anselma Heine, and Lou Andreas-Salomé.[6] The novelist Anselma Heine (1855–1930), known to her friends as Selma, believed that men feared the loss of women's mystique and viewed professional women primarily in terms of being their competitors. On this, Ellen Key agreed. Gabrielle Reuter's confessional novel *From a Good Family*, about an adolescent middle-class girl, had been a huge success. For three decades, she was one of Berlin's most prominent feminist writers. Ricarda Huch was a historian whose emphasis on the role of women in early German Romanticism led her to evoke the character and circumstances of a period rather than write about big events and military campaigns. She thereby opened a new chapter in German historiography. Of the four, the closest to Ellen Key was Lou Andreas-Salomé, a Russian-born psychoanalyst and writer remembered for her friendships with Nietzsche and Freud and for being the lover of the poet Rainer Maria Rilke (of whom Ellen Key was an early champion). These women represented the new modernist milieu of Berlin and made important creative contributions in early twentieth-century Germany. Any one or all of them would have provided Borthwick with stimulating company.

Meanwhile, Wright was on his way back to Berlin to address the delays and unforeseen problems with the Wasmuth portfolio. His desire to see Borthwick was surely another reason to make the transatlantic trip. It was probably she who somehow obtained tickets to Germany's cultural event of the year, the premier of Richard Strauss's opera *Der Rosenkavalier* in Dresden on January 26.[7] An immediate worldwide hit, the opera was so popular that special trains had to be arranged from Berlin. By the end of the year, the Chicago Symphony Orchestra was performing it in Orchestra Hall.

Wright did not leave Germany until mid-March even though a new contract with Wasmuth was signed on February 13. No doubt he wanted to spend the extra time with Borthwick and enjoy the cultural life of the city. Berlin's neighborhoods were themselves cultural attractions. As they had often done in Italy, they are likely to have gone exploring, shopping, browsing, and dining. One of their known destinations was the Paul Cassirer Gallery, from which they seem to have purchased several prints by German Secessionist artists.[8] The gallery also supported a bookstore of works by poets and thinkers. This may have been the "little bookshop in Berlin" where, according to Wright, Borthwick spied a small volume in German titled *Die Natur, ein Hymnus von Goethe* (*Nature, a Hymn by Goethe*).[9] Neither of them had heard of the work, although it was well-enough known for T. H. Huxley to have included it under the title "A Hymn to Nature" in the inaugural edition of *Nature* magazine in 1869. Unaware of this, Borthwick set about translating it with Wright's help in questions of expression. They labored over it until they had produced something they considered very special. Wright carried it with him for years.

The text appears to have been incorrectly attributed to Goethe. Goethe's young Swiss friend Georg Christoph Tobler claimed to have written *Die Natur* based on numerous conversations with Goethe, and it has been argued that the original source for the text was a collection of Orphic hymns written in the first centuries of the common era by devotees of Orpheus, the great poet-musician of the Hellenic world, believed to be the son of Apollo.[10] The hymn that may have inspired the text extols nature and the renewing power of love.

Unaware of these possible complications, Borthwick and Wright found the volume's phrases about love and eternal renewal to be reassuring and comforting. Until then, Wright had viewed nature as a standard for beauty and naturalness, something to be revered and imitated. The Orphic hymn presented nature as an all-pervasive, dynamic force whose essence, Time and Change, were manifested in contradictions, paradoxes, and opposing energies. Its further appeal for Wright, considering the high opinion he had of himself, was undoubtedly its description of Nature as having "Favorites upon whom she lavishes much and to whom she sacrifices much. Upon Greatness she has fixed her Protection." But what most compelled him to carry the translation in his breast pocket for years to come appears to have been its association with Borthwick and its emphasis on the centrality of love as an aspect of Nature ("Her crown is Love; Only through Love can we approach her").

Wright's stay in Berlin gave the pair time to strategize about what they would do after Borthwick returned to America. He planned to buy land in his mother's name in the Helena Valley in Wisconsin, near Spring Green and the hamlet of Hillside. This was where the Lloyd Jones family had prospered and also where he had spent a part of his boyhood. The land he purchased would become the site of an extraordinary house, a place where they could establish themselves and be protected from society's intrusion—or so they believed.

Two months after he left Berlin for America, Borthwick made preparations to return. On her way back, she planned to visit Ellen Key at Strand, which was now finished and ready to accommodate visitors. When the Joachimsthalsches Gymnasium's school year ended in early June, she left for Sweden and signed the guest book at Strand on June 9, 1911, making her name among the first of what eventually numbered four thousand. The house stands today as a memorial to Key and a retreat for women who have arranged a residency there. Its appearance is essentially unaltered.

If she had visited Alvastra during the winter, the seasonal change would likely have astounded her. In June, Lake Vättern had become a shimmering presence in a green valley flanked by forested slopes. Situated on a steep hillside among beech and fir trees, Strand looks out on the lake from a high vantage point. Key intended it to be a retreat for working-class women who might "enjoy sun and woods and lake, a good and beautiful home, happiness, cleanliness, and comfort [where they can] listen to the lapping of Wettern's [*sic*] waves [and] wander through the great light beechwoods . . . in the spring, when the anemones lie like blue and white islands under the bare branches."[11]

Borthwick is likely to have enjoyed nature walks and time spent with Key discussing the works to be translated. Her letters confirm that they strategized about how to handle Key's publisher, G. P. Putnam's Sons, and that Key sent Borthwick on the important mission of stopping at the Putnam headquarters in New York on her way to Chicago to meet with George Putnam himself.

Borthwick had changed. No longer the woman who had crossed the Atlantic and descended into the depths of despair in Nancy, she had found a new purpose. Her "little dim light" would grow bright as she brought Key's message to America. However, she was not as forthcoming with Key as she might

Ellen Key's home, Strand, on Lake Vättern, Sweden. Ellen Key's Strand.

have been about her plans for the future. Their later correspondence reveals that Borthwick made it sound as if the next step in her marriage depended on a choice she had yet to make.

Strand had been built to Key's specifications. It demonstrated her ideas for interior design with simple mats and runners on the floors, relatively plain-looking furniture, and reproductions of paintings ranging from contemporary back to the Renaissance. Its walls were off-white and pale-green painted wooden panels with accents in the blue-gray of Swedish classicism and the deep red colors of the rural tradition.[12]

In the spirit of a true devotee, Borthwick is likely to have taken in every detail and committed the place to memory. She seems to have spent several days there with Key before leaving for Copenhagen and her ship bound for New York. When she said goodbye, she passed through the front door beneath an inscription emblazoned in red letters: *Memento vivere*, Goethe's reversal of the Roman death motto: Remember to live.

PART IV

CHAPTER 22

HOME OF TOMORROW

The SS *United States*, with Mamah Borthwick on board, entered New York harbor at noon on June 27, 1911, amid a cacophony of ship's horns. In the distance, a giant woman held aloft the torch of liberty. Little had changed in the city's skyline since the last time Borthwick had seen it. The architectural transformation of New York had only just begun. The new Met Life Building rose only slightly higher than the pointed, forty-story Singer Building, and opportunities to build higher presented themselves wherever one looked.

On the pier as she disembarked, newsboys hawked their papers. If she bought a *New York Times* that day, she would have seen on its front page Bishop William Lawrence's advice to the new graduates of Radcliff to "stay by their own firesides" and not try to engage in civic reform: "A woman's efforts would be better confined to her home."

Fifth Avenue supported more car and bus traffic than two years earlier, but the street still had an unhurried pace. Once known as Millionaires Row, its posh residences had given way to early "skyscrapers" like the brand new sixteen-story Putnam Building, toward which she was headed. Built over the stables of the New York Cab Company at Fifth Avenue and Forty-Fifth Street, it symbolized New York's rise as the center of world publishing. All the great publishing houses—Henry Holt, E. P. Dutton, and others—had followed Putnam's north from Madison Square to the neighborhood above Forty-Second Street.

Key had asked her to meet with Putnam's president, George Putnam, about his interest in publishing more of Key's works, since it appeared that he might invest in more literature that addressed the so-called woman question. However, Borthwick was disappointed to find he was not in New York. The future spouse of Amelia Earhart had only just begun his first marriage, to Crayola heiress Dorothy Binney, and they were honeymooning in Europe. Her meeting with another Putnam executive was inconclusive. With all publishers still leery of much of Key's intellectual output, it would take Putnam himself to decide what titles they would issue.

Borthwick left New York having settled very little, not even the question of who besides herself was officially authorized to translate Key's work. She had sent proposals for her translations of three books to American publishers and had been turned down. Consequently, Wright had carried the manuscripts for *Love and Ethics*, *The Morality of Woman*, and *The Torpedo under the Ark* with him back to Chicago, where the publisher Ralph Fletcher Seymour had agreed to publish them if Wright would cover the cost.

Wright paid for the printing of Key's publications in Chicago, a measure of his commitment to Borthwick and to Key's philosophy. While it can be argued that they used the writings to publicly justify what they had done, they seem to have also sincerely believed that Americans would benefit from the translations. Apparently, neither Wright nor Borthwick understood that their unwelcome notoriety would be associated with Key's new, controversial ideas about sex and could overshadow her message.

Chicago's newspapers were starved for news about Borthwick. During her absence, a contrived photograph of her had appeared on the front page of the *Chicago Examiner* with a story that concluded that her relationship with Wright had ended and they would soon reunite with their families. Under the header "Cheney Loved and Trusted Wife," it praised Edwin's long-suffering loyalty. As it became obvious that Borthwick would not be returning any time soon, the appetite for news of her only grew.

Wright had not helped matters when he returned alone in the fall of 1910. He had a way of living in his own world. His client W. E. Martin, having consented to help him collect his luggage at the train station, found him wearing clothes like those of the man on the Quaker Oats package: a broad-brimmed hat, knee trousers, and long stockings. He seemed oblivious to the depth of hostility his actions had aroused and how he would inflame public opinion with the image he projected of an eccentric, strutting dandy. Even so, when the newspapers learned that he was back, the *Inter Ocean* ran a feature story about him with only Borthwick's face, not his, on the page.

It was not, however, a photograph of Borthwick. The image that appeared in many newspapers was a newspaper artist's impression of what she might look like based on the decade-old, cameo-like photograph that had been acquired by the *Chicago Tribune*. The arrangement of her hair aligns perfectly with the original done by Lily Wiltberger. Some newspaper artists made Borthwick appear exotic and seductive, but all of them used a cameo profile. Passed on from one newspaper to the next, by early 1912 her face had undergone considerable reworking by newsroom artists who, like reporters, were given license by editors to use their imaginations.

Having left her husband and children, Borthwick knew to expect public disapproval, but the vehemence of the reaction she encountered must have shocked her. The First Congregational Church of Oak Park expelled her as a member, and she and Wright were condemned from numerous pulpits. Even their children had suffered from the open disdain of classmates and teachers.

Wright managed to wheedle a slight change for the better from Orren M. Donaldson, the editor of *Oak Leaves*, who ran an article based on C. R. Ashbee's flattering introduction to the Wasmuth portfolio. Knowing that the liberal-minded *Leaves* editor would support him, Wright fed him some material for the article. It included Ashbee's observation that Wright had "given to the great city of the prairie something she had never had before, and what is equivalent to a new architecture." His admiring description of Wright was meant to reflect his friend's personal character as well as his architecture: "In the face of actual and fierce hostility, or the persecutions of 'that little knowledge, which is a dangerous thing,' he carved out a manner of his own and worked out his own principles."[1] Despite the coldness with which Oak Park greeted him, Wright promptly received a commission from one of its residents, Oscar B. Balch, to design a house.

Borthwick arrived in Chicago in early July, in time to see a feature story in the *Chicago Tribune* about Ellen Key's *Century of the Child*, a sign that her mentor was becoming better known in America. After meeting Wright, she proceeded (probably accompanied by him) to the hamlet known as Hillside near Spring Green, Wisconsin, where she was received by his sister Jane and her husband, Andrew Porter. Wright and his mother had purchased land next to them with financing made possible by Darwin Martin and had begun to build a home for himself and Mamah there. Borthwick remained with Jane for several weeks in her Wright-designed home Tan-y-deri (Welsh for "under the oaks").

Her priority was to reunite with her children. With Edwin Cheney's help, she had made plans to meet them in Canada in July.[2] One of the children involved was Jessie Pitkin, whom Borthwick and Cheney had raised since the death of Jessie's mother (also named Jessie), Borthwick's sister. It would have made sense, therefore, for Cheney to have approached young Jessie's uncle,

E. H. Pitkin, to ask if the family could use the Pitkin lodge on Sapper Island in Lake Huron. If this arrangement was made, it is likely that Borthwick took a train to Sault Ste. Marie, Ontario, not far from the wooded island, in order to meet them.

Built in 1902, the two-story summer cottage still stands on a rocky crag, its wraparound, first-floor veranda affording expansive views of Lake Huron. For Cheney, it would have been a bitter irony to have the family reunite in a place designed by Wright, and then only to finalize the terms of the divorce. This would be uncontested. Cheney retained full custody of their children; John was eight and Martha nearly six. Although Borthwick did not obtain a formal promise regarding her access to them, Cheney does not appear to have been obstructive. Near the end of July, he returned to Oak Park, leaving her and the children together. It gave her time to try to heal the wounds caused by her absence. Apart from spending time with them in summers, however, Borthwick could expect to see very little of them.

On August 3, Edwin Cheney entered a courtroom in Chicago and testified before a divorce judge that his wife had deserted him. In a perfunctory hearing, his mother and a neighbor provided corroborating testimony, making no mention of Wright in the process. Borthwick's attorney was present, but Borthwick herself was with the children in Canada. Everyone but the judge was apparently in the know. Cheney replied, "Yes, sir" when asked "Are the children now in your custody and control?"[3]

Reporting on the divorce, the *Chicago Examiner* took the opportunity to add the usual background about the scandal but focused on Wright's return to his family. Unaware of Borthwick's whereabouts, it only described her as "missing." The *Chicago Tribune* weighed in as well, maintaining its usual stance that divorce is usually the wife's fault. Its story featured Borthwick's face five times larger than Cheney's under the headline "Her Spiritual Hegira Ends in His Divorce." With scarcely veiled satisfaction, it declared that Wright had "tired of his new love, tired of a life without good ties, and returned to his family." By contrast, Borthwick was said to have "also repented and begged to be taken back, but to this extent her husband's love did not go."[4]

Two hundred miles north in Wisconsin, construction continued on the house Wright called Taliesin. Welsh for "shining brow," the name of the legendary sixth-century Welsh poet and bard, it would be one of the great houses of America. Work began in May and progressed rapidly. The dwelling emerges on the brow of a hill like a natural outgrowth of the landscape, its location

Taliesin in 1911. Photograph by Taylor Woolley. Used by permission, Utah State Historical Society.

chosen for its fine view of the valley. The carefully calculated placement began with a rending of the earth in a critical area just below the summit. The low house would then become, in Wright's words, "married" to the hill.

He had pondered Taliesin deeply before undertaking the project. Over months of examining Italian villas near Fiesole, he drew on traditional techniques and principles that he could realize in America, adapting them to ideas he had developed earlier. Taliesin embraces the natural world around it. Flowing water became one of the sounds of Taliesin as Wright engineered its storage and movement for practical and aesthetic purposes in courtyard and gardens.

Borthwick's influence on Wright's design choices, if there was any, is invisible and unknowable. She did not hesitate to say what she did not like aesthetically, as is evident in her critique of the Nielsen painting of Ellen Key, but since she had already seen how sensitive Wright could be to critiques of his work, it is unlikely that she intruded. Still, they had worked together on the design of Cheney House. She did not have the weight of a client, as she had had with Cheney House, but she served as an inspiration for both projects.

The biographer Ada Louise Huxtable describes how Wright created the house for Borthwick: "The land and the views, the light and the seasons, the scents and colors, the plantings and the man-made insertion of native quarried stone and sand-toned walls are all part of a total, immensely sensuous and

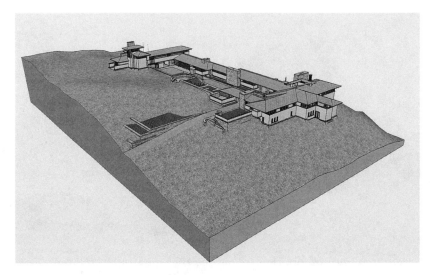

3-D rendering of Taliesin, 1911–1914. The residential area is in the foreground, the barn and stables in the rear. The slope of the hill held flower and vegetable gardens. Rendered by James McIntosh.

appealing design. . . . The house was, in fact, built for Mamah, as well as for himself. He makes it clear that the dream included her at its center."[5]

Taliesin was also an escape. Wright had built it to overlook the countryside from a commanding position like a stone fortress that would assure privacy. It was to be their retreat the way Fiesole had been, a high place from which to survey the landscape and pursue creative activities. But he could not escape his difficulties in Oak Park. Although he had quashed Catherine Wright's expectation that he would ever return to live with her, he still had to provide her with income. A remodeling project was underway to divide the house on Forest Avenue from the studio on Chicago Avenue, thus creating a rental unit. His mother still lived next door in the belief that the new house in Wisconsin was being built at least partly for her. Wright seems not to have informed her that it was really meant for him and Borthwick. Ever the architect, he was constructing a house of cards, discreetly positioning one person's interests against the other, even those of his fallback, Darwin Martin. The wealthy businessman was no fool; his correspondence with Wright indicates that he suspected subterfuge, but he went on indulging him with loans.

The remodeling project signaled that Wright's abandonment of Oak Park was permanent. In creating the apartment for Catherine Wright and their children, he sacrificed the studio, turning the impressive octagonal drafting room with its open two-story atrium into a living room with a lowered ceiling. This created a second floor squared off into four bedrooms for the children (Llewellyn, Catherine, David, and Frances; the two oldest sons were living on their own) and one for their mother. Over an adjoining garage he added yet another apartment.

Nothing could have better symbolized his double life than the wall he built through the middle of his house. It allowed him to live apart from Catherine while appearing to provide for his family. All the while, he was building an elaborate home for himself and Mamah in Wisconsin. It was only a matter of time before it would be known that she was there, but for the time being he was fooling everyone. Only one newspaper, the *Chicago Examiner*, had an intimation of what was really going on. Its front page announced, "Wright Divides Home to 'Protect His Soul.'"

> Mr. Wright [is] cutting in half that capacious, fascinating bungalow where for years—prior to his jaunt with Mrs. Cheney—he dwelt happily with his wife, Mrs. Catherine Wright, and their six children. The artist today is slashing apart the shell of his home just as two years ago the heart of it was separated. The larger half of this house divided against itself, according to all understanding, will be occupied by Mrs. Wright and the children, with Mr. Wright a frequent and ever welcome visitor. The other portion will be Mr. Wright's domain at such times as he is not out at Hillside, where the most exquisite architectural concoction that has ever grown from Mr. Wright's fancy is taking shape as his new studio home. The name of the ultimate chatelaine of this Hillside hacienda so far has been protected by silence, but revealed through insinuation.[6]

The *Examiner* added that "Mrs. Cheney remains abroad" teaching at "a young ladies seminary" in Berlin. It reported approvingly that she had been self-supporting since her departure and had lived separately from Wright. And yet the insinuation hung over the story that Wright was building the house in Wisconsin for her, where she would become the "ultimate chatelaine." Here was the potential for yet another headline if anyone cared to follow up. No Chicago reporter ventured out to Spring Green to see what was going on in the Hillside vicinity for another three months, though eventually Taliesin would become the center of a new controversy that would engulf Wright and Borthwick. To justify their right to live there together, Wright prepared a vague, polemical defense that alluded to his new home and lifestyle. "There is one thing of greater importance to mankind than the home of yesterday, and that is the home of tomorrow," he would say. "The home of tomorrow is not purified or dignified in maintaining blindly or religiously any artificial forms that preserve false face values in social life."[7] Little did he realize that the press would seize upon the term "home of tomorrow" as a mocking euphemism for his relationship with Borthwick and their cohabitation at Taliesin. But Wright understood the magic of the phrase and the effect it would have on his audience. He believed a Frank Lloyd Wright house should be seen to represent the future. With "the home of tomorrow" he sought to plant that seed in the public mind, oblivious to the fact that his lifestyle undermined his message. Wright and Borthwick were making the case for individual self-expression and self-fulfillment rather than nineteenth-century Protestantism's self-denial. Their argument would find acceptance in the coming era, but in 1911 ideas of individual rights and obligations were rooted in the past.

CHAPTER 23

⌣

A HOUSE DIVIDED

In mid-September, Taylor Woolley arrived from Utah, having been summoned by Wright to come help finish the work at Taliesin. Woolley found the site partially constructed, with walls and roofs in place and with a number of windows yet to be installed. No doubt Borthwick was delighted to see her old friend from Fiesole. By then a large work crew had become a daily presence, with a constant commotion of digging trenches; laying pipes; and hauling, cutting, and laying stone. As Borthwick described to Ellen Key, she had taken over from Wright's sister Jane Porter the burden of daily management and support for the workers.

Meanwhile Wright, having settled his differences with his colleague von Holst over what was due from the proceeds of his practice, spent much of the time in his Chicago office serving new clients and remodeling his home and studio in Oak Park. The remodeling project required a substantial sum of money, which he borrowed from Darwin Martin, a total of $16,000.[1] With so much ready cash in hand, he could not resist the temptation to buy a car worth $2,000, a 1911 Knox "raceabout" with a rumble seat in back,[2] and began using it to commute to Chicago. In July, he was arrested for speeding (twenty-nine miles per hour) on West Jackson Boulevard halfway between Oak Park and the Loop. It was his third "arrest" for speeding, the first two having been when he was driving the Stoddard-Dayton in 1909. According to the *Chicago Examiner*, he accused the policeman, A. F. Wentzlaff (perhaps an old nemesis), of having arrested him "for spite." The car compounded his problems a few days later. As he tried to start it with the engine crank, it backfired, causing the crank to kick back, striking his arm and fracturing it. Unable to drive because of the injury, he hired a chauffeur who called himself David Lawrence, although that was probably not his real name. In a matter of days, Lawrence backed the car out of the garage and disappeared with it. It was eventually discovered in St. Louis.³

These follies may have contributed to Wright's decision to bid adieu to Catherine and the children in October. Leaving her with a nearly empty bank account and mounting bills, he moved to Taliesin, where construction was not yet finished. Borthwick had already moved in. The Cheney household in Oak Park knew, of course, that she had returned to the United States, but they kept it a secret. Catherine Wright believed she was still in Berlin.

Wright had just completed his relocation when a letter arrived at Taliesin from his eight-year-old son Llewellyn, the youngest of his six children. Mailed from Oak Park on October 21 and addressed to "Mr. LL Wright, Hillside, Wisc.," the envelope displayed a child's looping, cursive handwriting. Its contents spoke volumes:

> Dear papa how are you I am feeling sad without you I love you very much. My room is sunny and pretty. I like my music lessons. I wont to play like you some day. James has gone home is it raining at Hillside now? I like to write you tomorrow is play day these are good night kisses o o o o o o
> From your loving little boy, Llewellyn Wright

Catherine Wright is likely to have overseen the writing of this letter. She knew that Wright's affection for his children was real if not always dependable. The boy's endearing hand-drawn kisses had the intended effect. Within three weeks of receiving the letter, Wright returned to his family in Oak Park, announced to the press that he had removed "the wall" that had divided his house, and told reporters to come witness that he had reunited with his family. His motives were, at best, muddled. At worst, they perpetrated a sham. When the reporters arrived at his residence on November 11, they found him seated with Catherine Wright before the always symbolic, glowing fireplace. They formed the very picture of unity and domestic tranquility. The *Chicago Examiner* gullibly supplied the headline "Wright Razes Wall: Reunited with Wife: Architect Who Deserted with Mrs. Cheney Happy Again in Undivided House."

> The last barrier separating the Frank Lloyd Wrights has been literally torn down. The Oak Park architect, who deserted his wife and children two years ago, so that he might enjoy a European trip with the since divorced wife of Edwin Cheney, has had the partition which divided the house into two distinct parts torn out. To all appearances the Wrights are enjoying domestic tranquility. . . .

Robert Llewellyn Wright. At age nine in 1912, he stands outside the Frank Lloyd Wright Home and Studio. Courtesy of the Frank Lloyd Wright Trust, Chicago.

Mr. and Mrs. Wright were seated before a roaring grate fire surrounded by their children, making a perfect family picture.[4]

As easily taken in as the *Examiner*, the *Inter Ocean* announced, "Architect Wright and Wife Reunited." Asked about the rumors of a divorce, Catherine Wright replied, "Well I suppose they have a right to say anything they wish but I wish they would leave us alone." The story ended: "And, hugging her children, she turned with a contented smile to Mr. Wright and the roaring fire."[5]

This scene took place in the living room that had been the drafting room of the studio. The reporters were unaware that the house had been extensively remodeled so that Catherine and the children could move into new rooms upstairs. The dividing wall had not been removed. The mystery is why Wright orchestrated such a deception, which proved to be short-lived.

That night, a historic, freak storm recalled as the Great Blue Norther of 1911 swept through the region, hitting major parts of Wisconsin, Illinois, and Indiana. A dozen lives were lost. In twenty hours, the temperature plummeted from 74 to 13 degrees Fahrenheit. Tornadoes ripped through communities, followed by a paralyzing blizzard. Southern Wisconsin near Taliesin saw extensive

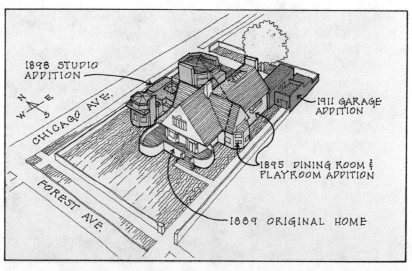

Frank Lloyd Wright home and studio in 1911. Shaded parts indicate what Wright divided from the rest of the complex with an interior wall. *The Home and Studio of Frank Lloyd Wright in Oak Park, Illinois, 1889–1911* published in 1982 by the Frank Lloyd Wright Home and Studio Foundation (now Frank Lloyd Wright Trust). Courtesy of the Frank Lloyd Wright Trust, Chicago.

damage. Wright seems to have returned at once to Taliesin to assess the situation. He remained there with Borthwick and did not return to Oak Park.

Catherine Wright wasted no time in responding. She helped Llewellyn send
another letter. As before, the child's expression was sincere, but he spoke on
behalf of the family as well as himself. He sent it on November 15.[6]

Dear Papa

This is my birth day I miss you very much Will you please eat thanksgiving
dinner with us. We are lone-some with out you. We are afraid you are sick. We
have snow now and sliding.

I hope you are warm as we are in the house. I am eight years old. good bye
from your loving son.

Llewellyn Wright

birthday kisses ooooooo

Wright's erratic behavior in this period with respect to his family, home,
and studio has gone unnoticed by his biographers. That he returned to Taliesin
right after the Great Blue Norther of 1911 can be inferred from the storm's
occurrence on the day he staged his family reunion followed by Llewellyn's
second letter, addressed to him at Taliesin, confirming that he rushed back
to assure himself Borthwick was unhurt and Taliesin undamaged. Catherine
Wright knew Llewellyn's letter would lash at her husband's conscience much
as her postcard to him in Berlin had in 1909. It is not known how Wright responded to the second letter, but apparently, he did not spend Thanksgiving
in Oak Park with his family.

He seems to have felt a profound sense of guilt from the episode. A puppet
theater that he had designed for Llewellyn in 1908 had never been built, but in
1914 he had the theater constructed and shipped to Llewellyn in Oak Park—
though not without first showing it in an exhibit with the Chicago Architectural Club. As if to foreshadow his future defiance of norms, he had emblazoned part of his 1908 drawing of the theater with Richard Hovey's words:
"We find for choosing the deeds to dare, the laws to keep."[7]

Meanwhile, "Mrs. Cheney" was trying to recover the right to use her maiden
name. In the guest book at Ellen Key's home, she had entered herself as Mamah
Bouton Borthwick, but under Illinois law the name was still not legally hers.
Through her attorneys (MacChesney, Becker, and Bradley), she petitioned the
Cook County Circuit Court to allow her to use it professionally and on legal
documents. The petition was approved in early December but at the cost of

Headlines, Inter Ocean, *November 13, 1911.* Describing Wright's alleged reunion in Oak Park with Catherine, the same edition reported the historic storm that sent him rushing back to Taliesin and Mamah.

drawing press attention. Reporters routinely scanned daily documentation from the courts for any possible story. The official notice of the name change was the first concrete news of her to have surfaced in two years. Her absence from the divorce hearing in August had fooled reporters into believing she was still in Berlin. Their suspicions should have been aroused by this new court action, but it only became an excuse to rehash the scandal. The *Inter Ocean* mocked the staid Oak Park community under the sarcastic headline "Oak Park: Model Suburb": "Every now and then something bobs up to emphasize this individuality of Oak Park. This time it is the suit of Mamah Bouton Borthwick Cheney who represents to the Circuit Court that the name Cheney now is distasteful to her and the associations and memories of that name are no longer pleasant to her. . . . Surely no place but Oak Park could furnish such a soulmate romance as that recalled by this suit."[8]

This renewed attention increased the risk that Borthwick and Wright would be discovered at Taliesin, but they continued to live there undisturbed. Local people sometimes saw them together and noticed that they seemed to be enjoying themselves. Once they were seen trying to find their way across a swollen stream until suddenly Wright picked Borthwick up in his arms and carried her across. On another occasion, they were reported to be ice-skating on a pond, laughing and cavorting.[9] With such stories floating about, their presence at Taliesin would become known further afield sooner or later.

Borthwick had written to Key upon arriving in Wisconsin but received no reply until early December. She responded with evident relief, "You cannot know the joy it was to receive a letter from you." She proceeded in businesslike fashion to answer all of Key's questions, one of which concerned a "pirated publication" (Borthwick's term) of *Love and Ethics* by the publisher B. W. Huebsch in New York: "Mr. Wright has written to Mr. Huebsch, perhaps something can be done." The problem, they would discover, was not with Huebsch but with Ellen Key.

Unaware that Borthwick had obtained a divorce, Key had expressed the hope that she would return to her family. Borthwick finally disabused her of that notion.

I have as you hope "made a choice in harmony with my own soul"—the choice as far as my own life was concerned was made long since—that is absolute separation from Mr. Cheney. A divorce was obtained last summer and my maiden name is now legally mine. Also I have since made a choice in harmony with my own soul and what I believed to be Frank Wright's happiness and I am now keeping his house for him. In this very beautiful Hillside, as beautiful in its way as the country about Strand, he has been building a summer house, Taliesin, a combination of sight and dwelling quite the most beautiful I have seen any place in the world. We are hoping to have some photographs to send you soon. I believe it is a house founded upon Ellen Key's ideal of love.

Mr. Wright's sister has looked after this all summer but when I came it was turned over to me. I have done very little of your work in consequence of the building. The house is now, however, practically finished and my time again free. Mr. Wright has his studio incorporated into the house and we both will be busy with our own work, with absolutely no outside interests on my part. My children I hope to have at times but that cannot be just yet. I had a good summer alone with them camping in the Canadian woods.

Mr. Wright said, after reading a part of your letter to me, "I feel as if I had lost a friend." He inferred from what you wrote that you would advocate my returning to my children and in that case necessarily to Mr. Cheney and was correspondingly disappointed.

It will be almost Christmas by the time this reaches you so I will wish you now a very happy Christmas and tell you that Frank is sending you a little

Hiroshige you may care to hang in your new home. I am grateful indeed for
your words of friendship and I trust I may live my life and I believe I am living
it so that you may not be ashamed of it as a testimony of faith in the beauty
and purity and nobility of Ellen Key's wonderful words.
  Your loving disciple
  Mamah Bouton Borthwick
  Spring Green
  Wisconsin USA[10]

The near breakdown she had suffered in Nancy was behind her. She had
reconciled herself to the choice she had made, quoting Key's phrase, "a choice
in harmony with my own soul." She thus placed her decision on a plane that
enabled her to justify her "absolute separation from Mr. Cheney." But Key
had implied that Borthwick's children should have priority in her life. This
wounded Wright. His generous gift to Key of a valuable print by Hiroshige
demonstrated his desire to retain her support. Weeks later, Borthwick wrote
again and reported that the print would be delayed because they had decided
to reframe it. She added, "Frank is sending also his photograph." At the bottom of the letter in cramped handwriting, Wright scribbled, "Mamah's photograph will follow soon! FLW."[11]

He apparently read each of Borthwick's letters to Key. In one, he went so far
as to cross out a word and substitute one he deemed better, thus suggesting
that he was signing off on her correspondence, including the observation in
her previous letter that Taliesin was "a house founded upon Ellen Key's ideal of
love." His agreement stands as important testimony to the centrality of Wright
and Borthwick's relationship to the conception and creation of Taliesin.

In expressing her hope that Key would not be ashamed of her, Borthwick
revealed her underlying concern. She knew that Key would worry that the controversy they had attracted might affect the acceptance of her ideas in America. It may have caused Key to have second thoughts about having chosen
Borthwick as her translator.

Borthwick and Wright received a prompt reply from B. W. Huebsch to
Wright's letter challenging his right to publish a rival translation of *Love and
Ethics*: "I have bought and paid for the sole rights to translate and publish the
book in England and America," he wrote. "Will you be good enough to recip-
rocate by informing me on what grounds you believe yourselves to be the
possessors of the American rights to the same book."[12]

Something clearly was amiss. The disadvantage of a lack of a written contract with Ellen Key had become all too apparent. Borthwick followed up

shortly with another letter to Key. Not wishing to openly confront her mentor about her rights, she enclosed the letter they had received from Huebsch and added, "Fletcher Seymour is publishing 'Love and Ethics' as the 'only authorized translation.'"

In mid-December, the Ralph Fletcher Seymour Company published Borthwick's translation of Key's *The Morality of Woman*. After months of delays and prevarication about the controversial material, the company had issued it under a gray cloth hardcover with black embossed lettering and gilt embossed design, a quality gift for Christmas. Their good friend Floyd Dell gave the book a positive review, but a new Scripps daily paper, *The Day Book*, called attention to it with the headline "'Spiritual Hegira' Ends in the Divorce Court: Eloping Wife Explains the Strange Ways of Love." It featured drawn caricatures of Borthwick writing and traveling with strategically placed quotes from Ellen Key such as "Love is moral even without legal marriage, but marriage is immoral without love."

This must have been disappointing to Borthwick, but to make matters worse, the Seymour Company had made two inexcusable errors in the publication. First, the title was incorrect. The *Morality of Woman* had been changed to *The Morality of Women*, the plural giving it an unintended sociological tilt.[13] Second, her name appeared on the title page with both her first and last name misspelled as "Namah Bouton Bothwick." Corrections were made in the second printing of the book, consigning the first printing to the fate of a collector's item, but the mistake may have been the result of sabotage. The publisher's own employees were unhappy with the controversial nature of the translations they were reading. Borthwick told Key that a proofreader for Ralph Seymour had stopped working on her other volume, *Love and Ethics*, and refused to be party to something he felt was immoral.[14]

On the morning of December 23, 1911, work on Taliesin had stopped for the Christmas holiday. Borthwick and Wright were there alone. A fresh blanket of snow outside seemed to provide assurance of peace and quiet. Borthwick was in the kitchen cooking breakfast when a knock came at the front door. Wright went to investigate and found a reporter for the *Chicago Tribune* standing in the cold. The reporter asked if he could come in to ask a few questions. Instead of slamming the door in his face, Wright allowed him to enter. He began by asking Wright his identity and whether the woman he had seen in the kitchen cooking breakfast was Borthwick. The newspaper reported in detail what followed.

Agitated and angry, Wright began to pace back and forth. "I'm Wright, but I won't say a word!"

Tabloid depictions of life at Taliesin. The discovery of Wright and Borthwick at Taliesin created new headlines, some with illustrations as in the *Chicago Examiner*, December 30, 1911.

"Is the woman living with you Mrs. Cheney?"

"That's none of your business! I won't say a word!"[15]

He then ordered the reporter to leave. An hour later, the telephone rang. Borthwick answered. Without identifying himself, the caller said, "I want to talk to Mrs. Cheney."

"I'm Mrs. Cheney," she replied. Realizing her mistake, she quickly hung up the phone, but it was too late; the reporter had what he needed.

They had been discovered.

CHAPTER 24

MISS CHICAGO

The *Chicago Tribune* newsroom came alive after the reporter telephoned his editor from Wisconsin to convey what he had learned. A second reporter was dispatched to Wright's home in Oak Park to ask Catherine Wright if she knew where her husband was. She replied that he was away on business, whereupon the reporter advised her that Wright was with Borthwick in Wisconsin.

It was a Saturday morning. Catherine immediately closed the door and called Sherman Booth, Wright's attorney. Finding that he was in his office downtown, she arranged to meet with him there and boarded the L train for the Loop. The reporter followed, keeping a discreet distance. When he saw her enter the American Savings and Trust Building where Booth's office was located, he waited until they emerged from the building. He then approached and challenged her again about her knowledge of Wright's whereabouts.

"Mr. Wright went north on business," she replied. "He built that bungalow as a home for his mother. If there is any woman there it is his mother."

"His mother would not dwell there in company with Mrs. Cheney?"

Booth interrupted. "I will say that I accompanied Mr. Wright to the Union Depot last Thursday night when he departed for Wisconsin. He was alone. There was no woman there, of that I am positive."

"Why did Wright divide the house in Oak Park? Is it true that his idea was to set up two establishments with Mrs. Cheney in one and Mrs. Wright in the other?"

"Absurd!" Booth answered.

"Why is the for rent sign on the studio part now?"

"Mr. Wright decided that the house was too large."

"Has Mr. Wright made any settlement upon his wife and family?"

"I will not discuss that."[1]

In fact, Booth had revealed quite a lot. He had admitted that Wright left for Wisconsin a few days before and that despite all the pretense of reconciliation with his wife, he had never torn down the wall in his house. Instead, as Wright later bragged, he had remodeled the studio into "one of the handsomest dwellings in the suburb," moved Catherine Wright and the children into it, and posted the "for rent" sign on the former residence.

The *Tribune* responded by sending a telegram to Wright at Taliesin demanding that he deny reports that he "had again deserted his wife and was living in a bungalow at Spring Green with the divorced wife of E. H. Cheney." Taking the bait, he fired a telegram back:

LET THERE BE NO MISUNDERSTANDING. A MRS. E. H. CHENEY NEVER EXISTED FOR ME AND NOW IS NO MORE IN FACT. BUT MAMAH BORTHWICK IS HERE AND I INTEND TO TAKE CARE OF HER.—FRANK LLOYD WRIGHT.

Again, a reporter rushed out to Wright's home in Oak Park, this time with a copy of Wright's telegram in hand to show Catherine Wright the proof of his and Borthwick's whereabouts. He was greeted at the door by her seventeen-year-old daughter, also named Catherine, who said her mother was not available. When he explained the situation and showed her the telegram, she responded light-heartedly that her father had been ping-ponging between the two locations.

Father was in town several days ago, Thursday, in fact, and I suppose he is in Milwaukee now. His business necessitates his being away from home a great deal, but he has been home several times within the last few weeks. Father did not come home to Oak Park on Thursday when he was here, but mother and we children went into the city and met him.

We expect him home over Christmas, but I really don't know whether he will be home or not. He has always told us to say nothing to the newspapers and for that reason Mama usually has refused to answer all questions. I'm sure she would not have anything to say in this matter.[2]

The reporter wandered over to Cheney House but, as usual, found no one available to provide a comment. The next day, Christmas Eve, the *Chicago Tribune* was triumphant:

Architect Wright in New Romance with "Mrs. Cheney"
Found at Spring Green Wisc. in Bungalow He Designed for Them Himself
Woman Changed Her Name
Old Spiritual Hegira Recalled

Wright's defiant telegram from Taliesin led the story. It was to be this way for days to come as he tried to explain and reporters egged him on. "We don't want to be social outcasts; we want to live and wed each other, but I—well, I have been the 'goat' in the affair," he told them. The *Chicago Examiner* described him as obviously agitated, "emphasizing his remarks by frequent gestures, the same time nervously running his fingers through his long iron-gray hair, combed in pompadour fashion." Wright claimed that the negative publicity had led to the cancellation of five of his contracts worth $100,000.[3]

Christmas Day arrived, and as in the previous two years, he and Borthwick, alienated from their spouses, were not with their children. Whatever pains of separation they might have felt were private, but the fact of their absence made for poignant, public news stories. Beneath the headline "Christmas Gloomy in Wright's Home," the *Inter Ocean* described a holiday with Dickensian overtones of Christmas Lost.

> With Christmas decorations lining the walls and brightening the windows of their beautiful Oak Park residence, Mrs. Wright and her six children waited in vain yesterday for the return of Frank Lloyd Wright, the eccentric architect who has again forsaken them to seek life's ultimate happiness with his fashionable affinity, Miss Mamah Borthwick, divorced wife of Edwin H Cheney. Festoons of evergreens and wreaths of holly, artistically arranged about their living room, bespoke holiday cheer which they did not feel.
>
> A Christmas tree, glittering with tinsel, lent no brightness to the home, which for the second time in the last two years has been disrupted by its founder's infatuation for a neighbor's divorced wife. Christmas Eve brought only regrets and unhappy memories. While his wife and children are spending their cheerless holiday in Oak Park, Wright is at the little bungalow he has erected as their Arcadia in a wooded glen near Hillsdale [*sic*], Wisconsin.

Meanwhile, at Edwin H. Cheney House, "Christmas decorations in the windows of the Cheney residence indicated that the two children of the divorced couple would receive a visit from Santa Claus this year in spite of the absence of their mother."[4]

The *Inter Ocean* was only getting started with this line of attack. Each day through the end of the month it carried a negative story about Borthwick and Wright, usually on the front page. They seem to have been oblivious to the terrible optics they were creating: an adulterous couple shunning their families at Christmas and over the holidays. Incredibly, instead of hiding out, Wright invited the *Tribune* reporter to spend part of Christmas day with them. Pacing back and forth in the Taliesin living room, he struggled to explain.

> The children, my children, are as well provided for as they ever were. I love them as much as any father could, but I suppose I haven't been a good father to them. Certainly I regarded it as a tragedy that things should have come about as they have, but I could not act differently if I had it all to do over again . . .
>
> I started out to give expression to certain ideals in architecture. I wanted to create something organic, something sound and wholesome, American in spirit and beautiful, if might be. I think I have succeeded in that. In a way my buildings are my children. . . .
>
> I wanted it to be what I had come to feel for some years I was. I would be honestly myself first and take care of everything else afterward. I felt I would find the strength and the way to help my family when I was strong with myself, and no man is strong until he is himself. I can do better by my children now than I could have done had I sacrificed that which was life itself to me and remained with them a sacrifice to duty, bound a slave and not a man, with coldness and falsehood in the atmosphere they breathed. . . .
>
> I have struggled to express something real to American architecture. I have something to give. It will be a misfortune if the world decides not to receive what I have to give. As for the general aspect of the thing, I want to say this: laws and rules are made for the average. The ordinary man cannot live without rules to guide his conduct. It is infinitely more difficult to live without rules, but that is what the really honest, sincere, thinking man is compelled to do. And I think when a man has displayed some spiritual power, has given concrete evidence of his ability to see and to feel the higher and better things of life, we have to go slow in deciding he has acted badly.[5]

The following day, the *Inter Ocean* committed its largest typeface headline to TAR AND FEATHER PARTY IS THREAT OF NEIGHBORS AGAINST FRANK L WRIGHT. The rumors overheard by an *Inter Ocean* reporter suggested a potential crisis. The community, it was said, was so incensed by the real purpose of the house that it was threatening to hold a "tar party."

One of the local citizens complained:

> There was no suspicion that there was anything wrong at the big new cottage across the river until the Chicago papers came out with the news that Mr. Wright's housekeeper is his affinity. Of course, there was considerable talk about the town when they were building such a fine house over there in the Grove. But it was passed up with the belief that Mr. Wright was only building a summer home for his family. When the woman went there to live at the house nothing was thought of it, as we were given to believe that she was only his housekeeper. She wore fine clothes and all that, but there was no reason to suspect the truth. In fact it was not known here that Wright was the man who eloped to Europe with another man's wife two or three years ago.

The newspaper suggested that people "knew where tar could be found and others said they had a plentiful supply of feathers left after their Christmas dinners."[6] Borthwick, not just Wright, was being threatened. Notorious in American history, the punishment of being covered with hot tar, then rolled in feathers, dates back to 1189 in England. A widely reported case of tarring a woman had just taken place that summer in Kansas. On August 7, a schoolteacher named Margaret Chambers (who just happened to be young and beautiful) had been stripped and tarred by a mob of men whose wives had falsely accused her of seducing a student.[7] Without missing a beat, the *Inter Ocean* continued the theme with an editorial that sanctimoniously deplored the idea of tarring and feathering Borthwick while simultaneously seeming to relish the prospect:

> Now, we deprecate the idea of tarring and feathering anybody under any circumstances. There is a legal way of dealing with every offense against public decency. But we must admit that when we think of the many points of resemblance between Wisconsin and Kansas, we are prepared for some very sensational news from Hillside.
>
> However, we trust that disapproval of the course of the Chicago couple that are now passing their second honeymoon, with the bar sinister, in a charming little bungalow will not hurry the indignant citizens of Hillside and vicinity into a repetition of the recent affair at Lincoln Center, Kansas. One case of tarring and feathering a woman is enough for a single century and for a single country. . . .

Of course, there is a certain rapidity in the process of tarring and feathering that chimes centrally with the mood of hasty zeal and indignation. But it should not be forgotten that this advantage is counterbalanced by the fact that a certain stigma is attached to the perpetrators of the act in the case of a woman.[8]

News reports suggested that Wright and Borthwick were about to be ousted by the local sheriff for violation of the marriage laws. Wright finally felt compelled to issue a statement. "We are here to stay. The report that the people of Spring Green are preparing to make a raid on us has no foundation in fact. I have received no notice from any law officer of the county and I do not expect to."[9]

The sheriff of Spring Green supported him: "I don't know yet just what charge can be brought against him. The citizens who consulted me do not want to take the law into their own hands. I told them I would do my best to thwart any attempt at tarring and feathering." The couples' friend Floyd Dell, the influential editor and book reviewer of the *Chicago Evening Post*, weighed in with an editorial deploring the "hunting and harrying" of Borthwick and Wright. "Let us not be under the illusion," he wrote, "that the ideal of monogamy can be implanted in people's hearts by sheriff's posses."[10] But no one else came to their defense.

By December 28, the tension had risen high enough to engulf even Wright's extended family. His cousin Richard Lloyd Jones, editor of the *Wisconsin State Journal* in Madison, inveighed against Wright in an editorial and convened a meeting of the Lloyd Jones family (not including Wright's mother) to discuss what was to be done. After all, among the potential casualties of Wright's behavior was the private Hillside School located very near Taliesin, founded and owned by his two aunts. Parents were threatening to withdraw their children. But Lloyd Jones succeeded only in issuing a statement that did little more than confirm the family's disapproval.

Years of speaking in lecture halls had accustomed Wright to receiving close attention from his audiences. By contrast, his long soliloquies in the newspapers struck readers as tedious. Editors dutifully printed the text he had handed reporters at Taliesin. Written in a convoluted style, trying to explain events from the very beginning, he referred to everyone in the third person (Mamah was "the woman," Catherine "the wife"). It required patience to decode. On December 30, he seemed to realize that he had only made matters worse, but he could not resist issuing a "final" statement that adopted a tone of weary resignation.

I am tired. The woman is tired. We are living the life that truth dictates. Our desire is to harm nobody. Our hope is that we may benefit humanity, our determination is to be true to our ideals at all costs. But it is impossible to escape responsibility in a certain sense to the public demand for an explanation. The established order in this case lost, and the unknown, untried, the daring struggle for a higher, more organic personal life won. There were no real obligations neglected. Neither the wife nor the children of the man had ever lacked or should ever lack anything that could be provided for their education or comfort. But the hue and cry of the yellow press was raised and from one end of the country to the other the "abandoned children," "deserted wife," the "affinity" and the "hegira" were proclaimed.

Finally, he put aside the written statement and simply placed the blame on Catherine Wright: "You must remember that things would have been all right if Mrs. Wright had only played fair. Mr. Cheney got a divorce and freed the woman wanted to be freed. Why does not Mrs. Wright free me? It is through the obstinacy of Mrs. Wright that the embarrassing condition that prevails has been brought about. Mrs. Wright has the situation entirely in her hands and it is for her to say whether or not I shall marry Mamah Borthwick."[11]

Borthwick remained silent throughout his press conferences. He claimed that she fully supported his statements. Perhaps she did, but she may also have decided there was no holding him back. Some accounts described her making brief, lighthearted admonitions to the reporters while he carried on. Whatever the truth may have been, an untruth about her son soon followed.

Little John Cheney Fights Lads Who Sneer at His Lost Mother.
Gallant Little Boy Clings to Love for the Woman Who
Deserted Him to Scandalize Wisconsin with Her Life with Her "Soulmate"

The opinion piece, disguised as a news story, appeared in papers as far away as the *Detroit Free Press*. It portrayed Borthwick's son as an outcast among boys in his neighborhood because of his mother, a woman who "makes her morals on the spur of the moment and defies conventions like any female Don Quixote flying uselessly against the flapping arms of windmills."[12]

Many were taken in by such stories, among them the *Inter Ocean* political cartoonist Harold Heaton. A leading illustrator who would eventually work for the *Chicago Tribune*, Heaton was a co-creator of the character "Miss Chicago," an icon of the 1893 World's Fair. Originally, he made her look like a

Victorian Amazon, but after 1900 he changed her to become an attractive, willowy symbol of virtue and morality.[13] Ultimately, like him, she was a prude. Having read enough about Borthwick and Wright, he decided to deploy Miss Chicago against them.

The *Inter Ocean* tar-and-feather stories had given Heaton the impression that the local Wisconsin community was up in arms over Wright and Borthwick. This inspired him to draw Miss Chicago refusing an indignant Miss Wisconsin's request to "take 'em back!" The cartoon appeared in the *Inter Ocean* on

Miss Chicago and Miss Wisconsin. Newspapers helped fan public outrage about Wright and Borthwick living together at Taliesin. The *Inter Ocean* cartoonist Harold Heaton drew Miss Chicago refusing Miss Wisconsin's demand to "take 'em back!" *Inter Ocean*, December 29, 1911.

December 29, the only time a Wright house was featured in a political cartoon. It shows Taliesin in the background belching smoke to create a cloud of "Scandal" overhead.

The image of the so-called Wright-Cheney bungalow thus was used to condemn and mock Frank Lloyd Wright years before the house would be recognized as a masterpiece. In time, the cartoon would fade from memory. But today, at first glance, Heaton's drawing of smoke pouring from chimneys and billowing over the house stirs a presentiment. Taliesin appears to be on fire.

CHAPTER 25

⁊⁊

MAMAH OF THE HILLS

A coterie of reporters gathered at Taliesin in the last days of December and in early January 1912 with the hope that Wright would deliver yet another impulsive outburst. Borthwick seems to have softened a few hearts among them. At least one reporter contrasted her calm detachment to Wright's speechifying earnestness. A story about her appeared in the *St. Louis Star* on January 3 based on interviews with the draftsmen and workmen at Taliesin.

> Mrs. Borthwick is indifferent [to the publicity]. She is a very remarkable woman. Her work suffices. She does it in a leisurely, concentrated fashion, working twenty minutes on a sentence of translation sometimes, and never counting the time lost. Near the big stone fireplace in the drafting room of the bungalow there is a settee, such a delightful old-fashioned settee, with a wide seat and cushions that were made to lie on. In that cozy corner the clever woman, whose fate has woven so intricate a web about her, may be found at nearly any hour of the day. She composes and translates, while the architect wrestles with elevations and the problems of architecture.[1]

The description of the drafting room at Taliesin is accurate insofar as it had a big stone fireplace. A settee like the one described appears in a photograph of the Taliesin living room taken four years later by Henry Fuermann and Sons. It is clear that she had won the hearts of the men who worked there: "There are five men working in the drafting room and about it. All these men are devoted to 'Mamah of the Hills.' She is so patient under the discomfort and incompleteness in the bungalow, so courteous to everybody, so easily pleased, so ready to laugh."[2]

This is the first published appearance of the expression "Mamah of the Hills." It was picked up by other newspapers and used in stories about her for years to come. Its origin remains unclear, but it may have begun with the arrival at Taliesin of the sculpture *Flower in the Crannied Wall at Taliesin* by Richard Bock. As described earlier, the figure of a nude woman contemplating an abstract object directly before her was completed in 1903 to stand in the entryway of Wright's Springfield, Illinois, masterwork, Dana-Thomas House. As it held great significance for the architect, he had a copy made and brought to Taliesin. Placed near a small garden that overlooked the house, it is unlikely to have arrived with a name assigned to it. Because of its prominent placement on the hill of Taliesin and Borthwick's obvious importance to Wright, the workmen presumed it was meant to be an evocation of her. So they began to call it "Mamah of the Hill" or "Mamah of the Garden."[3] The association with the hill would be in keeping with the observation by Wright scholar Neil Levine: "If Taliesin was Wright's alter-ego, the hill it was designed to consort with was its female companion. As much as he identified himself with the house, Wright identified Borthwick with the hill, the two so closely knit that 'hill and house could live together each the happier for the other.'"[4]

The *St. Louis Star* reporter preferred to use the more evocative plural, "Mamah of the Hills." In the end, there can be no certainty about the origin

Flower in the Crannied Wall at Taliesin, 1911. Richard Bock's sculpture had pride of place in the courtyard next to the Taliesin hill garden. In the studio directly across from it, Mamah worked alongside the draftsmen on her translations. They and others at Taliesin associated her with the statue. Photograph by Taylor Woolley. Used by permission, Utah State Historical Society.

of the expression, but it would seem to have reflected the affection and respect Borthwick inspired in those who came to know her. In the reporter's somewhat fanciful closing description, the contrast she presented to Wright was obvious.

> In this case the woman is the real philosopher. Wright himself is as nervous as a cat before a storm. He walks the roofs, so to speak. He can hear the wheels of a newspaper man's equipos scrouging and squeaking in the cold, crisp snow when the journalist outfit is 2 miles away. Wright concentrates on his work. He draws wonderful designs of oriental looking structures, but he does them with a forced expression that betokens his state of mind. The former Mrs. Cheney concentrates on her work and she forgets all else—except Wright.[5]

Newspaper accounts of life at Taliesin featured Borthwick so much that for a brief period she was a national celebrity. One version of her story was packaged and sold by a news service in a ready-to-print template with text, layout, and design. Adopted by newspapers around the country, it was occasionally altered to make her appear as a mysterious beauty who was writing a tell-all novel about her life. Another article, duplicated in the *Los Angeles Times* and elsewhere, glamorized her as the New Woman: "Mrs. Cheney is a beautiful woman still in the prime of her loveliness of person. She is a graduate of the University of Michigan. She has read much, traveled more, and associated with men and women of culture. Clever in speech and fluent with pen in expressing herself, she is a woman fitted intellectually and otherwise to hold her own in a drawing room."[6]

Borthwick had become the latest public incarnation of the New Woman typology that began in the 1890s. The term had a variety of meanings, but in her case, it implied someone whose travel, education, and sophistication, along with a controversial relationship with a man, had distanced her from ordinary life. It gave newspaper artists license to characterize her as anyone from a romantic heroine to a seductive temptress.

Whenever press attention flagged, something new would arise to stimulate curiosity. In January, Wright was seen traveling to Madison dressed in "a pair of riding breeches, high laced shoes, a Norfolk jacket, an automobile cap with goggles attached and a long flowing tie." Carrying a bundle of papers, he reportedly met with an unidentified man and woman who then left on the train for Chicago. This may have been Catherine and their attorney Sherman Booth, summoned by Wright in the hope of persuading her to give him a divorce.[7]

When it was discovered that he had purchased a life insurance policy for $50,000, a considerable sum at the time, he found himself on the defensive. Reporters asked if the beneficiary was Borthwick, to which he replied, "My wife and children are well cared for. They will never be in want. Now I am thinking of this woman. The moment that my right arm no longer protects her, she will be cast out on a pitiless, fickle world. The woman who is here with me is in a different position from any other woman in the world. I want her always to be surrounded with comfort and the artistic."[8]

The so-called yellow press kept stirring the pot. One headline declared that Borthwick was about to leave Wright because she had grown tired of the cuisine at Taliesin. While she could laugh at such stories, one in particular is sure to have bothered her. An article in the *Inter Ocean* stated that "friends of Ellen Key" believed she was tarnishing and distorting Key's message by "twisting it to her own soul mate doctrines." The "friends" were unnamed and probably not real. Key's network of contacts in America was limited, and her publisher, G. P. Putnam's Sons, had no incentive to encourage such stories.

Comfortable as a public speaker and amateur actor, Borthwick was no shrinking violet. Yet she demurred from making public remarks alongside Wright, probably because she viewed his effort as a fruitless endeavor. She wrote again to Key in early January 1912 to assure her that the press had exaggerated the public's reaction and that there would be no detriment to her work. She enclosed several clippings, including an article by the prominent author-editor Floyd Dell (who happened to be their friend) in which he staunchly defended them against the negative newspaper publicity.

The reference of Mr. Floyd Dell in the Post is to the unpleasant publicity the "yellow journals" gave to our situation here. They fabricated printed interviews and occurrences which of course never took place. The "officers of the law" was one of their fictions. You fortunately have in Europe nothing like our "yellow journals" which go to any lengths in order to invent something they can print as a sensation. Except for the newspapers we have been treated with every possible respect and uniformly courteous consideration. The local newspapers here were also kind and dignified in their expressions of real sympathy with us. Even the newspaper reporters who came here from Chicago said to Frank, "Personally you have our respect and sympathy and more, but our papers must print sensational news to please the people and sell the papers." It seems really very wonderful to me, knowing the American people, that our equivocal position should have been accepted as a dignified one so uniformly as it has been (except by the papers).[9]

This painted a too rosy picture of their situation. While a few Wisconsin newspapers were sympathetic to them, as already mentioned, Wright's own cousin Richard Lloyd Jones had denounced the couple in an editorial in the *Wisconsin State Journal*. So had W. R. Purdy, editor of the *Weekly Home News* in Spring Green, who wrote, "No man and no woman can live in the relation which these two brazenly flaunt and explain it to law-abiding, God-fearing people." He considered Wright and Borthwick to be "a menace to the morals of the community and an insult to every family therein."[10] He was not alone in this view. Ironically, an organization that had been founded years earlier by Wright's uncle Jenkin Lloyd-Jones, the Tower Hill Pleasure Company, held several meetings for the purpose of "protesting against the presence of the 'soul mates' in this neighborhood."[11]

By 1910, Americans had begun to use the expression "affinity relationship" to refer to an illicit love relationship like theirs. Preachers used expressions like "affinity fools" to denounce them. When Wright used words like "spiritual" and "soul mate" to justify their infidelity, it did not go unnoticed by Midwest newspapers that considered this usage tantamount to sacrilege. The *Scott County Democrat* of Benton, Missouri, editorialized: "The affinity idea is almost disgusting. It has been made to shield the most flagrant and wanton practices of adultery."

A movement to ban "affinity fiction" or "affinity literature" in America, inspired largely by the notoriety of Borthwick and Wright, attracted supporters. Borthwick admitted as much to Key: "The subject is being agitated especially just now because of the publicity, they tell us, given to our case. A delegation of men and women has been appointed to go down to New York to try to start some movement to legislate against 'affinity literature.'"[12]

The *Chicago Tribune* named her and Wright as the cause: "The Wisconsin Free Library commission is making a crusade against the circulation in this state of magazines containing 'affinity' fiction. A similar crusade is to be made against newspapers containing details of real affinity stories like that of architect Frank Lloyd Wright and Mrs. Cheney, the 'spiritual hegira' couple, who are living at his 'castle' at Spring Green."[13]

Borthwick hoped for a counterreaction. "Nothing could be better calculated to array all the *thinking* people in the country in an investigation of the morality of our social codes," she wrote. Her strongest feelings, however, were reserved for Catherine for her refusal to grant Wright a divorce. "You understand of course that everything would be condoned by the public *if only we* were married. *That* is the point. But Frank of course cannot marry as he has not been divorced. Neither of us has ever felt of course that that had the slightest possible significance in the 'morality' or 'immorality' of our action, but it has all the significance in the newspaper public consciousness."[14]

She wanted Key to understand that while she and Wright could not be diverted from their path, they would always conduct themselves according to her philosophy. She avoided pointing out that Key's philosophy was muddled when it came to real-world dilemmas like theirs. It advocated the right to leave a loveless marriage but provided no guidance if children were involved. Arrangements for joint custody in a divorce were not an option in 1912. Burdened by the tension between personal freedom and motherhood, Borthwick often mentioned her children to Key, perhaps to reassure her mentor that she had retained a mother's instincts.

In November 1912, she wrote again to try to reassure Key that the controversy at Taliesin had finally abated.

> You will be interested I think to know how our attempt to do what we believe right has succeeded. I can now say that we have, I believe, the entire respect of the community in which we live. I have never encountered a glance otherwise and many kind and thoughtful things have been done for us by the people around about here. I do not go to Chicago, but Frank goes and sees his children every week. My sister brought my children here for the summer during Mr. Cheney's absence in Europe for his wedding trip. He married a very lovely young woman, a dear friend of my sister's—and the children are very fond of her and she of them.
>
> The place here is very lovely; all summer we had excursion parties come here to see the house and grounds, including Sunday schools, Normal School classes etc. I will try to send you some new photographs—you will scarcely recognize them from the others.[15]

As she noted, the children were with her that August while Edwin Cheney was on his honeymoon in Europe. He had courted Lizzie Borthwick's friend Elsie Mellor during Borthwick's absence, and a year after receiving a divorce, he had married the public school teacher in his mother's home in Detroit. While Borthwick was pleased with how well Mellor got along with the children, she was relieved that Lizzie Borthwick stayed on as well, apparently devoted to her nieces and nephew.

Children at Cheney House. In this undated photograph, Mamah's niece, Jessie Pitkin, is reading to John and Martha Cheney on the terrace. Higgins family photograph.

Borthwick responded to Key's further questions about the situation.

> Your kind wishes and your interest touched me very much. Yes, Mrs. Cheney is very lovely with the children. My sister lives there you know, and no one but a mother could have the interest of the children nearer her heart (than a mother) than she has, and she thinks Mrs. Cheney wonderfully wise and lovely with them always. Only my sister's being there made my absence possible. I hope to go to Chicago to see them in a few days. Yes Frank was here when the children were here last summer and they love him dearly.[16]

The worst appeared to be over. The fact that Edwin had married Lizzie Borthwick's closest friend had improved the emotional atmosphere between him and Mamah. It appears he had agreed to allow her to meet the children in Chicago as well as at Taliesin. Catherine Wright's policy was the mirror opposite. One of her ways of punishing Wright was to prohibit their children from visiting him in Borthwick's presence.

Having never lost his knack for timing, Wright published one of his most remarkable works at this time. *The Japanese Print: An Interpretation* cemented his already strong reputation as an authority on the subject and boosted his credibility with the Japanese. It appeared just as a search had begun for an architect to design Japan's most prestigious hotel, the Imperial. The publication also drew the attention of two wealthy collectors of Japanese prints, the brothers William and John Spaulding in Boston. Aware of Wright's collection as well as his expertise, they invited him to visit them to discuss matters of collecting. The invitation coincided with Borthwick's need to go to New York to settle a question of her exclusive translation rights to Ellen Key's *Love and Ethics* with the New York publisher B. W. Huebsch. They decided to travel together as far as New York to settle the matter, after which Wright would continue to Boston.

Their meeting with the publisher was unsettling. Instead of backing down, Huebsch showed them Ellen Key's endorsement on the check he had given her for his right to have the translation of *Love and Ethics* done by someone other than Borthwick. Shocked, Borthwick wrote to Key upon her return to Taliesin to remind her of their agreement. By then, Key had upset her even more with a letter that implied she had exceeded Key's permission to submit certain works to publishers. In her reply, Borthwick demonstrated her readiness to challenge her mentor when necessary and to be emotionally open about it.

Your evident misapprehension and thought that I could give anything to anyone without your express command hurt me very much. I have before me your letter written to me in Italy; I quote it:

"I authorize you to commence with *Ibsen und die Frauen* (*Essais*) and *Liebe und Ethik* in two small volumes as you proposed. And translated from the German. In the meantime you study Swedish and when Putnam's has published *Ethik* and you are ready to offer him *Essais* translated by you from Swedish, I would be delighted to make you my only authorized translator in your language if you learn mine . . ."

. . . Now dear lady, no word of yours has been published through me that you did not give me express permission to use.

In this example and at other times, Borthwick showed a patient forbearance with Key and yet also real mettle in standing up to her, qualities that would have served her well in dealing with a man like Frank Lloyd Wright. But she ended with her usual warmth.

Forgive me for this long and uninteresting letter. I promise not to do it again,
but I had to get things straight. I dare only add one word to hope that many
years will bring blessings to you as you have brought blessings to us. I wish you
all happiness in many new years. With veneration and love,
> Mamah Bouton Borthwick
> Spring Green, Wis., Jan 5, 1913[17]

A comparison of Borthwick's translation of *Love and Ethics* with the one
published by Huebsch reveals that she (and Wright, who as discussed in chapter 19, was named as cotranslator despite his lack of German) was more highly
attuned to describing women and men in ways that did not imply male superiority. Nevertheless, Borthwick was willing to assess the differences between
the translations self-critically. She told Key that the publisher Ralph Seymour
had said the Borthwick-Wright translation was best.

> Frank and I compared the translations, sentence by sentence, I cannot say so
> unqualifiedly as Mr. Seymour that ours is a better translation. Huebsch's is
> clearer in many places and more concise, but because of its conciseness,
> perhaps partly, [it] is quite lacking in the richness and poetry of the original,
> which qualities I think our translation reproduces better. His translation is that
> of a man—very evidently—who gives a very clear statement of the thought,
> but as Frank said, "It is a poetry crusher, while ours shows it is a translation
> made with love and appreciation."[18]

The Huebsch translator was not male, however. Amalie K. Boguslawsky was
a woman who was given a privilege never accorded Borthwick. With or without anyone's permission, she provided an introductory "Note" to her version
of *Love and Ethics* that assured the reader that she was not ready to embrace
the revolutionary ideas she had translated: "Ellen Key points the way to these
higher values, without demanding that her revolutionary ideas of reform be
translated into immediate action. Conditions are not ripe for the radical changes
she suggests."[19]

The most significant difference between the two translations arose with respect to Charlotte Perkins Gilman. The prominent American feminist is singled out for criticism in Borthwick's translation but receives no mention at all
in Boguslawsky's. In Borthwick's translation, Key declares, "The American
feminist of the Charlotte Perkins Gilman type looks at all great problems of
life from an inferior point of view, when the question of self support becomes

the chief aim of the woman." This reference to Gilman does not appear in the German original text.[20] It is not something Borthwick would have added without Key's intervention and guidance (see chapter 21).

Havelock Ellis proved to be Borthwick's unseen enemy. He wrote to G. P. Putnam's Sons to complain that he was "particularly disappointed" in Borthwick's translation from Swedish of *The Woman Movement* (*Kvinnorörelsen*, 1909). Ellis, who did not speak or read Swedish, was to write the introduction to the book. Putnam advised Ellen Key of Ellis's comment and added that Borthwick had "worked very hard to make her translation as good as possible, and we feel that it is now in fairly satisfactory form. Frankly, we do not consider, however, that she is really a first class translator."[21] Key had an elaborate, convoluted style of writing that challenged all her translators. The lack of specificity in these gratuitous criticisms from sources lacking fluency in Swedish suggests that Borthwick was working in a hostile publishing environment in New York from the beginning.

After the meeting with Huebsch, Borthwick and Wright returned to Wisconsin separately. Wright continued on to Boston to meet the Spaulding brothers while she stayed in New York to meet with the publisher of *The American Magazine*, John Sanborn Phillips. He was presiding over the magazine's transition away from the public policy journalism pioneered by its star reporter, Ida Tarbell, to more popular material for a mass female audience. He thus showed little interest in the kind of articles Borthwick submitted on behalf of Ellen Key.

Wright, on the other hand, was a hit with the Spauldings in Boston. It was the beginning of one of the most lucrative relationships of his career, not to mention one of the most important in the history of museum collections of Japanese art. With the dual incentive of having a free hand to collect Japanese prints for the wealthy brothers and the prospect of the hotel contract in Tokyo, Wright prepared to go to Japan with Borthwick. Optimistic that he would be awarded the hotel contract, he wrote to Darwin Martin, "I am sailing for Japan tomorrow in search of the commission of consulting architect for the new Imperial Hotel, which the government is to build and operate. I have been in touch for some time—almost six months. The Mikado's death postponed affairs and now I have the trip to come. The building is to cost seven million dollars and a couple of years employment if I did—so wish me luck."[22]

CHAPTER 26

TAISHO TURMOIL

As their ship approached the seaport of Yokohama, Wright might have surveyed the scene with a professional eye, looking for signs of construction since his visit in 1905. The low, brick warehouses as well as the Western-style residences and hotels arranged alongside traditional Japanese houses testified to how Japan had changed. What had not changed was the forty-five-minute ride by train from Yokohama to the Shimbashi Station in Tokyo. From there it was a short rickshaw ride to the old Imperial Hotel.

They had left Taliesin for Seattle on January 12, 1913, accompanied by their Japanese servant, Satsu.[1] Despite a delay in their departure from Seattle, Wright had reason to be optimistic. Japan had become a land of opportunity for him. His dual mission was to buy high-quality, collectible prints for the Spaulding brothers and to land the contract for the Imperial Hotel. And yet the warning signs were present as they left the train station. The lingering smell of smoke from burned-out buildings, perhaps even the distant sound of a mass demonstration, is likely to have signaled the ongoing political unrest. Japan's restive population had begun to challenge the cozy relationship between its military and civilian leaders and the threat they posed to constitutional democracy. The turmoil may have come as a surprise to Wright because he was not well informed about modern Japan. Writing to Darwin Martin, he referred to the late Emperor Meiji as the Mikado, using an outmoded term generally avoided by Japanophiles even then. The political transition posed a risk to his contract: the selection of an architect for a building referred to as the Imperial and located on ground owned by the Imperial Household was sure to draw attention. For that reason, the survival of his commission through the earthquake of political unrest in 1913 is almost as noteworthy as the hotel's survival of the Great Kanto Earthquake ten years later.

He had been under consideration for the prestigious, lucrative commission for more than a year thanks to his friend and colleague Frederick W. Gookin, a Chicago banker and recognized expert in Japanese prints. Gookin knew the general manager of the current Imperial Hotel, Hayashi Aisaku.[2] The 1890 hotel, built by a German contractor in the French Second Empire style, was a joint venture among several parties in business and government, most prominently two wealthy businessmen, Shibusawa Eiichi and Okura Kihachiro. The hotel's age was showing. It needed to be replaced by a modern one, which to Meiji-era holdovers meant a design derived from the West. Gookin recommended Wright as the architect and, surprisingly, Hayashi responded that Wright would have first consideration. Hayashi just needed to be assured that the proposed design would not be too radical. There was no international design competition. It was simply a decision to be made by the hotel's board of directors. That seemed to make matters simpler, but only at first.

Wright assumed that decision-making about the new hotel had been delayed by a respectful mourning period following the death of the emperor, but the issues playing out were more fundamental. Pent-up demand for greater democracy in Japan was about to erupt. The Meiji era had officially ended, the Taisho era had begun—and with it a dangerous realignment of factional political power. The official two-year mourning period was intended in part to prevent traditional, seasonal celebrations in the countryside from appearing disrespectful, but it also served to discourage mass political demonstrations. As he and Borthwick arrived in Japan, Wright hoped that it would be just a matter of final consultations before he received the commission. Having told the press that in Tokyo he would "draw up plans and supervise the construction of a million dollar government building," he was to be disappointed.[3]

Their arrival date is uncertain, but on February 10, 1913, all normal daily activity ceased and progovernment newspaper offices and government buildings were assaulted and burned by mobs. Hundreds of police were injured. Wright made no mention of this turbulence, which suggests they arrived shortly after it had subsided. At the very least, he must have seen the destruction, but apparently he considered it to be of no lasting significance.

The power struggle underway pitted the army against the navy and both against democracy-minded politicians. By February 20, Prime Minister Katsura Taro had resigned, to be replaced by Admiral Yamamoto Gonbee. When Wright finally began to move freely about the city with Borthwick a few days later, they would have found ruined tram lines and burned buildings in areas near where they were staying. The "High City" of government and business

was more damaged than the poorer "Low City," where traditional life continued with fewer noticeable impacts. The latter part of town may have held
particular interest for Wright because of its historic role in the production of
prints, but even there, signs of growing Western influence were evident in
traditionally garbed men wearing boater hats.

The old Imperial Hotel was a de facto government guesthouse, perhaps
not what they had in mind for an extended stay. It is possible that they moved
somewhere that provided more of an experience of traditional Japan, perhaps
a house with a garden.[4] Still, Wright admitted that participating in traditional
customs tested his endurance: "On tortured knees . . . I have painfully participated in this 'idealized' making of a cup of tea following a Japanese formal
dinner, trying to get at some of these secrets if secrets they are. I confess that I
have been eventually bored to extinction by the repetition of it all and soon I
would avoid the ordeal when I could see an invitation coming. And I freely
admit, such a discipline is not for us. It is far too severe. Yes far too severe!"[5]

Enthralled by Japan's artistic traditions, Wright seems to have devoted his
attention to its visual and architectural heritage. The contemporary cultural
changes shaking the foundations of Japanese society may have mostly escaped
him, but Borthwick may well have noticed the public discussions going on
about the concerns of Japanese women and the attention in newspapers and
periodicals paid to "the New Woman" movement. A Japanese translation of
Ellen Key's *Love and Marriage* had just been serialized in the new feminist
literary publication *Seito*, whose founder and editor, Hiratsuka Raicho, led the
fledgling Japanese feminist movement. She, like Borthwick, had found a powerful awakening and new identity in discovering Ellen Key's work. In her autobiography, written decades later, Hiratsuka explained, "I came to see the need
to liberate women not only as human persons but also as sexed women. This
was a totally new philosophical problem for me. My guide and moral support
at the time, my source of ideas and hints as how to proceed, was the book by
Ellen Key [*Love and Marriage*]."[6]

Premiering in Tokyo in September 1911, Ibsen's *A Doll's House* had jolted
Tokyo much as it had Chicago in 1905 when Ethel Barrymore played Nora. It
inspired interest in modern drama and the rights of women in Japanese society. The feminist literary organization Seitosha, cofounded by Hiratsuka,
occupied the center of the debate. Journalists labeled its members "Japanese
Noras" and "New Women," terms intended as pejoratives to warn that such
women were troublemakers. The assertively curious Seitosha members even
began to explore bars, normally out of bounds, causing men to react just as the

Inaugural cover of Seito, *September 1911.* The title of the feminist magazine *Seito* was a rendering in Chinese characters of "blue stocking," a pejorative term used in Europe for intellectual women. Cover design by Chieko Naganuma.

Reverend Frederick Hopkins had done in his campaign against the "tippling ladies" of Chicago.

Hiratsuka had declared that 1913 would be the "Year of the Woman Problem" in Japan, but her articles in *Seito* did not advocate social initiatives. Rather, she sought to inspire women to seek greater self-definition. Popular periodicals picked up themes she raised, broadening the attention given to the New Woman movement. Whether Borthwick was able to meet and interact with women like Hiratsuka is unknown, but since her stay in Japan coincided with the peak of the Taisho women's movement, and she is known to have written a letter to Key from Japan describing their experience, it seems quite possible. The letter has been lost, but after Borthwick returned to America, she urged Key to accompany them when they next returned to Japan.

Borthwick may have spent much of her time accompanying Wright on excursions in search of prints. The two clients who had supplied him with formidable buying power, the wealthy Spaulding brothers of Boston, trusted him to buy prints for them using his best judgment. He did not disappoint them. He used this time to add substantially to his own valuable collection as well. The sales of prints would support his future income along with the commissions he earned as a buyer and dealer.

His well-connected friend Shugio Hiromichi provided vital assistance in this enterprise by introducing Wright to sellers. Wright had stopped in London on his way home from Europe in the fall of 1910 not only to see Robert Ashbee but to spend time with Shugio, who was then a representative of the Japanese government. In Tokyo, Shugio provided him an entrée among elite sellers and was equally useful in conducting negotiations. He continued to buy on Wright's behalf after the latter returned to America.

But even Shugio may have been of little help in navigating the issues involved with the contract for the Imperial Hotel. The land where the hotel was to be located was owned by the Imperial Household Ministry, which was also the largest shareholder in the hotel. It was also occupied by the residence of the home minister, which had to be removed. Thus, the hotel's board had to be exquisitely sensitive in managing the transition while maintaining the hotel's positive image. Their choice of an architect for the hotel was fraught with risk. Whether it was necessary or even appropriate to choose a foreigner remained an open question.

By 1913, Japan had a number of well-trained architects who could have competed in a national design competition for the hotel, but for reasons unknown, the board had decided not to hold one. From the outset they seem to have preferred Wright despite receiving an unsolicited competing design from the Japanese architect Shimoda Kikutaro (1866–1931). He proved to be so aggressive in the matter that he later accused Wright of stealing his ideas. There is no record of the board's deliberations, which were not transparent. The chairman of the board, Okura Kihachiro, had achieved the rank of baron due to the role his business empire played in enabling Japanese operations abroad. A man of considerable influence, he became one of Wright's strongest supporters in Japan, but the volatile political environment required him to tread carefully.

With the contract still uncertain, Wright sought to better understand the site conditions before leaving Japan. The ground in that part of Tokyo was notoriously unstable and magnified the risk to the hotel in an earthquake. He found eight feet of soft soil covering seventy-five feet of softer alluvium. Groundwater rose to within two feet of the surface. The solution, as he famously declared, was to design the hotel to float like a ship on the underlying soil on short piles rather than anchor it deeply. This approach is said to have enabled it to withstand the Great Kanto Earthquake of 1923. In fact, compared to other buildings in the area, some of which withstood even more severe shaking, the hotel's structural performance "might be termed good, but not outstanding," according to one study.[7]

Wright's solution may not have been the best one for surviving earthquakes, but it was only part of what he had in mind for the hotel. He aimed to integrate the country's culture and artistic vision within a modern structure. Whether or not he succeeded has been a subject of debate, but the guest rooms clearly reflected an attempt to combine efficiency, utility, and minimalism in the furnishings and features.

The Imperial Hotel was demolished in 1968 amid worldwide expressions of dismay. A masterpiece of innovative design, its low-rise, low-density profile was impractical in the heart of high-priced downtown Tokyo. The deciding factor in its demise, however, was the deep layer of "mud" that Wright found lurking beneath the site in 1913. Nothing could change that. The hotel's owners in the 1960s gave up on the building in the face of unremitting repairs as it continued to settle in the soft earth.[8]

All of that was in the future, however; the contract was still unsigned when Wright and Borthwick left Japan in May 1913. The architect was disappointed but nevertheless remained optimistic. He felt he still had a good chance to land the hotel contract despite a new storm on the horizon. A serious diplomatic

The Imperial Hotel, Tokyo, 1930s. Photograph courtesy of IMPERIAL HOTEL.

dispute was brewing between Japan and the United States over Japanese immigration into California. It had caused so much resentment in California that a powerful movement was underway for state legislation to restrict Japanese ownership of land. The openly racist Alien Land Law was seen by the new Taisho government in Tokyo as a combined threat and insult. Even before Wright's arrival in Japan, its government had threatened that if the proposed legislation was passed, they would withdraw funding support for the Panama–Pacific International Exposition planned by San Francisco. Nevertheless, on May 1, 1913, the California senate gave its approval to the Alien Land Law. Japan reacted with a surge of anti-American resentment. Journalist Soho Tokutomi began a campaign against what was termed "white snobbery" (*hoku batsu*). In a famous speech in Kyoto, Dr. Ichimura Sanjito of the Imperial University complained, "White men are full of racial pride and conceit. When they gain an inch they grasp a mile. To make a concession to them is to lay up a store of humiliation."

In this atmosphere, the Imperial Hotel board risked public outrage were it to choose an American architect over a Japanese candidate. Located in Tokyo, Japan's "showcase" city, the partly government-sponsored hotel was one of several buildings representing Japan's image to the world. Its industrial counterpart was Tokyo Station (Marunouchi Station), "Gateway to the Imperial Capital" (Teito no Genkan). Occupying the very center of the Imperial railway system, the station fronted a wide, straight avenue, the "Triumphal Return Boulevard" (Gaisen Doro) used by Japan's returning military leaders to parade in triumph directly to the moated Imperial Palace. Tokyo Station was completed in record time in early 1914, a full two years before Wright received his contract. Located not far from the hotel, it suffered no comparable delay. Its advantage was clear: its architect was Japanese. Tatsuno Kingo, the dean of Japanese architects, was hardly a controversial choice.

The political minefield likely accounts for why the Imperial board delayed the decision on the contract for the hotel for three more years. Unaware of how long the deliberations would last, Wright left for home somewhat deflated, opting to travel via San Francisco. It's unknown why Wright and Borthwick chose this route, as it was longer than necessary; possibly Wright wanted to make contacts in the Bay Area, which was still in the midst of a building boom following from the devastating 1906 earthquake.

As if choosing a metaphor for their social exile, they sailed on the SS *Siberia*. Its manifest shows them occupying adjoining cabins, numbers 2526 and 2527, rather than a single suite. Borthwick registered as "Mrs. Hannah B. Bostwick," which suggests that they may not have presented themselves as a married couple in Japan the way they had in Italy. On the other hand, the press routinely scrutinized ship's manifests for names of celebrities, which may explain her use of a sound-alike alias. Like her mother seems to have done (see chapter 2), she hid her family name with a change of spelling that could pass as an innocent clerical error.

As they arrived in San Francisco on June 2, a headline in the *San Francisco Call* announced Japan's reaction to the Alien Land Law: "Envoy Decries War Talk: Japanese Statesman Urges Calm." Wright remained unconcerned. His interest had shifted to the newspaper's owners, the Spreckels family, who had let it be known that they intended to replace the San Francisco Call Building with a new one on the corner of Market and Fourth. He had learned of the project before leaving for Japan and worked on a design while still at Taliesin. However, after reaching San Francisco, he learned that the commission had been awarded to someone else. Making the best of it, he contacted a reporter from the *Call* and invited him to meet him at the elegant St. Francis Hotel, where he and Borthwick were staying. Unsurprisingly, his presence was announced the next day in the *Call* with an excessively flattering description of his work:

Frank Lloyd Wright, an architect of international note, whose home is in Chicago, has just returned from Japan, where he is superintending construction of a new hotel in Tokyo, which will be the largest in the island empire. Mr. Wright, who is a guest at the Saint Francis, has built hunting lodges and summer homes of the royal family of Germany, as well as for many of our most wealthy Americans. The hotel now being built in Tokyo is the first of a chain of large hostelries to be erected in Japan. Mr. Wright is also superintending the construction of several buildings for the emperor.[9]

This is the kind of exaggeration that came easily to Wright when talking to reporters without Borthwick present to serve as a check on him. The design for a narrow, towering Call Building in San Francisco continued to intrigue him even as the Imperial Hotel design developed on the drawing tables at Taliesin. He was restless and impatient to get on with large commercial projects, unaware that he would soon receive the commission for Chicago's outdoor entertainment complex, Midway Gardens.

Borthwick and Wright returned to Chicago during the second week of June. Edwin Cheney brought the children to Wisconsin to stay with their mother while Wright spent a few days at his office in Chicago. When finally he returned to Taliesin, he summoned his draftsman Emile Brodelle to come from Chicago to join them. Borthwick began translating again for Ellen Key. They had hoped that their absence would allow the scandal to recede in the public memory, but the *Inter Ocean* hoped to revive it with the news of their return. It incorrectly informed its readers that the couple had "figured in a series of elopements" and had "returned from Europe," while its reporters sought reactions from Catherine Wright and Cheney. They both refused.

As the publicity subsided, Borthwick began to settle in at Taliesin. She wrote to Key about the beauty that surrounded her as she enjoyed the summer flower and vegetable gardens and worked on translations. At last, it seemed that she and Wright could look forward to a quiet life there.

CHAPTER 27

THE WOMAN MOVEMENT

Borthwick had not heard from Ellen Key for six months. Upon returning to Taliesin, she received a card from her and was much relieved. In reply, she wrote the following letter.

Dear Ellen Key, Beloved Lady:

I received your card a short time ago and was more delighted than I can say, I thank you so much for the prospect of the Putnam volume of Essays, and for the article on Romain Rolland. I have not yet finished it, but expect to send it in very shortly. I had just returned from Japan when your card came and as our Japanese servant was delayed I have been my own cook since then.

I have a great fear that I have missed again a letter of yours. The one I lost in Italy has been a continual regret to me. Frank's sister, Mrs. Porter, said she thought she forwarded to me, in Japan, a letter from Sweden, but I received none. The card is the only word I have had from you since last December. I have written twice since then. I wrote again for I wanted you to know of our delightful trip to Japan. Frank is to build the Imperial Hotel in Tokio and a few other things, not the property of the Emperor, so less important. The main object of the trip was, however, Japanese Prints, of which you know Frank is a collector. I have a dream of your coming to America, visiting us, and then of our going over to Japan together. Will you realize it, do you think possibly? Frank must go again in connection with the hotel, so we expect to have a little house there where you would again be our guest, during your stay in Japan. Would you consider it? Of course you would be perfectly independent to make whatever side trips you might wish.[1]

Here, she suddenly stopped typing, flipped the page, and wrote on the back, "Frank's mother has just telephoned me, she has a letter so I must run over there—Pardon haste. With dearest love, Mamah."

In 1913, Anna Lloyd Wright lived close to Taliesin, probably with her two sisters at their residence at their private school, Hillside. Mamah Borthwick's relationship with Anna can only be guessed at from this hurried note. Whether their telephone conversation was cheerful or an abrupt summons for Borthwick to come at once, Anna Wright was notoriously possessive of her only son and unhappy when she had to share him. More ominously, her personal history reveals someone whose husband decades earlier was so troubled by her dangerously violent treatment of her stepchildren that he asked her brothers if there was a history of mental illness in the family.

Anna Wright knew that Mamah Borthwick had effectively replaced her in the house Frank had originally promised would be hers. While he had included a small apartment for her in Taliesin, it was less than what she had expected. His subterfuge from the outset may have negatively impacted her disposition toward Mamah, but there is no evidence that Anna created for Mamah anything like the hell she made for Catherine. Borthwick is likely to have managed her with the same tact and tolerance she showed with Ellen Key, who was sometimes surprisingly testy and duplicitous with her disciple. Key even complained about having to pay a small amount of postage due on receipt of Wright's generous gift of the Hiroshige print. Borthwick responded patiently and sent her the money. Wright's mother may have required similar forbearance.

Indeed, Mamah's patience was impressive. Upon reviewing her correspondence with Key as part of his history of Taliesin, journalist Ron McCrea concludes:

> No one could have asked for a more dedicated, patient, consistent, cooperative, hardworking and loyal translator than Mamah Borthwick. She was constantly at work, translating many more essays than were published and always asking for more. Key, suspicious, complaining, and controlling, would not give Borthwick or Wright any freedom to market or repackage her work. Mamah emerges as the soul of charity, never disrespectful but earnest, considerate, and obedient. She is so grateful for the personal liberation Key has helped her find, and so happy with her life, that no abuse by Key can dampen her warmth or temper her high spirits.[2]

In late July, Wright traveled to Boston to meet with the Spaulding brothers, who were eager to open the shipping crates full of Japanese prints that had just arrived from Japan. When he got there and opened them, the outpouring of treasures dazzled his clients. The prints eventually became the foundations for several great collections in American museums.

Once back in Chicago, he had clients of a different kind to court. Taliesin's distance from "Miss Chicago" may have given him a certain satisfaction, but the two-hundred-mile train trip discouraged interaction with potential clients. So he kept an office at Orchestra Hall, and upon returning from Boston invited his sons John and Lloyd to join him there with other draftsmen.

High on the top two floors of the same building, the Cliff Dwellers still occupied their prime space. Having expelled Wright as a member three years earlier because of the scandal, they found it awkward to encounter him in the Orchestra Hall elevators. He was still on uncertain ground with them. Some had never liked him in the first place; he had not been invited to join any other honorary organization, unlike his friend, the Cliff Dwellers president, Hamlin Garland. A master of networking, Garland was a member of the New York–based National Institute of Arts and Letters and its offspring, the American Academy of Arts and Letters. The latter, styling itself as the nation's preeminent arts institution, included composers, artists, writers, and architects. Wishing to make Chicagoans aware of their (and his) importance, Garland made headlines by leaving for New York and arranging, under the auspices of the Cliff Dwellers, for the two organizations to hold a special joint session on November 13–15, 1913, in Chicago. The Cliff Dwellers even sponsored a special train for academy members to travel to the event in Chicago from Boston via New York, Philadelphia, and Washington. Upon their arrival, the club hosted the opening and closing banquets and all the luncheons in the Cliff Dwellers' club rooms atop Orchestra Hall.

Wright clearly regretted his expulsion from the Cliff Dwellers Club. When Hamlin Garland felt a twinge of guilt and enlisted Hyde Park architect Henry K. Holsman to drop by and see whether he would be interested in rejoining the club (at least that is how Wright interpreted the visit), he jumped at the chance. When Garland failed to follow up, Wright wrote to him on April 20, 1914:

My Dear Hamlin Garland,
    Some time ago Holzman [*sic*] came to see me with a brotherly message from you asking if I cared to rejoin my old companions among the "Cliff Dwellers."
I replied that nothing gives me greater pleasure and that I would gladly do so if I would not in so doing cause any trouble in the club—but nothing was said as

to how I was to "come back," whether my resignation would be withdrawn—
or whether I should make a new application for membership or just drop in as
though nothing had happened and pay my dues from then on.

Perhaps none of these things—I have had no word from Holsman since and
the matter may have dropped of its own weight?

Sincerely your friend,

Frank Lloyd Wright[3]

Contrary to what this letter suggests, Wright had not resigned from the
Cliff Dwellers. His phrase "as if nothing had happened" told the real story. He
had been quietly booted from the club because of the scandal. There is no
record of Garland's reply, but it can be inferred that he admitted to having
miscalculated, having been unable to engineer Wright's readmission. Tactfully
laying the matter to rest, Wright replied on April 24.

Dear Hamlin Garland,

I am sorry to have forced the admission. Having heard nothing I thought to
possibly check if you were waiting for me. It was incredible to me that all the
elements in the "Cliff Dwellers" could be harmonized upon such a proposition
even from Hamlin Garland. So—while I regret somewhat this phase of the
situation I realize that one may not "have his apple and eat it too" and I need
mine—in my system. That you cared to have me with you again is what really
matters. I am glad you enjoyed the exhibition!

As always sincerely yours,

Frank Lloyd Wright[4]

Wright's experience with the Cliff Dwellers has been ignored by his biographers, but it was significant for two reasons. The first is that, clearly, this
membership genuinely mattered to him. He showed little interest in belonging to most organizations, including the Chicago Architectural Club, but the
Cliff Dwellers was different. Its membership brought professional and social
connections at the highest level. It represented the pinnacle of midwestern
professional achievement. In contradiction to his posturing as a nonconform-
ist at a distance, his effort to rejoin the Cliff Dwellers demonstrated how much
he craved its level of approval in 1914.

Second, his failure to be reinstated was not only owing to the moral disapproval of some members. Included among the Cliff Dwellers were a number

of members of the Chicago Architectural Club.[5] A controversy had erupted over the exhibition Wright mentioned at the end of his letter to Garland, the annual exhibition at the Art Institute by the Chicago Architectural Club. Some of its members had withdrawn their exhibition entries in protest. As had happened in the past, the show had committed the "sin" of featuring Wright's work in a special display that attracted the most attention. If some of the protesters belonged to the Cliff Dwellers, they or perhaps as few as one key member may have blocked Wright's efforts to be reinstated.[6]

It must have galled some that Wright's part of the show was indeed the most impressive, and he knew it (he did not even include one of his masterpieces, Taliesin, in it). His model for the San Francisco Call Building towered over one area while a model of the Midway Gardens complex dominated another. In effect, the exhibit shouted, "I'm back!" to his critics. He proceeded to rub their noses in it by providing this quote to the *Chicago American*: "Let them talk. Let them say what they will. What do I care. I have three walls for my work. I am erecting the Imperial Hotel at Tokyo and I am doing other big work in the world. Both the scandal and what I am doing artistically will bring us greater crowds. Let them talk, let them talk."[7]

Wright had grown jaundiced and openly scornful toward those he perceived as prosaic copycats. In May, he created even more hard feelings when he lashed out at his critics and the alleged imitators with an essay in the *Architectural Record* titled "In the Cause of Architecture." Supposedly an update to a 1908 essay, it offered mostly a tendentious rehash of old complaints against unnamed rivals.

As the controversy boiled, his workload in Chicago increased. The commission for Midway Gardens, the expansive outdoor concert complex along the lines of the traditional German Biergarten, had an impossibly demanding schedule that required it to be ready by summer. In his absence from Taliesin, Borthwick renewed her efforts to find publishers for Key's works and tried to untangle the confusion Key had created with her vague authorizations of translations.

The Woman Movement was Borthwick's most important translation for Key. Published by Putnam's in late 1912, its focus shifted from love and marriage to issues involving the feminist movement itself. The book seemed to catch the rising tide of the movement. Two weeks after Borthwick's return to Taliesin, Illinois governor Edward Dunne signed into law a bill giving women the right to vote for president as well as for local offices. It would be another seven years before the Nineteenth Amendment was added to the US Constitution, but Illinois had become the first state east of the Mississippi River to give women the right to vote for president. It created a new air of optimism and sense of momentum for the feminist movement in the Midwest despite the failure of a 1911 statewide referendum in Wisconsin.

But events in Europe would overshadow the "woman movement." In the cultural ebb tide that followed World War I, Key's book would be left stranded on the beach. Until then, she engaged in a constructive debate with Charlotte Perkins Gilman, who laid out her argument against Key in early 1913 in her periodical *The Forerunner*. While it was ostensibly a response to Borthwick's translation of *The Woman Movement*, it is also possible that Key's pointed criticism of Gilman in *Love and Ethics*, possibly encouraged by Borthwick, drew Gilman's ire. She made clear that she had always admired Key but that this book was a bridge too far:

> That great Swedish thinker and lover, Ellen Key, in her book on "The Woman Movement," translated by M. B. Borthwick, and published here by G. P. Putnam's Sons, has voiced with power and beauty her conception of woman's place in life. In the course of her book she gives special attention, and opposition, to what she names "the amaternal theory," using the Greek prefix, as in the word "asexual," and in this opposition my name and work is mentioned. When lecturing in Europe in 1904 and 1905 I was told that Ellen Key considered my work as in strong antithesis to hers, but I was unable to see why, as I found myself in full agreement with so much, so very much, of her teaching. Neither in "The Century of the Child," nor in "Love and Marriage" did I find such antithesis made clear, but in this book it comes out so strongly that a definite discussion is possible.[8]

Feminists like Gilman took issue with *The Woman Movement* for asserting that working outside the home was a detriment to a woman's personal fulfillment and to the nurturance of her children. Key's views on the subject opposing Gilman were ill-timed in light of the vast number of women that would soon work in industry and agriculture during World War I. She changed her position near the end of the war, but until then she and Gilman sparred vigorously. Gilman was especially concerned that Key's position would only further confine and isolate women. In what Dolores Hayden calls "material feminism,"[9] Gilman supported the need for new physical structures and arrangements to allow women to pursue economic independence and social equality.

*Charlotte Perkins
Gilman, ca. 1900.*

Overlooked was Key's effort to change the terms of the debate. She wanted to focus on society's economic undervaluation of motherhood and was among the first to argue that "only when society recompenses the vocation of mother, can woman find in this a full equivalent for self supporting labour."[10] Her view was thus not far removed from Gilman's later statement, "Until 'mothers' earn their livings, 'women' will not."[11] Further, Key represented a European perspective that decried the oppressive conditions for women working in modern industry. As examples, she pointed to the grim, late nineteenth-century paintings by Constantin Meunier of *hiercheuses*, female coal miners.

Trapped between her pursuit of personal fulfillment and her desire to be a responsible mother, Borthwick gave no indication of whose argument she favored. She had come to terms with her own unique circumstances and refused to extrapolate for others. When Key sent one of her more controversial pieces to be translated, *Mißbrauchte Frauenkraft* (*The Misuse of Woman's Strength*), Borthwick responded with alacrity that she would devote herself to it.[12] She saw herself not as a critic but as the vehicle by which Key's thought would reach the widest possible audience. The text was controversial in that it highlighted a division between "old school" feminism, focused exclusively on achieving parity with men, and those who felt liberated by the permission Key gave them to identify themselves uniquely as women, free to fall in love with either sex.[13] In *The Woman Movement*, Key reiterated her view that the feminist movement's aims should not be limited to "equality with man's work, man's studies, and the accomplishments of man" but should include spheres defined by women.

Two works by Key, *Century of the Child* and *Love and Marriage*, had already been translated and widely distributed. They were promoted on speaking tours in the United States by the Dutch national Emma V. Sanders, who held a PhD from the University of Amsterdam. Sanders spent the summer of 1913 at Strand with Key, who hoped Sanders and Borthwick would someday meet. Apparently unaware of Sanders's speaking schedule, Borthwick missed her when she came to Chicago in late 1913.

Although Sanders occasionally gave interviews to newspapers, it was mostly through book reviews that Key's ideas, in summary form, reached a larger American audience. Perhaps with this in mind, Borthwick's former teacher Robert Herrick weighed in with a review of her translation of *The Woman Movement* in the *Chicago Tribune* in early 1914. He admired the book's attempt to describe "what direction it [the movement] is heading today" and described Ellen Key as "the feminist whom women of culture and intelligence prefer. In after years it will be Ellen Key rather than Mrs. Gilman who will be remembered as the greatest influence toward liberation of spirit, which is at the bottom of the feminist movement."[14]

Feeling perhaps not on solid ground with this last observation, he quickly moved on to complain about how limited the efforts by novelists had been in presenting women's perspectives. It allowed him to end his essay with a gracious endorsement of the new novel *Hagar* (1913), by Mary Johnston (1870–1936). In his review, Herrick twice used "feminist," a word that had only begun to appear in the American vocabulary. It was rapidly catching on, along with "feminism," as a replacement for the outmoded expression Woman Movement.

Meanwhile, in Oak Park the Cheney household had settled into its routine of school and work. Lizzie Borthwick still lived there with Edwin Cheney and his new wife, Elsie, and the three children. In a nearly seamless transition, the membership lists of the Nineteenth Century Club in Oak Park and the Chicago College Club again included a "Mrs. E. H. Cheney."

As May approached, a large contingent of women in Oak Park prepared to march under their own special banner in a large suffrage parade on Michigan

Avenue. Lizzie Borthwick and Elsie Cheney probably joined in. Hailed as a great success, the march on May 2 was an auspicious start to a Chicago summer featuring all-stars of the feminist movement, including Charlotte Perkins Gilman. She may have had a dual purpose in mind when she accepted an invitation to speak at a fundraising event for a new Women's Building in Spring Green, Wisconsin. She knew that Frank Lloyd Wright had designed it and that it would be just a stone's throw from Taliesin, where she would have the opportunity to meet not only Wright but also Ellen Key's translator.

FINAL PORTRAIT

By the early summer of 1914, Taliesin had passed the third anniversary of its groundbreaking. The freshly upturned earth that had surrounded it in the initial frenzy of construction had disappeared into the landscape of the hill. Only a handful of workers remained on duty to indulge Wright's perpetual urge to tinker with the design.

Nothing like it had been seen before in America, certainly not as a private residence. Appropriately, much has been made of its Prairie Style heritage and its incorporation of centuries-old lessons from Fiesole of house, garden, and landscape. In contrast to Cheney House, the other inaccessible house built for Borthwick, Taliesin seems fortress-like from afar but also exudes a sense of repose, seemingly taking the landscape within its expansive embrace.

Wright's larger mission at Taliesin was one of comprehensiveness, a total plan for a self-supporting, working farm. Thus, the elevated corridor cutting across the working end of the complex did not just balance the design, it was a serviceable haymow placed exactly where it was needed for resident cows and horses, yet allowing vehicles to pass underneath. Gardens were situated agreeably around the buildings, their water distributed from a reservoir at a higher level.

Not that Taliesin was a particularly comfortable place to live year-round. In winter the cold penetrated, and in summer there was no real refuge from the heat. Borthwick admitted as much when she wrote to Ellen Key on July 20, 1914:

> Dear Ellen Key,
>   Beloved Lady,
>   You cannot believe how happy you made me with your letter; it gave me great relief as well as joy in itself . . .

The fact that she addressed Key by her full name was not unusual. Another of Key's friends, the young poet Rainer Maria Rilke, addressed her as "Frau Ellen Key" even though she was not married. Rilke felt that to use "Fräulein" (Miss) would be disrespectful of her stature. Borthwick similarly sought to maintain that tone of respect: "Strand must be lovelier than ever now. You are to be envied its coolness if nothing else. It is nearly 90 degrees in the room as I write, with every prospect of reaching 100 very soon. It is of course extremely enervating."[1]

This was to be her last letter to Key. She began with the business of trying to untangle lines of communication between them and other translators. One translator had written to Borthwick contesting her right to translate an article by Key on the French writer and peace activist Romain Rolland.[2] After *The Woman Movement* was published, only a few essays by Key remained for Borthwick to translate. It remained to be seen what kind of project she might undertake next. Wright perhaps recalled that the author of *Woman of the Hour* had assigned herself the role of a newspaper editor, meaning that the playwright (in all probability Borthwick) likely had dreamed of being one. So he offered to buy the newspaper in Spring Green and to make Borthwick its editor. It may have been half in jest, but she apparently encouraged him to look into it.

Writing to Key, she added in an offhand way a significant item: "Charlotte Perkins Gilman has been here to see us a couple of times recently—an extremely interesting woman of course, with a terrifyingly active brain."

The seemingly casual observation was, of course, loaded with implication. Gilman's intellectual opposition to Key, while not bitter, was widely known, and Borthwick seemed eager to avoid keeping Gilman's visit a secret or placing herself between them. At the same time, as we have seen, she did not shrink from working with Key to insert critical language in her translation of *Love and Ethics* that targeted Gilman by name.

Accompanied by the novelist and playwright Zona Gale, Gilman had come to Wisconsin in June after addressing the Twelfth Biennial of the General Federation of Women's Clubs in Chicago. She and Gale traveled first to Madison to participate in a suffrage workshop, and they may have then visited Borthwick at Taliesin, which lies about forty miles west of Wisconsin's capital city. They came again in early July for the benefit that was held in support of the Women's Building in Spring Green. The acquaintanceship noted carefully by Borthwick to Key is confirmed elsewhere; in his autobiography, Wright mentions meeting Gilman and Gale at Taliesin. The two may have stayed overnight there at least once.

Borthwick's description of Gilman as "an extremely interesting woman of course, with a terrifyingly active brain," reflected Gilman's wide-ranging interests. In Chicago her presentation "The New Art of City Making" suggests she had an overlapping interest with Wright in the area of city planning. She who had said that "to be surrounded by beautiful things has much influence upon the human creature: to make beautiful things has more" would have been impressed by Taliesin.[3]

The presence of Gale and Gilman together must have made for lively dinner conversations at Taliesin. They were a natural team onstage. Their performance at the benefit for the Women's Building in Spring Green was a great hit with the audience. Wright and Borthwick may have been there to support the building project, which had been initiated by Jane Porter, Wright's sister, but as he was often in Chicago working on Midway Gardens, he may have missed at least some of their celebratory visit. In her letter to Key, Borthwick mentioned his work: "Frank has been very busy; had a special exhibit of his work in the Art Institute this winter, which attracted a great deal of attention. I am taking the liberty of sending you one of the articles on some Concert Gardens he has just built."

Midway Gardens had opened with great fanfare with a large, black-tie event in June. According to Wright, it was "as brilliant a social event as Chicago ever knew. Unforgettable to all who attended, the architectural scheme and color, form, light, and sound had come alive. Thousands of beautifully dressed women and tuxedoed men thronged the scene."

But the work was not finished. Even as daily attendance exceeded all expectations, decorations around the main entrance remained incomplete. The towers lacked their final touches, and many other details required his attention, including sculptures, furnishings, and lighting to create the "total art experience." As a result, he was constantly called to Chicago to work on site with his son John.

Midway Gardens will be forever linked in history with Taliesin by the name of someone besides Frank Lloyd Wright. Julian Carlton, recommended by John Vogelsang Jr., the caterer for Midway Gardens, became the butler for Taliesin. Wright also employed Carlton's wife, Gertrude, as his cook. Carlton was thought to be from Barbados, but it seems more likely that he was descended from an enslaved Black family in Alabama.[4] The couple arrived at Taliesin in early June, after which dissatisfaction with the cooking ceased to be a problem, suggesting that Gertrude Carlton at least lived up to expectations.

be there tonight—don't miss the gala evening at

MIDWAY GARDENS

THIS will be a wonderful occasion; you'll surely want to be there. The opening of Midway Gardens is the dedication of the first permanent home of high class summer music Chicago has ever had.

The National Symphony Orchestra

Sixty men from the best orchestras in America—under the gifted leadership of Max Bendix. Such an orchestra under such a director has not given summer concerts in Chicago since the days of Thomas in the old Exposition Building. For music lovers who come for the concerts only, 500 orchestra chairs have been reserved at the front.

Arrange to Dine at the Gardens

Advertisement, gala opening of Midway Gardens. Chicago Tribune, June 27, 1914.

There were, however, some indications of problems with Julian Carlton, with some of Taliesin's white residents and employees finding him cooperative but others finding him difficult.[5]

In trying to arrange for her children to spend part of the summer at Taliesin, Borthwick found it hard to coordinate their schedules. John Cheney had a friend in the Belknap family with whom he would go on a short trip that summer. He could not come to Taliesin until early August. His sister could join him then, but their cousin Jessie could not. She had expected to come to Taliesin with her friend Verna Ross Orndorff, but Verna's father had objected. He was uncomfortable with the presumed "goings on" at Taliesin. Instead, Jessie and the

new Mrs. Cheney joined Verna and her parents on an excursion to Delavan
Lake, sixty miles north of Chicago.

It was around this time that Carlton's general demeanor and attitude are said
to have changed. Telling Gertrude that he had to go see a dentist in Madison,
he walked from Taliesin to the train station in Spring Green. The next she heard
from him was in the form of a telegram saying he was in Chicago. Returning
without revealing what his purpose had been, it is possible that he received a
reprimand from Borthwick for having suddenly disappeared. A few days later,
on August 7, he walked again into Spring Green, entered the apothecary shop,
and bought a small bottle of muriatic (hydrochloric) acid, saying that it was
needed for the farm's supplies. Gertrude later reported that he was acting
strangely. She sometimes found him staring out the window at night holding
a hatchet. If this was symptomatic of a psychological disorder, he seems to
have successfully masked it during the day.

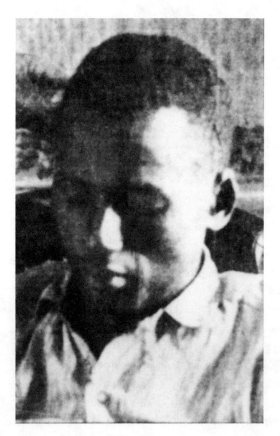

Julian Carlton. The only
surviving image of
Carlton is this newspaper
photograph taken in a
courtroom. *Dodgeville
Chronicle,* August 21, 1914.

Carlton had no previous history of violence or work-related problems until August 12, 1914, the day the draftsman Emile Brodelle ordered his horse saddled and Carlton refused. An altercation erupted, during which Brodelle berated Carlton using racial epithets, and this may not have been the first such confrontation between the two. But Carlton was already planning to resign and leave Taliesin. He had told Gertrude to inform Borthwick that she was homesick and that they wished to return to Chicago. The specific date of their planned departure is unclear, but it appears to have been August 15.

Meanwhile, the Chicago newspapers were full of foreboding news about Europe on the brink of war. As tensions that eventually led to World War I grew, different, far more domestic elements, seemingly unrelated, began to converge a world away at Taliesin. Midway Gardens would soon call Wright to Chicago, a racist draftsman would have his final argument with Carlton, workmen would carelessly leave a shingling hatchet lying around, and children who were rarely present would arrive for the summer.

Borthwick wrote to Key in anticipation of seeing her children: "We have had some other interesting people here lately, editor of The Dial, artists, etc., but best of all my children come in a day or two to spend the summer with us." A bit further on, she added, "Frank said a few days ago he was going to send you a photograph of me if you still care to have it. I should be so happy to have a word from you when you can spare me one. With dearest love . . ."

There was no signature. It is the only letter she left unsigned.

The photograph to which Borthwick referred is extraordinary. The photographer, William Louis Koehne, knew Wright well. He had commissioned Wright's Oak Park studio to design a house for him and his wife, Zila, in Palm Beach.[6] During a half century as Chicago's preeminent portrait photographer, Koehne made memorable portraits of Chicago celebrities like Louis Sullivan, James Deering, and Harold McCormick. Much of his studio's work was prosaic, often carried out by his assistants, so that nearly all his photographs are unsigned. But he signed his portrait of Borthwick.

Whose idea it was to have the photograph taken, and whether it really was a "surprise" for his birthday, as Wright later described, will never be known. Koehne's studio at 104 South Michigan Avenue was only a block from Wright's office in Orchestra Hall. No account exists of how Koehne worked with Borthwick to create the portrait. But the image is distinctively modern for its time. The print, measuring seven by four and a half inches, shows that Koehne was aware of the modern portrait photography being practiced by the American Secessionist Edward Steichen (and published by photographer Alfred Stieglitz).

Mamah Bouton Borthwick, 1914. Photograph by William Louis Koehne. National Library of Sweden, MS L 41b:17:6:2:2, archival photographer, Ann-Sofie Persson.

Koehne has not received the kind of accolades Steichen has, but his portrait of Borthwick is worthy of the comparison. His rare signature confirms that he took pride in it.[7]

In that era, women usually posed with the pretense of distraction or with a sentimental expression. Instead, Borthwick interrogates the camera with an earned, assured sense of self. Her pose is unconventional, her clothing open and simple. Possibly designed by Wright, the dress exposes her front and back without the customary covering of lace. Unlike the 1890s portrait she had made dutifully for Edwin Cheney, showing half her face and less than half her personality, in 1914, she turned to the camera to reveal the person she had become.

The timing of the Koehne photograph, ostensibly made for Wright's birthday, was prescient. If this was how she wished to be remembered, she could not have imagined how timely the gift would be.

It was mid-August by the time her letter reached Sweden and found its way to Ellen Key, who opened the envelope to find it unsigned. Weeks later, she opened another letter, this one from Frank Lloyd Wright, with Borthwick's photograph enclosed. By the time she eventually stored Borthwick's unsigned letter, she knew the truth. On it she mournfully wrote Borthwick's name in black ink near where the signature was missing. At the top of the page, she made the sign of the cross and above that, in Swedish, the words *nu mördad*. Murdered.

CHAPTER 29

LIGHTNING

The story of the Taliesin tragedy of August 15, 1914, has been told often enough to require no great elaboration. The salient facts ring out loudly and overwhelm everything else. Without warning, Julian Carlton murdered Mamah Bouton Borthwick and six others, leaving Taliesin in flames. This shocking, seismic event in the life of Frank Lloyd Wright was, according to him, the equivalent of being struck by lightning.

The sequence of the attacks is uncertain, but Carlton's method was clear. Wielding a hatchet and a can of gasoline, he sprinted between two widely separated rooms whose occupants were waiting for him to serve them lunch. Instead, he brought death. By 1:00 p.m., with Taliesin ablaze, Borthwick lay dead along with her two children. Also dead or dying were three workmen and the thirteen-year-old son of one of them.

A commonly accepted version of events has Carlton entering the family dining room where Mamah sat with John and Martha. It is said that he caught her unaware, killing her instantly with a blow to the head. Evidence to the contrary appeared in the Moline, Illinois, *Dispatch*, whose circulation manager was Wright's cousin Ralph Lloyd Jones. Vacationing at Spring Green at the time of the murders, he helped place Borthwick's body in a pine casket. It is likely that he was the one who provided the details of her wounds. (His editor probably added the term "love castle.")

There were no witnesses to the murder of Mamah Borthwick and her two children. The three were seated at luncheon in the family dining room at the end of the north wing of the "love castle." The outer door was found locked and it is believed that Carlton entrapped Mrs. Borthwick and the children as he did the others. The room was destroyed by fire, but the passage connecting the two dining rooms is not burned, showing that Carlton set each dining room afire in turn. It is believed that he also threw gasoline upon the three in the family dining room. Mrs. Borthwick had been struck on the head and breast with the hatchet, it was found. Her daughter, Martha, was cut and burned in the neck. Fire removed all trace of the wounds in the boy John.[1]

If this account is correct, it can be concluded that Borthwick rose to confront Carlton before he struck her down. Perhaps trying to defend her children, she received a blow to the breast prior to a fatal blow to the head. All other newspapers imagined her death in predictably vivid, gruesome terms, but the only reliable description of her wounds and the burn pattern of the crime scene appears to be that of Ralph Lloyd-Jones in the *Dispatch*.

Carlton inflicted even more carnage in the men's dining room in the southeast corner of the residential section. After surreptitiously locking the men in, he poured gasoline under the door and set it alight.[2] Two of those trapped in the inferno, Herbert Fritz and Emile Brodelle, escaped by breaking through a window. Carlton killed Brodelle just after he exited, but Fritz managed to get away. The remaining four were Tom Brunker, David Lindblom, William Weston, and his thirteen-year-old son, Ernest. All but the elder Weston died from Carlton's attacks.

From the kitchen located halfway between the two rooms, Gertrude Carlton, having witnessed Carlton starting the fire outside the men's workroom, fled down a flight of stairs to the basement and from there out through a window. By then Carlton's effort to kill so many had failed. Three men had escaped. Carlton could hear shouts of alarm in the distance as Lindblom and Weston reached a group of threshers in a nearby field. He realized they would arrive soon and begin looking for him. Checking to make sure he still had a bottle of acid in his pocket, he raced down to the basement, where a furnace offered him an unlikely hiding place. Its empty boiler was a large enough space to crawl into. He planned to wait there until night and escape.

Meanwhile, Lindblom, who would soon die of his wounds, ran to a neighboring house to telephone for help. Weston returned to Taliesin with the field workers to extinguish the fire, but they could not save the residential section. Fritz joined them, and with the help of others, they managed to recover Borthwick's body along with what little remained of John's. Martha's burned remains were found in the courtyard, where she had fled before being cut down.

The telephone calls placed from nearby farms brought the sheriff and the fire department, along with an incipient lynch mob. Although Gertrude Carlton was picked up a mile away hiding in bushes near a road, there was no sign of Julian Carlton until someone thought to check the furnace. He was pulled out, still holding the hatchet, rasping that he had drunk "acid." With considerable effort, the sheriff, John T. Williams, and his deputies, pistols drawn, held back the lynch mob. They pressed Carlton into a car and took him to the county jail in Dodgeville to begin what would be a farrago of investigative blunders and confusing testimony. In the weeks ahead, Carlton, weak and barely able to speak, would slowly starve to death from a burned throat and esophagus.

A motive for the attack may be inferred from two testimonies: Harper Harrison, one of the deputies who captured Carlton, testified that Carlton told him that Brodelle had been abusive, and that had motivated his actions. Dr. Wallis G. Lincoln, who treated Carlton in the jail, said Carlton told him of "an altercation on Saturday [August 15] morning, during which Brodelle abused me for more than a half hour. I told him I would 'get him,' and I waited for my chances."[3]

In light of this, the idea that Carlton began by attacking Borthwick instead of Brodelle makes little sense, although one analyst, William Drennan, tries to make the case.[4] In truth, little can be established with certainty at this distance from the crime. The exact sequence of events, Carlton's state of mind, and his motives were and remain murky, but—as ever after a tragedy—there was still more to do for those who remained.

Wright had to be informed. The task fell to Frank Roth, a friend of his in Madison, who called Wright at Midway Gardens. John Wright saw his father leave to take the call in another room. He returned in silence, his face ashen. Leaning against a table, he groaned. Taliesin had burned, he said. Roth had not told him that Borthwick and the children were dead. Adding to the alarm and confusion, a telegram arrived. Signed only "M.B.B.," it summoned Wright to come at once because "something terrible" had happened. The timing of the telegram at around 2:00 p.m. led him to believe she was still alive, since he had been told that the fire happened around noon. It is likely that the telegram came from someone in Spring Green who had taken it upon themselves to alert Wright using Borthwick's initials, which were sure to get his attention.

The next train to Spring Green would not leave until early evening and would take hours to get there. Wright and his son made their way to Union Station, stopping at the Orchestra Hall office, where he found the phone ringing with frenzied calls from reporters. He called his lawyer, Sherman Booth, and asked him to join them on the train. Edwin Cheney, too, had been informed and rushed to board the train, although, like Wright, he had not been given the worst of the news, only that there had been a fire at Taliesin. Silently appalled to meet one another on board, the two men shook hands, and, with John and Sherman Booth, they found a private compartment away from prying reporters. Their agony worsened with each station stop. John later recalled, "I have often tried to erase from my mind the anguish that was in Dad's face in that feebly lighted compartment when he learned the ghastly details from reporters and heard them shouted from the throats of newsboys along the way."[5]

By the time they arrived in Spring Green, they knew the worst. As they disembarked, Wright was so shaken he was barely able to stand. It was nearing midnight. They took a car to his sister Jane Porter's home, Tan-y-Deri, where the dead lay covered with sheets. Exhausted but sleeping little, Wright is said to have been overheard sobbing in his room. The next day, he walked over to the smoldering ruins to confirm the extent of his material loss. He knew he must bury Mamah and decided to harvest her flower gardens for her grave. The man who had spent his youth on a farm would have gone to the barn and returned with a long-handled scythe, the European style of scythe used in Wales for cutting hay, taking rhythmic swings like the Grim Reaper exacting his toll on zinnias and dahlias, perhaps in tears and rage as he reached the area planted in the University of Michigan's blue and yellow.

As the day wore on, he went to see Edwin Cheney, who was taking the remains of his children to Chicago. Addressing one another in a simple, respectful goodbye, they shook hands in the knowledge they would never see one another again.

Borthwick's grave was prepared in the Lloyd Jones family cemetery next to its Unity Chapel. A simple pine casket was fashioned and a bed of flowers laid in it for her body. They gently placed her on the flowers, piled more over her until she was covered, and sealed it. Together, Wright's son John and young cousins Orin and Ralph Lloyd Jones loaded the casket on a wagon and heaped more flowers on it. They hitched it to a pair of matched sorrel horses, their favorites, Darby and Joan, and the little procession walked slowly down the hill to the chapel.

After the casket had been lowered into the grave, Wright asked the others to leave. He recalled the moment in his autobiography in vague, mystical terms: "The August sun was setting I remember on the familiar range of hills.

Dimly, I felt coming in far-off shadows of the ages struggling to escape from subconsciousness and utter themselves . . . Then—darkness . . . I filled the grave—in the darkness—in the dark."[6]

There had been no ceremony, no final words of any kind spoken. There was no gravestone, no marker. Only a pine tree stood nearby.

It began to rain.

CHAPTER 30

ALL THAT REMAINS

An unmarked grave is cruel in the way a forgotten history is cruel. Frank Lloyd Wright meant no cruelty to Mamah Borthwick in leaving her grave unmarked. He just gave no consideration to what it might mean to others. All that mattered to him was that that memory itself had become unbearably cruel. "Why mark the spot where desolation ended and began?" he wrote.[1]

Initially he isolated himself in the part of Taliesin that had survived and would not speak to his family, not even to his mother. Briefly, his skin broke out in boils. The shock was profound, but his outward signs of grieving soon ceased. In September, he hosted the annual picnic of Sauk County rural mail carriers, at which everyone is said to have had enjoyed themselves. Deplored by some of his biographers as evidence of his emotional shallowness, the event would have been scheduled long in advance, and he said he preferred the company of strangers at the time. It was also an expression of gratitude toward the community.

On August 20, 1914, he published an eleven hundred–word letter "To My Neighbors" in the local Spring Green newspaper. While it expressed gratitude for their support, it also adopted the angry, defensive tone with which he had addressed the press years earlier. It was the letter of a man in pain who began to adopt the embittered resentment that would characterize his remaining years. It began, "To you who have rallied so bravely and well to our assistance—to you who have been invariably kind to us all—I would say something to defend a brave and lovely woman."

And it ended:

Mamah and I have had our struggles, our differences, our moments of jealous
fear for our ideals of each other—they are not lacking in any close human

relationships—but they served only to bind us more closely together. We were more than merely happy even when momentarily miserable. And she was true as only a woman who loves knows the meaning of the word. Her soul has entered me and it shall not be lost.

You wives with your certificates for loving—pray that you may love as much and be loved as well as was Mamah Borthwick! You mothers and fathers with daughters—be satisfied if what life you have invested in them works itself out upon as high a plane as it has done in the life of this lovely woman. She was struck down by a tragedy that hangs by the slender thread of reason over the lives of all, a thread which may snap at any time in any home with consequences as disastrous.

And I would urge you upon young and old alike that "Nature knows neither Past nor Future—the Present is her Eternity." Unless we realize that brave truth there will come a bitter time when the thought of how much more potent with love and action that precious "Present" might have been, will desolate our hearts.

She is dead. I have buried her in the little Chapel burying ground of my people—beside the little son of my sister, a beautiful boy of ten, who loved her and whom she loved much—and while the place where she lived with me is a charred and blackened ruin, the little things of our daily life gone, I shall replace it all little by little as nearly as it may be done. I shall set it all up again for the spirit of the mortals that lived in it and loved it—will live in it still. My home will still be there.

Frank Lloyd Wright[2]

The reference to "our struggles, our differences, our moments of jealous fear" was an admission that their relationship had endured some rocky moments but indicates also that it was characterized by strength and equality. His comment that she chose not to "devote her life to theories or doctrines" fits with Borthwick's reluctance to more actively proselytize on Ellen Key's behalf. He also discredited newspaper reports that she had been "struggling against remorse for her past conduct"[3] and noted that it had irritated her the way people expected her to be sad when she wasn't. He assiduously avoided giving her death a meaning.

Along with his letter to the community, he published Borthwick's translation of "Hymn to Nature" in the newspaper. It had survived the fire only because he carried it in his pocket. His quote in his letter, "Nature knows neither Past nor Future—the Present is her Eternity" was taken almost verbatim from it.[4]

Destruction at Taliesin, 1914. View of the courtyard and burned residential section.
Wisconsin Historical Society, WHS 55871.

Only in a rare comment to his sister did he suggest that he had been brought
down for having reached too high, but rather than seeing himself as having
suffered for his hubris, in the style of Greek tragedy, he portrayed his loss more
in the medieval style, as happiness destroyed by Fortune. Without framing
it in so many words, he did not understand his personal failings as the cause
of his misfortune. Wright's grief over Mamah Borthwick echoed the lament
of the anonymous medieval poet, "The falcon hath taken my make [mate]
away."[5] The same sense of tragedy resonates in the prophecy that Taliesin is
said to have made at the end of his life, that all would be lost, all except Wales.[6]
Wright would gather the remnants, rebuild, and remain productive, but he
would never lose his sense of vulnerability, of being subject to the irrational,
unseen forces of nature, especially the element of fire.

If Wright was correct in believing that "tragedy . . . hangs by the slender
thread of reason . . . a thread which may snap at any time," the slender thread
that snapped in Julian Carlton did so with extraordinary timing. Taliesin had
been an object of public anger, a symbol of its owner's alleged iniquities. The
fact that much of it burned to the ground when it did, through human agency,
no less, raised eyebrows. In the months leading up to the murders, during a
period of intense animosity, Wright had thumbed his nose at many, including
members of the Architectural Club. Nevertheless, the notion that anyone but

Carlton was involved in the crime finds no support in the evidence. In response to questioning by the sheriff, he explained that his effort to kill so many was an attempt to eliminate witnesses. Despite his comment that he had secreted a bag of clothes in the woods to use in his escape, the sheriff apparently did not try to recover it as evidence. Brodelle, who seems to have been the first to die, was likely his foremost target. And yet while Brodelle's racist attack on August 12 must have antagonized him, it may have been only the last straw. By then he had already purchased the acid with which to kill himself in case his plan failed.

When the sheriff prodded him repeatedly with the proposal that his motive had been to take revenge on Brodelle, he finally answered unconvincingly, "I guess you've solved the question." Until the very end, Carlton seems to have believed it was in his interest to keep the court guessing about his motive and even about his sanity. Nothing about him before or after the event struck observers as abnormal. His only complaint against his victims was that he had been "imposed upon." He said nothing to suggest that he considered himself to be the instrument of God's vengeance.

The haze of uncertainty around what motivated the crime was exacerbated by the statements and actions of some of the actors involved. For example, former deputy sheriff George Peck stated ominously that, on the basis of his experience of having once been a guard at Taliesin, "Mr. Wright has many enemies."[7] Carlton's unexplained trip to Chicago and an utterance he made upon his arrest, that he would only reveal the full story if he was allowed to live, helped keep rumors alive. Finally, Gertrude Carlton's testimony raised more questions than it answered. She seems to have suspected that her husband was planning something wicked. After two weeks of questioning, she was put on a train and never heard from again.

The murders were announced in headlines across the nation, with some newspapers implying that justice had been served. The judgmental righteousness with which the press told their story infuriated Wright. He sequestered himself at Taliesin and waited there through the rest of the year.

In his initial shock and grief, Wright retreated even from Mamah. He admitted that she occupied the opposite side of a rift in time: "Strange! Instead of feeling that she, whose life had joined mine there at Taliesin was a spirit near, that too was utterly gone. After the first anguish of loss, a kind of black despair seemed to paralyze my imagination in her direction and numbed my sensibilities. The blow was too severe."[8]

Borthwick's grave in the Unity Chapel cemetery remained unmarked. Its barrenness testified to the shock and desolation in which it had been made.

Ogden Standard, *September 5, 1914.* Newspaper stories confused Catherine Wright's face with Mamah Borthwick's, as shown here. The judgmental tone of the stories infuriated Wright.

His son John observed the impact that it had on him: "Something in him died with her, something lovable and gentle that I knew and loved. . . . As I reflect now, I am convinced that the love that united them was deep, sincere and holy in spite of its illegality—I am convinced that the woman for whom he left home was of noble character."[9]

It was a telling tribute by someone who would have been justified in feeling bitter toward Borthwick. John Wright's observation of his father after her death was reflected in Wright's first public statement, his letter to the community, in which he complained about the press. His long-standing propensity to feel resentful indignation, as historian Anthony Alofsin has observed, "would figure into the defensive and arrogant person into which Wright would grow."[10]

But the Frank Lloyd Wright who exhibited these traits in the mid-twentieth century was not the younger Wright who fell in love with Borthwick. During that earlier time, he was a happier person. This became clear in his autobiography, first published in 1932, when, surprisingly, he broke his silence about Borthwick and wrote about their life in Fiesole.

> Walking hand in hand together up the hill road from Firenze to the older town, all along the way in the sight and scent of roses, by day. Walking arm in arm up the same old road at night, listening to the nightingale in the deep shadows of the moonlit wood—trying hard to hear the song in the deeps of life. So many Pilgrimages we made to reach the small solid door framed in the solid white blank wall with massive green door opening toward the narrow Via Verdi itself. Entering, closing the medieval door on the world outside to find a wood fire burning in the small grate. Estero in her white apron, smiling, waiting to surprise Signora and Signore with the incomparable little dinner: the perfect roast fowl, mellow wine, the caramel custard—beyond all roasts or wines or caramels ever made, I remember.[11]

One of the many accounts he could have offered, it shows how rich their life together had been. Borthwick, it seems, had remained ever-present in his mind.

In a letter he wrote to Ellen Key from Taliesin on December 8, 1914, he vowed that Borthwick's spirit would appear in his future work.

> Dear Ellen Key,
>   Your kind words of Mamah are like balm to my heart. You will receive her picture under a separate cover. I am sending it today. It was made as a surprise

for my birthday last June. There is nothing to say. The lightning struck—why,
no one can say. All that remains to be done is to keep it from sinking in so
deep that my usefulness will be gone. Or rather to take it as the heart of her
would have me and put the soul of her into the forms that take shape under
my hands. We *lived*—richly. She was taken—suddenly—without warning or
pain to her I am sure. Just as we were beginning to feel that the bitter struggle
was giving place to the quiet assurance of peace and the place we coveted
together. I hope I can see you some time and we can talk of her. You have been
strength and comfort to us both and we have blessed you often.

 With love and regard, Faithfully yours

 Frank Lloyd Wright[12]

Ellen Key was the only person to whom he could have written such a letter.
In responding to her condolence, he confirmed how important she was to
him. The Hiroshige print he had given her is evidence of the special tie he felt.
But with Borthwick's death, he lost his connection to Ellen Key. The spiritual
triad of Borthwick, Wright, and Key had been broken.

His letter to the community had ended with his vow to rebuild Taliesin,
a vow that he kept, replacing it with slightly different versions as the years
passed. But the spirit of Taliesin in the summer of 1914 could not be rebuilt.
Its original, unaffected rusticity and sense of possibilities with Borthwick had
been lost.

Something was lost within the feminist movement as well. The mobiliza-
tion of women's labor during the war had bolstered the cause of women's suffrage, but the cultural debates over motherhood and work lost momentum.
Across the Atlantic, the war's carnage left a generation of women embittered
and spiritually exhausted. In England, Vera Britain could not bear to write and
publish *Testament of Youth*, her classic memoir about loss and caring for the
wounded, until 1933. By then a younger generation, lacking awareness of what
she and her contemporaries had endured, showed little interest.

Ellen Key, in despair over the war despite all the efforts, including her own,
in support of peace, wrote to her close friend Lou Andreas-Salomé, "Alas, my
dear Lou, will not all the golden bridges that the peoples of the world have
constructed be washed away in blood and fury?"[13] She withdrew for a time,
full of pessimism and misanthropy, before once again regaining some of her
former optimism. Her death in 1926 was noted in Europe but received little
attention in the United States. Even more quickly than Vera Britain, she and
her generation receded into the mists of time.

The proportion of women to men in colleges peaked briefly just after the war, followed by a long downward trend. Key might not have been surprised had she been present in Ann Arbor in 1917 at the twenty-fifth reunion of Borthwick's class. All the remarks made for the record were given entirely by men. It was their career progress, not that of the female graduates, that was duly noted in their report to the class.[14] Edwin Cheney attended the reunion; it was said he never missed one. His face in the group photograph is a smiling, frozen enigma. In 1926, he moved with his wife to St. Louis to work for Wagner Electric. He died in 1947, survived by a daughter and two sons, all born after the loss of John and Martha.[15]

Borthwick seems to have aspired to make her mark beyond translation. Her tutelage under Robert Herrick suggests she wanted to be a novelist. Alternatively, if her authorship of *Woman of the Hour* gives any indication, she entertained the idea of becoming the editor of a newspaper or magazine.[16] In any case, she kept her own identity throughout her trials. She loved Frank Lloyd Wright, but she appears not to have lost herself in him the way the women who married him did.

After Catherine Wright finally granted him a divorce in 1922, Wright married a sculptress named Miriam Noel, whom he began seeing not long after Borthwick's death. He married her only to quickly divorce her amid further sensational headlines. His detractors who cited this relationship as evidence that he had quickly forgotten Borthwick were unaware that Noel wrote him a bitter letter complaining that he "worshipped the ghost of a dead woman."[17]

He soon followed with a more successful marriage to Olga Ivanovna Lazović, originally from Montenegro and known as Olgivanna. It was she who helped him finally organize his affairs and stay afloat financially. She too, however, felt Borthwick's abiding presence. After Wright died in 1959, she had an inexpensive sandstone headstone placed flush with the ground over Borthwick's grave, but the name chiseled boldly on it, Cheney, was the one Borthwick had specifically, publicly renounced. The small, porous stone eroded rapidly and eventually cracked in half.

At his request, Wright was buried close to Borthwick, but Olgivanna's will directed that upon her death his body should be exhumed, cremated, and taken away. Without forewarning, in 1983 the body of Frank Lloyd Wright was indeed removed and cremated, his ashes shipped to Arizona and enshrined with hers. Robert Llewellyn Wright, Wright's youngest son, called it "an act of vandalism." A memorial rock now shows where Frank Lloyd Wright was buried.

With a view to establishing an appropriate memorial for Mamah, the Borthwick family asked permission to replace her misbegotten headstone. The Lloyd Jones family readily assented. Less than a mile from Taliesin, her head-stone now bears her correct, full name. Engraved below it are Wright's words, in his handwriting, from his letter to Ellen Key:

We *lived*—richly.

NOTES

ARCHIVAL SOURCES

The Ellen Key Archive of the National Library of Sweden holds ten letters from Mamah Borthwick to Ellen Key (designated as MMB to EK) and one from Frank Lloyd Wright to Ellen Key (designated FLW to EK). They are quoted here with permission. The folder numbering system of the archive is included in the letter citations with an indication of the order of the letters.

The Kappa Alpha Theta Fraternity archive located in Indianapolis, Indiana, holds letters and published materials concerning its members, including Mamah Borthwick and Mattie Chadbourne.

The Bentley Historical Library at the University of Michigan has holdings related to Borthwick's time at Michigan. These include files devoted to her, Mattie Chadbourne, and Edwin Cheney. Also in Michigan, the Special Collections of the St. Clair County Library System were of assistance in exploring Borthwick's time in Port Huron.

Other facilities that provided advice and consultation include the Chicago Historical Museum, the Chicago Public Library, the Oak Park River Forest Public Library, and the Frank Lloyd Wright Trust. Wright's correspondence, drawings, photographs, and other works are consolidated mostly at the Avery Library of Columbia University. His correspondence with Hamlin Garland is held by the University of Southern California Libraries Special Collections in the Hamlin Garland Correspondence, 1864–1941. Correspondence between Darwin D. Martin and Frank Lloyd Wright is housed in the archival and manuscript collections of the State University of New York at Buffalo. The Marriot Library of the University of Utah holds manuscripts and the photographs of Taylor Woolley, Wright's draftsman. Other Woolley photographs are held by the Utah State Historical Society. William Norman Guthrie's correspondence with Wright is held by the Andover-Harvard Theological Library, Harvard Divinity School. Margaret Belknap Allen's memoir is located in the Margaret Belknap Allen Papers, 1943–1991, Berea College Special Collections and Archives, Berea, Kentucky.

PREFACE

1. "The Terrible Fate of Mamah Borthwick in Her Bungalow of Love," *Ogden Standard*, September 5, 1914, Magazine Section, 1.

CHAPTER 1. WOMAN OF THE HOUR

1. The Nineteenth Century Club is regularly misnamed in Wright literature as the "Nineteenth Century *Women's* Club." Its name today is the Nineteenth Century Charitable Association.

2. Mamah Borthwick will be referred to by her first name and surname, respectively, depending on context. She used her maiden name, Mamah Bouton Borthwick, professionally. Her married name, Cheney, will be used as needed for consistency with public records.

3. Allen, *Family Memories of Four Sisters*, 25.

4. See Ashbee, *Janet Ashbee*.

5. "Newspaper Farce," *Oak Leaves*, May 2, 1908, 20–21. Quotes and details of the play described in this chapter appear in the article.

6. By the late nineteenth century in America, certain food choices had come to be associated with socioeconomic status. According to one study, "eating onions, leeks, or garlic marked one as a lowerclass individual." Purnell, *Sensational Past*, 203.

7. In the list of characters Borthwick provided to *Oak Leaves*, her description of Sappho as "loved and sung" is followed in parentheses by "not carried upstairs." This was a tongue-in-cheek reference to the novel *Sapho* (1884) by Alphonse Daudet about French life and customs. It refers to a scene in which a courtesan is scandalously carried upstairs in the arms of her lover. Retained in the novel's theatrical adaptation on Broadway, the scene outraged moralistic observers in the early twentieth century.

CHAPTER 2. HEARTLAND

1. Clinton, "Equally Their Due," 41.

2. Almira's birth in Charlottesville is confirmed in a handwritten note preserved by Jessie Borthwick Pitkin Higgins. I am indebted to Rhea Higgins for this information.

3. Another family in the Charlottesville area spelled its name Bowcock. They were also Presbyterians but not as prosperous as the Bococks; they could not have afforded to send a daughter to Lyons Female College.

4. The notion that Mamah's name was originally Martha may have arisen because that was the name she gave her daughter. However, Martha Cheney was named for Martha (Mattie) Chadbourne (later Brown), Borthwick's close friend. In turn, Chadbourne Brown named her daughter Mary in recognition of Mamah's original given name.

5. H. Borthwick and W. Borthwick, *The Borthwick Family*, 61.

6. "A Pioneer Gone," *Daily Times* (Davenport, IA), February 13, 1895, 3.

CHAPTER 3. DAKOTA TERRITORY

1. Lewinnek, *Working Man's Reward*, 12.

2. "Charles Henry Felton," *Album of Genealogy and Biography, Cook County, Illinois: with Portraits* (Chicago: Calumet Book & Engraving Co., 1897), 491.

3. Mamah's sister Lizzie Borthwick is mentioned in newspaper accounts as having contributed financial support for her sister's university education. This may have been a confusion with her cousin Lizzie Felton, who was in a far better position to provide such help.

4. Rury, "Schools and Education."

5. "Our Cows Must Behave," *Oak Park Reporter*, August 24, 1899, 6.

6. "Oak Park," *Cicero Vindicator*, August 22, 1885, 4. Oak Park was one of eight communities at the time under the jurisdiction of the township of Cicero. Not until 1902 did Oak Park manage to secede from Cicero and incorporate as its own municipality. No information is available about who the other members of the party were.

7. "Oak Park," *Cicero Vindicator*, August 22, 1885, 4.

8. "Pipestone," *Saint Paul Globe*, November 6, 1885, 5.

9. Wright, "In the Cause of Architecture" (1908), 157.

10. Kittredge, "Cross Saddle Riding for Women."

11. *The Northern Pacific Railway Business Directory, 1883–84.* See also John Caron, "Fargo, North Dakota: Its History and Images," NDSU Archives.

12. Describing the entertainment during a large church benefit, a reporter took note of "a recitation by Miss Mamah Borthwick, which by the way was beautifully rendered, and enlisted an encore." "Oak Park," *Cicero Vindicator*, October 17, 1885, 4. Her performances on other occasions are also noted in the "Oak Park" sections of the *Inter Ocean*, June 14, 1885, 14, *Cicero Vindicator*, June 13, 1885, and *Lake Vindicator*, December 26, 1885, 2.

13. Richard James Browning, "Early Fargo Theaters."

14. "Oak Park," *Cicero Vindicator*, September 12, 1885, 4. The sisters told the story about fishing with pitchforks to the *Cicero Vindicator* reporter. It provides confirmation that Devils Lake was their destination. The only record for such a practice in America is at Devils Lake in winter and only through the year 1885 (R. T. Young, *Biology in America*, 101).

15. "Oak Park," *Cicero Vindicator*, September 12, 1885, 4.

16. "Oak Park," *Lake Vindicator*, December 26, 1885, 2.

Chapter 4. The Prophecy

1. Sheffield, "Student Life," 107.

2. *Michigan Alumnus* 6, no. 47 (October 1899): 1–2.

3. Mattie Chadbourne's father, Alexander Scammel Chadbourne, was a grain merchant and coal dealer in Vinton, Iowa, with family roots in Michigan. Near the end of his life, he was chairman of the Peoples Savings Bank in Cedar Rapids, whose building was designed by Louis Sullivan.

4. Edward L. Walter, chairman, Department of Romance Languages and Literature, University of Michigan, letter of recommendation for Mamah Borthwick, May 11, 1893, Ann Arbor, Michigan, Archives of Kappa Alpha Theta Fraternity.

5. Dykhuizen, "John Dewey and the University of Michigan," 520–21. Dewey also served on the faculty committee that oversaw Borthwick's pursuit of her master's degree.

6. Smith-Rosenberg, "Female World."

7. Letter to school boards from Professor Isaac N. Demmon, University of Michigan, Ann Arbor, May 16, 1893, Archives of Kappa Alpha Theta Fraternity.

8. Smith-Rosenberg, "Female World."

9. "Literary Class Day," *Inter Ocean*, June 29, 1892, 2.

10. Borthwick, "Prophecy," from which all quotes that follow are taken.

11. Sutton, *House of My Sojourn*, 86.

12. Buchanan, *Regendering Delivery*, 62.

13. F.R.S. presumably refers to Fellow of the Royal Society.

14. See Hoffmann, "Meeting Nature Face to Face," 94, for discussion of the exchange between Wilhelm Miller and Frank Lloyd Wright concerning Miller's use of the term "Prairie Style." Miller was one of two men in Mamah Borthwick's class at Michigan who would come to know Wright personally. The other, of course, was Edwin Cheney.

Chapter 5. A Nobler Womanhood

1. Borthwick pursued her master's degree during the first year of the graduate school's separation from the main college (1892–93). She would have been one of the first cohorts to go through the new school. Graduate students pursued an area of study based on their interests within the "seminar system" introduced by President Angell, requiring them to write papers and attend seminars overseen by a committee of the chairmen of departments. Thus, a master of arts degree was awarded without designation of a specific discipline. Borthwick's area of concentrated study is not recorded. I am indebted to Jacob Nugent of the Bentley Historical Library, University of Michigan, for this information.

2. Sheffield, "Student Life," 119.

3. Weimann, *Fair Women*, 261.

4. Broude, "Mary Cassatt," 36

5. Letter from Gertrude Hull to Carrie A. Bean, Ann Arbor, Michigan, May 25, 1893, Archives of Kappa Alpha Theta Fraternity.

6. Turk, *Bound by a Mighty Vow*, 4, 168.

7. Frederick Jackson Turner, "The Significance of the Frontier in American History," paper read at the meeting of the American Historical Association in Chicago, July 12, 1893, during the World Columbian Exposition.

8. Slotkin, "Nostalgia and Progress."

9. Quoted in Weimann, *Fair Women*, 261.

10. Larson, *Devil in the White City*, 286.

Chapter 6. Mrs. Jarley and Mrs. Cheney

1. Gaffney, *Port Huron, 1880–1960*, 10.

2. "Board of Education," *Times Herald* (Port Huron, MI), July 10, 1896, 7; "The Public Schools," *Times Herald* (Port Huron, MI), August 27, 1896, 7.

3. "Former Port Huron Teacher Put to Death along with Five Others," *Times Herald* (Port Huron, MI), August 17, 1914, 1.

4. Marcus Borthwick's obituary in 1900 lists his three daughters as his survivors but not his son, Frank.

5. *Biennial Report of the County Superintendent of Schools* (Chicago: Dept. of Public Instruction, Cook County, Illinois, 1898/1900), 77. In 1896, $85 had an equivalent value of approximately $2,600 in early twenty-first-century U.S. dollars.

6. *Peterson Magazine* 6, no. 8 (August 1896): 823.

7. Ward, *Bicycling for Ladies*, 12–13.

8. "Don't Miss Them!," *Oak Park Reporter*, May 14, 1897, 4.

9. Bartlett and Bentham, *Mrs Jarley's Far-Famed Collection*, 12.

10. Bartlett and Bentham, *Mrs Jarley's Far-Famed Collection*, 8.

11. Secrest, *Frank Lloyd Wright*, 193.

12. In 1906, Cheney became president of the Fuel Engineering Company. At the beginning of 1909, he was named Chicago District Manager of the Wagner Electric Manufacturing Company. *Electrical Review and Western Technician*, February 27, 1909, 415.

13. Secrest, *Frank Lloyd Wright*, 316.

CHAPTER 7. WESTWARD HO

1. Lewinnek, *Working Man's Reward*, 9.

2. *Western Golf*, August 1899, quoted in "Golf in Oak Park," *Oak Park Reporter*, August 24, 1899, 5.

3. "Westward Ho Golf Club," *Oak Park Reporter*, July 27, 1899, 1.

4. *The Chicago Blue Book 1901*, 450. The *Blue Book* notes where club membership by a couple is entered under the man's name. Lizzie appears separately but incorrectly as Bostwick. All club membership lists were collected during the year prior to the *Blue Book* publication, meaning that the three were members of the club in 1900.

5. Anthony was also a member of the Glen View Club.

6. Hecker, *Golf for Women*.

7. Westward Ho charter members are unevenly documented. Some were also members of the River Forest Golf Club. Jean Guarino names Wright as a charter member of Westward Ho (*Yesterday*, 120). He does not appear in the later listings of club members in the Chicago *Blue Book*, although the lists do not include honorary members. Wright was not a golfer but he would have used his charter membership to his advantage.

8. "Among Local Golf Clubs," *Chicago Tribune*, March 31, 1901, 18.

CHAPTER 8. MODERNS IN TRANSITION

1. Several reporters were present in 1911 when Wright described the moment he met Mamah Borthwick. The *Pittsburgh Press* (December 31, 1911, 4) provides a slightly different quote than the *Chicago Examiner*, as does the *Seattle Star* on January 4 and other newspapers with the byline E. C. Rogers.

2. Ashbee, *Janet Ashbee*, 122.

3. Ashbee, *Janet Ashbee*, 143–44.

4. The wealthy Pitkin family discouraged Albert's efforts to see his daughter, Jessie, in subsequent years (personal communication, Rhea Higgins, Jessie's daughter-in-law, n.d.).

5. Jessie Borthwick Pitkin's brother-in-law, the businessman E. H. Pitkin, built a cottage on Sapper Island near Sault Ste. Marie in Canada. The architect for the project was Frank Lloyd Wright.

6. Edwin Cheney's passport contains a note directing its delivery to the named ship on the day of departure.

7. The source of this data, Newspapers.com, includes entire pages in all sections. While the two newspapers were roughly comparable in total page space in the Progressive Era, their real estate sections may account for part of the difference. The word "modern" was a potential selling point for a house in the greater Chicago area.

8. Moore, *Chicago*, 71, 84.

9. Menocal, "Taliesin," 74.

10. J. L. Wright, *My Father*, 27.

11. Delap, *Feminist Avant-Garde*, 7–9.

CHAPTER 9. LOCAL HERO

1. "Chicago's Art under the Lash," *Chicago Tribune*, December 6, 1900, 1.

2. Wright biographer Meryle Secrest raises the possibility that Ashbee met Wright in Chicago in 1896 (Secrest, *Frank Lloyd Wright*, 160). While Ashbee visited the United States in 1896, he did not venture as far west as Chicago at that time (Hasbrouck, *Chicago Architectural Club*, 271).

3. "City Too Busy for Art," *Chicago Tribune*, December 7, 1900, 5.

4. "City Too Busy for Art," 5.

5. Ashbee, *Janet Ashbee*, 56.

6. "New Idea for Suburbs," *Oak Park Reporter*, July 18, 1901, 4.

7. "New Idea for Suburbs," 4.

8. Twombly, *His Life and Architecture*, 223.

9. "New Idea for Suburbs," 4.

10. Jacobson, "Idea of the Midwest," 237.

11. "Wright Demolishes Idols," *Oak Park Reporter*, October 17, 1902, 6.

12. Personal communication, Mary Ann Porucznik, secretary, Nineteenth Century Club, March 13, 2021. Neither Borthwick's mother nor her sisters were members of the club.

13. Sources provide conflicting evidence of the address of the Cheney residence from 1900 to 1903. The *Oak Park Directory* published on January 1, 1903, gives the address as 628 East Avenue. The address given for Mamah Borthwick, Lizzie Borthwick, and Edwin Cheney by the 1903 *Blue Book* is 133 South Scoville Avenue. The latter source was probably out of date.

CHAPTER 10. CHENEY HOUSE

1. According to "Certificate of Registration of American Citizen," 20933, Mamah Bouton Borthwick, Berlin, Germany, September 19, 1910.

2. Steiner Index: References to the Architecture of Oak Park and River Forest, compiled by Frances H. Steiner, 1999.

3. J. L. Wright, *My Father*, 80.

4. Magda Frances West, "Homes Crushed by Elopement Saved by Sacrifice," *Chicago Examiner*, August 4, 1910, 3.

5. Kahneman, *Thinking Fast and Slow*. This perception is also referred to as the "availability heuristic."

6. Schrenk, *Oak Park Studio*, 161n18. The reason for Hardin's departure is hearsay and undated.

7. The preliminary floor plans for Cheney House are discussed in Nissen, "Taliesin," 114–21.

8. G. Wright, *Moralism and the Model Home*.

9. The redefinition of the modern household in association with spatial features of the house is explored in Friedman, *Women and the Making of the Modern House*, 18.

10. Cheney House presents a symmetrical facade with two entrances, one on each side. The main entrance is on the right. The house is rare among Wright's Prairie Style houses for having a symmetrical plan.

11. Levine, "Frank Lloyd Wright's Own Houses," 31.

12. Allen, *Family Memories*, 25.

13. Hildebrand, *Wright Space*, 43.

14. Allen, *Family Memories*.

15. *Kappa Alpha Theta* 20 (January 1905): 133–34, Archives, Kappa Alpha Theta Fraternity.

16. "A New Year's Eve Party," *Oak Park Oak Leaves*, January 7, 1905, 11.

Chapter 11. Modern Drama

1. Matthews, *Development of the Drama*, 311.

2. Moi, *Henrik Ibsen*, 25.

3. Durbach, *A Doll's House*, 22; DiCenzo, "Feminism," 45.

4. "Faith in Their Cooking," *Chicago Tribune*, November 3, 1901, 42.

5. The popularity among adults of the stage play *Peter Pan*, by J. M. Barrie, reflected a new sentimentalism about a safely rebellious childhood. Changing views of childhood are discussed in Cunningham, *Children and Childhood in Western Society*.

6. "Wants Equality in Marriage," *Chicago Tribune*, January 23, 1905, 6.

7. Guthrie took an interest, for instance, in new poetry written by women. His lecture in the summer school of the University of Chicago in 1903 was titled "Woman's Poetic Self-Expression: Emily Bronte, Johanna Ambrosius, Ada Negri." His grandmother was the Scottish-born abolitionist and feminist Fannie Wright.

8. W. L. Hubbard, "Sarah Bernhardt as She Appeared Last Night in Camille," *Chicago Tribune*, November 22, 1905, 8.

9. "Bernhart Talks of Art," *Inter Ocean*, November 22, 1905, 3.

10. Guthrie, *Modern Poet Prophets*, 242–43.

11. "Ladies to Study Modern Drama," *Oak Leaves*, March 31, 1906, 11.

12. Cheney, "Installation of Alpha Iota Chapter," 168.

13. In 1906, Wright rode Kano as far as Janesville, Wisconsin, one hundred miles from Oak Park. "On Horseback from Oak Park," *Janesville Daily Gazette*, June 18, 1906, 1.

14. Schlereth, "H. H. Richardson's Influence," 59.

15. Twombly states that Borthwick "left her children with a nurse or at boarding school" (*An Interpretive Biography*, 101). The family used a nurse (nanny) but never a boarding school. After 1914, Borthwick's niece Jessie was sent by the Pitkin family to a boarding school in Kentucky.

16. "Chicago Welcomes Gayest Christmas in All Its History," *Inter Ocean*, December 25, 1906, 1.

17. "German Dramatists," *Oak Leaves*, January 19, 1907, 20–21. The newspaper's summary apparently uses lines from Guthrie's address.

18. Ellis, "Woman in the Modern Drama," 302.

19. Goldman, *Social Significance*, 94.

20. "Class in Modern Drama," *Oak Leaves*, February 23, 1907, 8.

21. "Swedish Authoress' Ideas on Marriage Sensation of the Day in Germany," *Chicago Tribune*, April 30, 1905, 40.

CHAPTER 12. LUNCH AT MARSHALL FIELD'S

1. The Alice Wadsworth in Kappa Alpha Theta is not to be confused with the infamous leader of the national anti-suffrage movement of the same name.

2. Beaumont and Fletcher, *Works of Francis Beaumont*, 367.

3. Turk, *Bound by a Mighty Vow*.

4. Remus, "Tippling Ladies," 752.

5. See, for example, "Queerest Divorce Suits in the World," *Chicago Tribune*, June 23, 1907, 42.

6. "Queerest Divorce Suits," 42.

7. Personal communication, Mary Ann Porucznik, secretary, Nineteenth Century Club, March 13, 2021.

8. "Cliff Dwellers in Chicago," *Chicago Tribune*, November 7, 1907, 8.

9. Smith, *Wright on Exhibit*, 24–25, 36.

10. Hamlin Garland, president of the Cliff Dwellers, was an outspoken critic of the Armory Show, which included Duchamp's *Nude Descending a Staircase No. 2* and Braque's *Violin and Candlestick*. While Wright did not embrace modern art movements like Cubism, he and Borthwick were enthusiastic about German and Austrian Secessionist artists. See Alofsin, *Frank Lloyd Wright, Art Collector*.

11. In *No Place of Grace*, T. J. Jackson Lears describes antimodernism in the Progressive Era as a complex phenomenon but essentially an embrace of past traditions and a search for an imagined "authenticity."

12. "Monday Night, Feb. 24, at Unity House," *Oak Leaves*, February 22, 1908, 2.

CHAPTER 13. WISCONSIN ROAD TRIP

1. "New York-Paris Racers in Oak Park," *Oak Leaves*, February 29, 1908, 6.

2. "Most Automobiles," *Oak Leaves*, February 17, 1906, 27–28, provides an exhaustive list of Oak Park car owners and their machines. Frank Lloyd Wright is notably missing from the list. Secrest (*Frank Lloyd Wright*, 147) states without evidence that around this time he had a Stoddard-Dayton roadster custom built to elaborate specifications.

3. "Society," *Wisconsin State Journal*, August 18, 1908, 5. John O. Holzhueter ("Frank Lloyd Wright's Designs for Robert Lamp") makes note of the trip but wrongly concludes that Catherine Wright was the fourth person in the car. The item in the *Wisconsin State Journal* refers specifically to "Mr. Cheney's mother of Chicago," confirming that the fourth passenger was Armilla, not Catherine. In all probability, Robert Lamp provided this information to the newspaper.

4. Margaret Belknap Allen mentions Cheney owning a Studebaker, but that may have been later. As previously noted, her memoir is error prone and conflates time periods.

5. Wright, *An Autobiography* (1992), 1:126.

6. See Hertzberg, *Frank Lloyd Wright's Hardy House*.

7. Wright, *An Autobiography* (1943). In the 1932 edition of *An Autobiography*, the article "the" appears before "disturbance." Wright's attention to this sentence in his 1943 revision is significant in light of its possible implication.

8. Frank Lloyd Wright, letter to Anna Lloyd Jones Wright, July 4, 1910, Avery Architectural & Fine Arts Library, Columbia University, New York.

9. "Wright Lays Bare Entire Hegira Story," *Inter Ocean*, December 31, 1911, 1–2. Wright indicated that September 1908 marked the beginning of what he believed to be his one-year waiting period with Catherine Wright before obtaining her agreement to a divorce. If his July 4, 1910, letter to his mother is to be believed, he thought Cheney had insisted that Borthwick marry him before she went away with him: "She told her husband one year before she went away with me that she would go with me married or not whenever I could take her. Marriage was never a condition with her any more than it was with me—except that in order to work I felt this must take place when it might if it might. *It seemed at one time (owing to requests of her husband solely) as though this were to be made a condition*—and I so misunderstood it myself for a time but this was never her stipulation nor did she ever hide behind it" (emphasis added).

10. Smith, *Wright on Exhibit*, 27.

11. Alofsin, *Lost Years*, 11–12.

12. "Pope Sobs as He Greets," *Chicago Tribune*, September 17, 1908, 2.

13. Frank Lloyd Wright to Darwin D. Martin, December 2, 1908, Darwin Martin and Martin Family Papers, State University of New York, Buffalo.

CHAPTER 14. HYDE PARK HIDEAWAY

1. Wright's name appears among the permanent residents of the Chicago Beach Hotel in the 1909 edition of *The Chicago Blue Book* (311). The data for the 1909 edition were collected during 1908. Although he is not listed as a resident in the 1910 edition, he may have kept the apartment in the first half of 1909.

2. Graduate School, University of Chicago, transcript of Mamah Borthwick Cheney, matriculation on October 1, 1908.

3. Nevius, *Robert Herrick*, 167.

4. Nevius, *Robert Herrick*, 181–82.

5. In an interview, Robie confirmed that he bought the house lot on May 19, 1908, and that he began discussing the project with Wright that summer. By winter, Wright

had produced enough drawings and ideas for Robie to proceed with the project (Hoffmann, *Frank Lloyd Wright's Robie House*, 17, 26).

6. Twombly, *Interpretive Biography*, 61–63.

7. *Landmark Designation Report*, Shoreland Hotel, 5454 S. South Shore Drive Preliminary and Final Landmark Recommendation adopted by the Commission on Chicago Landmarks, July 1, 2010. Landfill has since increased the distance to the beach from where the hotel was located.

8. "Wright's Soul Mate Is Slain," *Mason City Globe Gazette*, August 17, 1914, 1.

9. Guarino, *Yesterday*, 79. This may further indicate that their relationship was not yet widely known. Had the cat been out of the bag, the Nineteenth Century Club would surely have shunned Mamah.

10. Ashbee, *Janet Ashbee*, 105–20.

11. Ashbee, *Janet Ashbee*, 122.

12. Ashbee, *Janet Ashbee*, 122.

13. Guthrie, *Beyond Disillusion*.

14. F. R. Wright, *Frank Lloyd Wright*, 163.

15. Huxtable, *Frank Lloyd Wright*, 109.

16. Letter from Frank Lloyd Wright to Eric Lloyd Wright, September 14, 1953, *Whirling Arrow*, September 14, 2017, Frank Lloyd Wright Foundation.

CHAPTER 15. FLIGHT

1. Herrick, "Our Predecessors," 23–31.

2. Regnery, *Cliff-Dwellers*, 21.

3. Although he was a charter member of the Cliff Dwellers in late 1907 (chapter 12), Wright was dropped as a member in late 1909. This is confirmed by his omission from the first official list of members published in early 1910. The list notably does not include Louis Sullivan either, even though in 1907, he, like Wright, was a charter member. Sullivan eventually became an honorary member. The club rebuffed Wright's attempt in 1914 to be reinstated (chapter 27).

4. It is inferred here that by early 1909 they had decided to go to Europe once the waiting period had ended. Wright signaled as much when he wrote to Ashbee on January 3, 1909, that it was "a great temptation" to accept his invitation to Europe and "desert" Oak Park (Crawford, "Ten Letters," 66). Borthwick continued to be active in the Nineteenth Century Club in early 1909. On April 7, she made a presentation on drama to its members just two days after Catherine Wright had made one ("Nineteenth Century Club," *Oak Leaves*, April 3, 1909, 24).

5. "On Ornamentation," *Oak Leaves*, January 16, 1909, 20.

6. F. L. Wright, *Frank Lloyd Wright*, 163.

7. Frank Lloyd Wright to Darwin D. Martin, September 16, 1909, MS 22.8, Frank Lloyd Wright—Darwin D. Martin Papers, 1888–1979, University Archives, State University of New York at Buffalo.

8. "News of the Schools and Colleges," *Inter Ocean*, March 25, 1909, 7.

9. Two newspaper announcements, likely placed by Edwin Cheney or Lizzie Borthwick, confirm that Mamah Borthwick took all three children with her to Boulder:

"Mrs. E.H. Cheney of Fair Oaks has taken her three children to Colorado for the summer." *Oak Leaves*, July 3, 1909, 2; "Summer Wanderings," *Chicago Tribune*, July 11, 1909, 19. Hendrickson (*Plagued by Fire*, 178) believes that her niece, Jessie, was not included. Having raised her from birth, Mamah treated Jessie as if she were her child. Wright confirmed this when he remarked to the press that she had three children. Secrest (*Frank Lloyd Wright*, 194) mistakenly views his comment as meaning that he did not know how many children she had.

10. The excellent train service of the era permitted Lizzie Borthwick to have her sister's luggage picked up in Oak Park by Union Pacific and checked through to Denver. Station accommodations could often be found designated especially for women and children.

11. Karl Baedecker, *United States*, xx.

12. Hendrickson, *Plagued by Fire*, 181.

13. The start of school on September 6 is noted in "School Monday," *Oak Park Oak Leaves*, September 4, 1909, 4. Borthwick and Cheney had an agreement that she must give up the children in time for them to be in Oak Park and ready to attend school in late August. Wright confirmed this in "Wright Reveals Romance Secret," *Chicago Tribune*, December 31, 1911, 4.

14. Borthwick's expression of the hope that she will have access to her children appears in an undated, unidentified newspaper clipping in her personal file held by the University of Michigan's Bentley Historical Library.

15. MBB to EK, January 5, 1913, L41a (letter no. 8).

16. Meech, *Frank Lloyd Wright*, 61.

17. Grant Carpenter Manson states that Wright made an "overnight decision" to leave and that he was dramatically rushed in his departure. As he awaited Borthwick's telegram from Boulder, it is more likely that there was confusion and uncertainty over *when* to leave rather than *whether* to do so. Manson, *Frank Lloyd Wright to 1910*, 212.

18. Secrest, *Frank Lloyd Wright*, 204.

19. Frank Lloyd Wright to Catherine Wright, July 4, 1910, Frank Lloyd Wright Foundation Archives (The Museum of Modern Art | Avery Architectural & Fine Arts Library, Columbia University, New York). Reproduced in Schrenk, *Oak Park Studio*, appendix D.

20. "Little Locals," *Boulder Daily Camera*, September 24, 1909, 4.

21. "Frank Lloyd Wright of 500 Forest Avenue Oak Park, left Thursday for Germany where he will spend a year in travel." "News of the Society World," *Chicago Tribune*, October 3, 1909, 23. Wright wrote to Ashbee a year later that he left Oak Park on September 20, but in the letter to his mother of July 4, 1910, he gave the date as September 23.

22. The press gleefully reported that Wright had taken Borthwick on the itinerary he and Catherine Wright had followed in Germany on their honeymoon in 1899, but the Wrights had honeymooned in Wisconsin, not Europe. In fact, Borthwick may have taken Wright on part of the itinerary of *her* honeymoon.

23. Despite occasional press descriptions of his work as "bizarre," evidence that his reputation had become far-reaching less than three years after the scandal appears in

the description of Wright as "the father of the new American style of architecture" ("Home Building Grows," *Salt Lake Tribune*, February 18, 1912, 2). However, Levine (*Architecture of Frank Lloyd Wright*, 443n14) believes his reputation was more limited. Professional architectural clubs like the Chicago Architectural Club played the principal role in promulgating new architectural ideas, including Wright's, to wider audiences. He believed that his Wasmuth portfolio would boost his reputation.

CHAPTER 16. BERLIN SETUP

1. Ashbee's house, sometimes called "the Whistler house," is described in "Possibilities of Beauty in the City House," *The Craftsman* 12, no. 3 (June 1907): 336. It was destroyed during the bombing of London in World War II.

2. Quoted in Andrew Saint, "Wright and Great Britain," 127. Ashbee's architectural office at 37 Cheyne Walk was also a residence for his mother and sister. His dates of residence at nearby Number 74 are uncertain, and it is possible that Wright was looking for Number 37. In any case, he and Borthwick passed by a house on Cheyne Walk in Chelsea that he assumed was Ashbee's residence. He may also have stopped in London to meet with an old acquaintance, Hiromachi Shugio, an important advisor to Wright on buying Japanese art who was on a temporarily assignment for the Japanese government.

3. Endell, *Beauty of the Metropolis*, 59.

4. Newham-Davis, *Gourmet's Guide to Europe*, 221.

5. Secrest concludes that the informant was someone in Chicago: "The ostensible explanation for the article was that an alert foreign correspondent had discovered the false hotel registration. Since the possibility of a newspaper reporter's scanning the hotel registers in any city in pursuit of irregularities is remote, one is left to conclude that someone in Chicago wanted the elopement exposed and told the newspaper where to start looking." Secrest, *Frank Lloyd Wright*, 329.

6. "Leave Families; Elope to Europe," *Chicago Tribune*, November 7, 1909, 1.

7. "Leave Families; Elope to Europe," 1.

8. "Mrs. Alden H. Brown," *Daily Camera*, October 16, 1909, 2.

9. Smyth (*Wright on Exhibit*, 250n68) discusses the unplanned nature of Wright's Wasmuth venture, confirmed by his impromptu decision to summon Lloyd to help with it.

10. Their overall European itinerary is described in Alofsin, *Lost Years* (see 35–40 for the visit to Darmstadt).

11. MBB to EK, November 10, 1912, L41a (letter no. 7). There is no likely scenario by which Borthwick spent a night in Nancy alone without Wright. None of her possible train travel itineraries alone in Europe required Nancy as an overnight stop. Their visit to Nancy seems to have occurred just after the Nancy Exposition concluded and while the pavilion by Vallin was still intact.

12. Descouturelle et al., *Nancy 1909*, 146–47.

13. Key, *Love and Marriage*, 348–49.

14. Friedman, "Frank Lloyd Wright and Feminism," 144.

15. MBB to EK, November 10, 1912, L41a (letter no. 7).

16. Werner, *Transatlantic World*, 187–88. Borthwick is not listed among the Americans in Werner's compilation "American Students at the University of Leipzig, 1781–1914." In any case, reports that Borthwick taught at the University of Leipzig are mistaken. No woman, let alone a foreign woman, was allowed to serve on the faculty.

17. According to his autobiography published more than two decades later, Wright found himself alone in Paris in November 1909. Alofsin suggests Wright was mistaken on the date, that instead he was there in late January 1910, during the great Paris flood (Alofsin, *Lost Years*, 40). Wright did note at the time that the Seine was "*most of the time* over its banks" (emphasis added), suggestive of the "small floods" along the Seine in November through December 1909 (cf. Jeffrey H. Jackson, *Paris under Water*), but not the catastrophic flood of late January. To walk the Paris streets through the night as he described having done would not have been possible in January during the great flood, when his likely location was traversable only by boat. In a letter, his daughter congratulated him on having avoided the Paris flood. In short, this itinerary takes Wright at his word: he was alone in Paris in November 1909.

CHAPTER 17. HOME FRONTS

1. "Leave Families; Elope to Europe," *Chicago Tribune*, November 7, 1909, 4.
2. "Cheney Champion of Runaway Wife," *Chicago Tribune*, November 9, 1909, 7.
3. "Cheney Champion of Runaway Wife," 7.
4. "Leave Families; Elope to Europe," 4.
5. "Pastor Rebukes Affinity Fools," *Chicago Tribune*, November 8, 1909, 10.
6. "Leave Families; Elope to Europe," 4.

CHAPTER 18. MISSION TO STOCKHOLM

1. Inferred from Wright's letter to his mother, July 4, 1910, in which he refers to "Aunt Nell's word on Christmas received in Paris."
2. That Borthwick met Key in Sweden in early 1910 is confirmed in a comment made by Wright's assistant Taylor Woolley about their relationship (Alofsin, *Lost Years*, 41n59). Her contact with Key must have occurred in January or February. In March she moved to Fiesole, where she received a letter from Key confirming details of the agreement they had reached in Sweden.
3. Personal communications to the author by Maja Rahm, director, Ellen Key's Strand, October 15, 2019, and by Hedda Jansson, PhD student, Stockholm University, October 29, 2019, who also provided information based on Key's correspondence with Ellen Michelsen.
4. Madeleine Z. Doty, "Women of the Future: In Sweden the Genius," *Good Housekeeping*, August 1918, 34, 108–10.
5. Doty, "Women of the Future."
6. Wägner, *Penwoman*, 20–21.
7. Borthwick thanked Key for this article in her first letter of record, which is undated. The article must have been published in conjunction with the Stockholm Peace Conference that Key addressed in early August 1910. This indicates that Borthwick's letter was written in the latter part of 1910.

8. Nyström-Hamilton, *Ellen Key*, 77.

9. De Angelis, "A Biography of Ellen Key," 243–44n48.

Chapter 19. Love and Ethics

1. Henderson was the wife of the wealthy photographer John Cruickshank (1852–1918), who had commissioned a large Arts and Crafts mansion, Coombe Head, in Surrey. For a discussion of Wright in Italy at this time, see Fici, "Frank Lloyd Wright," 4–17.

2. See Alofsin, *Lost Years*, 334n54.

3. Crawford, "Ten Letters," 67.

4. Dreiser, *Traveler at Forty*, 395.

5. Ambjörnsson, "Ellen Key," 134.

6. Key, *The Torpedo under the Ark*, 17.

7. Friedman, "Frank Lloyd Wright and Feminism," 146.

8. Quoted in Alofsin, *Wright and New York*, 23.

9. Key, *Love and Ethics*, trans. Borthwick, 16.

10. The book consists of three essays: "The Morality of Woman," "The Woman of the Future," and "The Conventional Woman."

11. Levine, *Architecture of Frank Lloyd Wright*, 445n52.

12. F. L. Wright, *An Autobiography* (1992), 2:221, which reproduces Wright's expanded 1943 version. In his original 1932 biography, he used the adjective "Roman" for the road they traversed.

13. Quoted in McCrea, *Building Taliesin*, 43. Sasha is the Russian nickname for her husband, Alexander. Translation from the French by Jonah Hacker.

14. Amberg, *Piireissä*. See also "Kaikkien rakastama Mascha" (Mascha, Loved by All), *Antiikki & Design* (Helsinki), November 24, 2016, https://antiikkidesign.fi/blogit/kaikkien-rakastama-mascha.

15. Quoted in Alofsin, *Lost Years*, 52.

16. Frank Lloyd Wright to Anna Lloyd Jones Wright, July 4, 1910. I am grateful to Keiran Murphy for providing a typed transcript of this letter, the original of which is in the Frank Lloyd Wright Foundation Archives (The Museum of Modern Art | Avery Architectural & Fine Arts Library, Columbia University, New York).

17. 318–04.866 Register of Passenger Fees, line Rotterdam–New York (westbound): August 1, 1910, until August 31, 1910. I am grateful to Fillipo Fici for his discovery of Lizzie Borthwick's return journey in 1910 (Fici, "Frank Lloyd Wright").

Chapter 20. Secession

1. Frank Lloyd Wright, Duplicate Passport Application, no. 255, National Archives and Records Administration, issued by United States Embassy, July 20, 1910, Rome, Italy.

2. Alofsin believes Wright lacked the resources to use the passport (Alofsin, *Wright and New York*, 27). A check of the relevant repositories in Turkey for foreign visitors in this period, including the Ottoman state archives, does not produce the name of Frank Lloyd Wright. I am grateful to Dr. K. Mehmet Kentel, Istanbul Research Institute, for this information.

3. Alofsin, *Lost Years*, 19. Cf. 339n144.

4. Alofsin, *Wright and New York*, 32.

5. Alofsin, *Wright and New York*, 339n143.

6. Alofsin, *Wright and New York*, 56.

7. Key, *Verk Och Manniskor*, quoted in Nyström-Hamilton, *Ellen Key*, 74.

8. *Bruckmann's Illustrated Guide* (1910) indicates the performance dates in September. They would have seen the performance scheduled for September 11.

9. "'Art Mates' Bare Souls," *Chicago Examiner*, December 31, 1911, 3. In a prepared statement with Borthwick present, Wright declared, "The woman remained to work in Berlin in communication with her husband and her children. She was prepared to remain alone until the legal divorce, which she insisted upon, was granted."

10. She indicated to the consulate that she was a student, possibly to avoid a regulatory restriction on her employment.

11. Alofsin, *Frank Lloyd Wright, Art Collector*, 24.

12. MBB to EK, October–November 1910, L41a (letter no. 1). In her letter to Key, "conventionalization" means abstraction. Wright often used the word for that purpose.

13. After visiting Wright and Mamah in Fiesole, the von Heiroths created a travel scrapbook, now held by the Finnish National Board of Antiquities, containing a photograph of the painting. A note by a family member has been added next to the photograph. Written in Swedish, it reads: "Tavlan köptes 1910 av den berömda arkitekten Frank Lloyd Wright ([unclear] 1985)" (The painting was bought in 1910 by the famous architect Frank Lloyd Wright [(unclear) 1985]). *Mascha Von Heiroth, Kuvia Fiesolesta Ja Jäljennös Alexander Von Heirothin Maalauksesta*, finna.fi. An additional entry in French by Mascha von Heiroth describes the painting as a "Japanese" tree at the Villa Bardi near Fiesole. If the painting hung in the residential section of Taliesin I, it would have perished in the fire of 1914.

14. For her Berlin consular record, Borthwick gave the Amalienhaus address, Mohrenstraße 11, as her initial residence.

15. See *Special Reports on Educational Subjects*, vol. 19, *School Training for the Home Duties of Women*, part III, *The Domestic Training of Girls in Germany and Austria* (Great Britain: Board of Education, H. M. Stationery Office, 1907), 62.

16. The return address on Borthwick's first letter to Ellen Key, written after she had moved from Amalienhaus, was "Schaperstraße 2–3, Pension Gottschalk." The historic building that housed the teachers of the Joachimsthal Gymnasium still stands at Schaperstraße 23. The dash Borthwick placed between the 2 and 3, if preserved today, would not significantly alter its location next to the school. Pension Gottschalk may have been its unofficial name in 1910.

Chapter 21. Berlin to Alvastra

1. These presumed circumstances of Key's housing are based on personal communication to the author by Maja Rahm, director, Ellen Key's Strand.

2. MBB to EK, October–November 1910, L41a (letter no. 1).

3. Strand was not entirely finished when Key moved into it in late December 1910. She did not receive guests there until spring 1911.

4. Gilman, "New Motherhood," 17–18.

5. Doty, "Women of the Future."

6. De Angelis, "Biography of Ellen Key," 228.

7. Alofsin, *Lost Years*, 348n98.

8. Alofsin, *Frank Lloyd Wright, Art Collector*, 24.

9. Sometimes called a hymn or rhapsody on nature, the text, ascribed at the time to Goethe, was viewed with a certain reverence in Germany. It was published in the early twentieth century by Mandruck A. G. Munich in one hundred small, handmade, leather-bound volumes under the title *Die Natur*. The collector's edition published in Darmstadt in 1910 under the title *Die Natur, ein Hymnus von Goethe* was likely the one found by Borthwick and Wright in the bookstore. An initial page within it carried the traditional title from a 1783 version written in the hand of Goethe's secretary Seidel, *Die Natur: Fragment (Nature: A Fragment)*.

10. Kistler, "Goethe-Tobler Fragment"; Trevelyan, *Goethe and the Greeks*. The hymns were found by Giovanni Aurispa in Constantinople and brought to Venice in 1423.

11. Nyström-Hamilton, *Ellen Key*, 168. Vättern is misspelled in Putnam's translation.

12. Johannesson, "Ellen Key," 127. See also Lane, "An Introduction," 26.

CHAPTER 22. HOME OF TOMORROW

1. "An English Critic," *Oak Leaves*, June 24, 1911, ii–iii.

2. In a letter to Key, Borthwick referred to it as "camping in the Canadian woods," an expression that did not necessarily mean the use of tents. Camping commonly referred to cottage rental in a remote area.

3. Superior Court of Cook County, Certificate of Evidence, Edwin H. Cheney vs. Mamah Borthwick Cheney, Gen. no. 288,177, Term no. 10,901, August 3, 1911. Reproduced in Nissen, "Taliesin."

4. "Cheney Divorces Wife Who Eloped," *Chicago Sunday Tribune*, August 6, 1911, 3.

5. Huxtable, *Frank Lloyd Wright*, 129.

6. "Wright Divides Home 'To Protect His Soul,'" *Chicago Examiner*, November 8, 1911, 1.

7. "Elopement Is Modern Right, Says Affinity," *Springfield Republican* (Springfield, MO), December 26, 1911, 1.

CHAPTER 23. A HOUSE DIVIDED

1. Schrenk, *Oak Park Studio*, 182.

2. Herink, *Car Is Architecture*, 3–4, 25.

3. The incidents are reported in three news accounts: "Speeder in Third Arrest," *Chicago Examiner*, July 12, 1911, 8; "Chauffeur and Auto Gone," *Chicago Examiner*, September 1, 1911, 13; *Oak Park Oak Leaves*, July 22, 1911, 7. The unusually precise traveling speed cited in the report probably reflected a practice used at that time by police: waiting with stopwatch in hand and noting the amount of time it took for a car to reach them from a particular point.

4. "Wright Razes Wall: Reunited with Wife," *Chicago Examiner*, November 13, 1911, 1.

5. "Wright Family Reunites and Divorce Is Off," *Inter Ocean*, November 13, 1911, 1–2.

6. Llewellyn's letters are quoted from Hendrickson, *Plagued by Fire*, 97–98.

7. Alofsin, "Taliesin," 48.

8. "Oak Park: Model Suburb," *Inter Ocean*, December 11, 1911, 6.

9. The stories were reported later in articles such as "Architect Wright in New Romance with 'Mrs. Cheney,'" *Chicago Tribune*, December 24, 1911, 1.

10. MBB to EK, est. December 7, 1911, L41a (letter no. 2).

11. MBB to EK, est. early January 1912, L41a (letter no. 4). Wright's link to Ellen Key through the Hiroshige print went undiscovered for decades. It hung in Key's home at Strand unremarked until the researcher Lena Johannesson took it down and discovered Key's note on the back: "A gift from the great American architect Frank Lloyd Wright." This led the researcher to find Borthwick's letters in the National Library of Sweden. Johannesson, "Ellen Key," 129.

12. B. W. Huebsch to the Ralph Fletcher Seymour Company, December 7, 1911. The letter was included with MBB to EK, December 1911, L41:58 (letter no. 3).

13. The full, correct title was *The Morality of Woman: And Other Essays*.

14. The possibility of sabotage is proposed by McCrea, *Building Taliesin*, note 85. Johannesson ("Ellen Key," 131), on the other hand, believes the error was an attempt by Borthwick to disguise her identity with a pseudonym. The latter explanation is unlikely given that all the errors, including her name's misspelling, were corrected in the second printing.

15. "Architect Wright in New Romance with 'Mrs. Cheney,'" *Chicago Tribune*, December 24, 1911, 1.

CHAPTER 24. MISS CHICAGO

1. "Wright Renews Cheney Romance," *Chicago Tribune*, December 24, 1911, 4.

2. "Wright Renews Cheney Romance," 4.

3. "Wife Shackles Me to Ruin, Promised Divorce, Wright Says," *Chicago Examiner*, December 30, 1911, 3.

4. "Christmas Gloomy in Wright's Home," *Inter Ocean*, December 25, 1911, 3.

5. "Spend Christmas Making 'Defense' of 'Spirit Hegira,'" *Chicago Tribune*, December 26, 1911, 1–2.

6. Tar and Feather Party Is Threat of Neighbors against Frank L. Wright," *Inter Ocean*, December 26, 1911, 1.

7. Fitzwater, *Esther's Pillow*.

8. "Hillside and the Wright-Cheney Case," *Inter Ocean*, December 27, 1911, 6.

9. "Wright in Castle Fearless of Raid," *Chicago Tribune*, December 28, 1911, 1.

10. *Chicago Evening Post Friday Literary Review*, December 29, 1911, fig. 110, quoted in McCrea, *Building Taliesin*.

11. "Wright Lays Bare Entire Hegira Story," *Inter Ocean*, December 31, 1911, 2.

12. *Detroit Free Press*, December 28, 1911, 6.

13. Szuberla, "Yesterday's City."

CHAPTER 25. MAMAH OF THE HILLS

1. "Architect Wright Plans to Keep Mum," *St. Louis Star and Times*, January 3, 1912, 2.

2. "Architect Wright Plans to Keep Mum," 2.

3. Nissen, "Taliesin," 6–7. Nissen notes that "Wright's later wife Olgivanna removed the statue." The iconography of the sculpture and its meanings for Wright are discussed in Menocal, "Taliesin," 66–82; and Levine, "Frank Lloyd Wright's Own Houses," 30.

4. Levine, "The Story of Taliesin," 20. Elsewhere, Levine observes that the sculpture may also have represented the Welsh goddess of nature, Ceridwen (Levine, *Architecture of Frank Lloyd Wright*, 100).

5. "Architect Wright Plans to Keep Mum," 2.

6. "Forms Profane, Spirit Sacred," *Los Angeles Times*, January 7, 1912, 4.

7. "Wright Mysterious in Trip to Madison," *Chicago Examiner*, January 9, 1912, 3.

8. "Insures Life for Soul-Mate," *La Cross Tribune*, January 5, 1912, 9.

9. MBB to EK, January 1912, L41a (letter no. 4).

10. "A Prophet Is Not without Honor Save in His Own Country," *Weekly Home News*, December 28, 1911.

11. "Family Murdered Love Palace Gone Children Killed," *La Crosse Tribune*, August 17, 1914, 6. The article states incorrectly that the Tower Hill Pleasure Company was founded for the purpose of protesting Wright and Borthwick's presence at Taliesin. It was founded in 1890 by Jenkin Lloyd-Jones to support Spring Green recreation and educational programs. Titus, "Historic Spots in Wisconsin," 326.

12. MBB to EK, January 1912, L41a (letter no. 4).

13. "Fight on 'Affinity' Fiction," *Chicago Tribune* January 13, 1912, 9.

14. MBB to EK, January 1912, L41a (letter no. 4), (emphasis in original).

15. MBB to EK, November 10, 1912, L41a (letter no. 7).

16. MBB to EK, January 1913, L41a (letter no. 8).

17. MBB to EK, January 1913, L41a (letter no. 8).

18. MBB to EK, January 1913, L41a (letter no. 8).

19. Boguslawsky, "Note."

20. The publication of *Liebe und Ethik* by the German publisher Wilhelm Borngraeber appeared in hardbound edition ca. 1905 and softbound ca. 1910. No other version was published. It is the only original text either translator would have used.

21. Johannesson, "Ellen Key," 134.

22. Wright to Darwin Martin, January 10, 1913, Wright-Martin Papers, SUNY Buffalo.

CHAPTER 26. TAISHO TURMOIL

1. "Soulmates Go to Japan," *Oshkosh Daily Northwestern*, January 14, 1913, 5. Alofsin believes they departed from San Francisco on January 11, which appears to be too early (Alofsin, *Wright and New York*, 268). McCrea states that they departed from Seattle, having missed the boat there on January 15, and sailed two weeks later (McCrea, *Building Taliesin*, 149). If the latter is correct, they may have arrived in Tokyo just after the riots.

2. The customary practice of placing family name first will be used for all Japanese names.

3. "Dodgeville News," *Mineral Point Tribune* (Mineral Point, WI), January 23, 1913, 5. After their return, Borthwick wrote to Ellen Key on July 8, "the main object of the trip, however, was Japanese prints."

4. Borthwick wrote to Ellen Key that they expected to live in a small house when they returned to Japan (MBB to EK, July 8, 1913, L41:58). This remark is the only documentation suggesting that they may have lived in one when they were there.

5. Wright, *An Autobiography* (1943), 200.

6. Yusa, "Zen-Feminist Raichō," 622. Hiratsuka's given name was Haruko, but she was generally known by her pen name, Raicho, which means "snow goose" or "thunder bird," a variety of grouse in Japan.

7. Reitherman, "Frank Lloyd Wright's Imperial Hotel," 147.

8. Wright's history with the Imperial Hotel project is described in Kathryn Smith, "Frank Lloyd Wright and the Imperial Hotel: A Postscript."

9. "Hotel News," *San Francisco Call*, June 8, 1913.

CHAPTER 27. THE WOMAN MOVEMENT

1. MBB to EK, July 8, 1913, L41:58 (letter no. 9). Borthwick refers to having written a letter to Key from Japan describing their experience there. That letter is not present in the Borthwick correspondence preserved in the National Library of Sweden.

2. McCrea, *Building Taliesin*, 173–74.

3. Frank Lloyd Wright to Hamlin Garland, April 20, 1914, the Hamlin Garland Correspondence, 1864–1941, USC Libraries Special Collections, University of Southern California.

4. Frank Lloyd Wright to Hamlin Garland, April 24, 1914, the Hamlin Garland Correspondence, 1864–1941, USC Libraries Special Collections, University of Southern California.

5. Hasbrouck, *Chicago Architectural Club*, 420.

6. Wright was not bitter toward the Cliff Dwellers for expelling him, but in a letter recently discovered in the club archives, he subtly alluded to their apparent amnesia concerning his history with the club.

Dear Cliff Dwellers:
   I am pleased to be honored by the club that honored Sullivan. And I hope that I may occasionally warm his chair there. A fine thing the Cliff Dwellers did for him.
   I was a charter member of your group. Hamlin Garland, Daniel Burnham and the novelist at Chicago U Robert Herrick got us together. I remember, if some of you do not?
   I hope to see you all occasionally and would like to see you at Taliesin.
   Sincerely yours,
   Frank Lloyd Wright, July 12, 1947

7. "Architects Quit Big Exhibit," *Chicago American*, April 9, 1914, 68.

8. Gilman, "On Ellen Key."

9. Hayden, *Grand Domestic Revolution.*

10. Key, *Woman Movement,* 163.

11. "Maternity Benefits and Reformers," *Forerunner* 7 (March 1916): 65–66.

12. MBB to EK, est. early December 1911, L41a (letter no. 2). The response to *Miß-brauchte Frauenkraft* by Borthwick's character in the novel *Loving Frank* is exactly opposite to what she stated in this letter.

13. The impact of Key's 1896 work *Mißbrauchte Frauenkraft* is discussed by Edward Ross Dickinson in his survey of the movement in Germany, *Sex, Freedom, and Power in Imperial Germany, 1880–1914.* Birgitta Holm's "The Third Sex" addresses the text's different impact in Scandinavia. The lasting bitterness with which German suffragists viewed Key was assimilated by the American writer Katherine Anthony, who attended the universities of Heidelberg and Freiburg. She famously called Key a "wise fool" (Anthony, *Feminism and Scandinavia,* 213–14), a view that was not generally shared outside Germany.

14. Robert Herrick, "What Women Say of Selves; Ellen Key on 'Soul Hunger,'" *Chicago Tribune,* May 17, 1914, viii.

Chapter 28. Final Portrait

1. MBB to EK, July 20, 1914, L41a (letter no. 10).

2. Borthwick's translation of Key's "Romain Rolland" was published posthumously by her friend Margaret Anderson in *Little Review* 2 (October 1915): 22–30.

3. Gilman, *Women and Economics.*

4. Hendrickson, *Plagued by Fire,* 190.

5. Drennan, *Death in A Prairie House,* 139.

6. The house, known as Villa Zila, since demolished, was a multilevel house built in 1913/14 that bore similarities to Wright's Oscar B. Balch House (1911) in Oak Park. The architect's name is blocked out on a floor plan that was donated by Marion Mahony to Northwestern University's Block Museum. The design is attributed to Mahony, but Koehne claimed that he commissioned it from Wright. Galicki and Stamm, "The Villa Koehne in Palm Beach."

7. The National Library of Sweden holds the only known original print, which was conveyed to it by Ellen Key's Strand. A later print from the same negative, which Koehne signed more boldly, is held by Getty Images (an inch and a half is missing from the bottom). The latter print appears to have been removed from Wright's files at Taliesin in 1925. Getty Images adds the note, "1925–Original caption reads: Mamah Borthwick Cheney, Frank Lloyd Wright's mistress." The year 1925 is when Wright's third wife, Olga Ivanovna Lazović (Olgivanna), began to reside at Taliesin.

Chapter 29. Lightning

1. *Dispatch,* August 17, 1914, 12. This description also answers William R. Drennan's confusion (*Death in a Prairie House,* note 90) about the location of the men's dining room. Carlton followed an indirect "passage" of sorts totaling sixty feet that connected the family dining room to the men's dining room in the southeast residential area, not the studio area. In addition to the account in the *Dispatch,* the *Wisconsin State Journal,*

August 16, 1914, notes the proximity of threshers nearby and the behavior and appearance of Gertrude Carlton.

2. A survivor of the attack, William Weston, said a burning rug was placed at the door. Carlton's initial alibi was that the fire broke out by accident when he was using gasoline to clean a rug. His wife testified that he was cleaning a rug just before the attack ("Bury Victims of Mad Negro's Fury," *Muscatine Journal*, August 17, 1914, 10). Hendrickson (*Plagued by Fire*) states there is no evidence to support Carlton's use of a gasoline-soaked rug.

3. Drennan, *Death in a Prairie House*, 141–43.

4. Drennan, *Death in a Prairie House*, 95–101.

5. J. L. Wright, *My Father*.

6. F. L. Wright, *An Autobiography* (1992), 2:240.

CHAPTER 30. ALL THAT REMAINS

1. Wright, *An Autobiography* (1932), 190.

2. "Frank Lloyd Wright to His Neighbors," *Weekly Home News*, August 20, 1914.

3. "Wright's Soul Mate Is Slain," *Mason City Globe Gazette*, August 17, 1914, 3.

4. Goethe (attributed), "Hymn to Nature," 32. Published in October 1914 by their friend Margaret Anderson in her avant-garde journal, *Little Review*, the attribution for the translation was given only as "by a strong man and a strong woman whose lives and whose creations have served the ideals of all humanity in a way that will gain deeper and deeper appreciation." Anderson apparently felt a need to withhold their names in light of the recent headlines.

5. Benjamin Britten, "Corpus Christi Carol" (Unison), from "A Boy Was Born," Oxford University Press, Catalogue No: 978019351079. Based on a medieval poem.

6. "Prophecy of Taliesin," *Cambro-Briton* 2, no. 16 (1820): 185–88. See also Borrow, *Wild Wales*, epigraph.

7. "Enemies of Wright Are Blamed," *Cincinnati Enquirer*, August 18, 1914, 9.

8. F. L. Wright, *An Autobiography* (1992), 2:240.

9. J. L. Wright, *My Father*, 85.

10. Alofsin, *Wright and New York*, 26.

11. F. L. Wright, *An Autobiography* (1992), 2:220.

12. Frank Lloyd Wright to EK, Taliesin, December 8, 1914, L41a (letter no. 11).

13. Holm, "The Greatest Movement."

14. Bishop, *The Quarter Centennial Reunion*.

15. The oldest child of the Cheney household, Jessie Pitkin, survived by being absent from Taliesin on the fateful day. Years later, she married Roger Higgins and moved to Amherst, Massachusetts, where she taught dance and eventually took care of her beloved aunt Lizzie Borthwick. The latter died there in 1946.

16. Storrer states that Borthwick had written a biography of Goethe and that her manuscript was lost in the fire (*Architecture of Frank Lloyd Wright*, 164). This seems unlikely. She gave priority to translation and had limited opportunity to conduct extensive research on Goethe.

17. "Marriage Assailant Divorced," *Buffalo Times*, December 24, 1922, 64. Noel's letters to Wright were stolen by a discharged servant and sold to the newspapers.

BIBLIOGRAPHY

Allen, Margaret. *Family Memories of Four Sisters.* Calcutta: Lake Gardens Press, 1976.

Alofsin, Anthony. *Frank Lloyd Wright, Art Collector: Secessionist Prints from the Turn of the Century.* Austin: University of Texas Press, 2012.

———. *Frank Lloyd Wright—The Lost Years, 1910–1922: A Study of Influence.* Chicago: University of Chicago Press, 1993.

———. "Taliesin, to Fashion Worlds in Little." In *Wright Studies*, vol. 1, *Taliesin 1911–1914*, edited by Narciso G. Menocal, 44–65. Carbondale: Southern Illinois University Press, 1992.

———. *Wright and New York: The Making of America's Architect.* New Haven, CT: Yale University Press, 2019.

Amberg, Anna-Lisa. *Piireissä: Mascha von Heiroth 1871–1934.* Helsinki: Siltala, 2016.

Ambjörnsson, Ronny. "Ellen Key and the Concept of Bildung." *Confero* 2, no. 1 (2014): 133–60.

Anthony, Katherine. *Feminism in Germany and Scandinavia.* New York: H. Holt, 1915.

Ashbee, Felicity. *Janet Ashbee: Love, Marriage, and the Arts and Crafts Movement.* Syracuse, NY: Syracuse University Press, 2002.

Baedecker, Karl. *The United States: With an Excursion into Mexico.* New York: Charles Scribner's Sons, 1904.

Bartlett, George Bradford, and William Gurney Bentham. *Mrs. Jarley's Far-Famed Collection of Waxworks.* London: S. French, 1873.

Beaumont, Francis, and John Fletcher. *The Works of Francis Beaumont, and Mr. John Fletcher.* London: Printed for J. and R. Tonson and S. Draper, 1750.

Bishop, William Warner. *The Quarter Centennial Reunion: Class of Eighteen Ninety-Two, University of Michigan.* Ann Arbor: University of Michigan, 1919.

Boguslawsky, Amalie K. "Note." In *Love and Ethics*, 5–6. New York: B. W. Huebsch, 1911.

Bolon, Carol R., Robert S. Nelson, and Linda Seidel, eds. *The Nature of Frank Lloyd Wright.* Chicago: University of Chicago Press, 1988.

Borrow, George Henry. *Wild Wales: Its People, Language, and Scenery.* 3rd ed. London: J. Murray, 1872.

Borthwick, Halsey M., and William S. Borthwick. *The Borthwick Family: A History and Genealogy of the Family of Borthwick, Chiefly in Scotland and America.* Cornwallville, NY, 1936.

Borthwick, Mamah Bouton. "Prophecy." *The Commencement Annual of the University of Michigan* 12 (June 30, 1892): 111.

Broude, Norma. "Mary Cassatt: Modern Woman or the Cult of True Womanhood?" *Woman's Art Journal* 21, no. 2 (2000): 36–43.

Browning, Richard James. "Early Fargo Theaters: Record of the Professional Theatre Activity in Fargo, Dakota Territory from 1880–1888." *Fargo History Project*, North Dakota State University, Fargo, ND, 1979. http://fargohistory.com/2012/11/17/vaudevillian-culture-in-fargo/.

Bruckmann's Illustrated Guide: Oberammergau and Its Passion Play 1910. Munich: A. Bruckmann's Verlag, 1910.

Buchanan, Lindal. *Regendering Delivery: The Fifth Canon and Antebellum Women Rhetors.* Carbondale: Southern Illinois University Press, 2005.

Cheney, Mamah B. "Installation of Alpha Iota Chapter." *Kappa Alpha Theta*, March 1907, 167–68.

The Cliff Dwellers: An Account of Their Organization, the Dedication and Opening of Their Quarters, Constitution and Bylaws, Officers, Committees, and List of Members. Chicago: Ralph Fletcher Seymour, 1910.

Clinton, Catherine. "Equally Their Due: The Education of the Planter Daughter in the Early Republic." *Journal of the Early Republic* 2, no. 1 (1982): 39–60.

Crawford, Alan. "Ten Letters from Frank Lloyd Wright to Charles Robert Ashbee." *Architectural History* 13 (1970): 64–76, 132.

Cunningham, Hugh. *Children and Childhood in Western Society since 1500.* New York: Routledge, 2014.

De Angelis, Ronald William. "A Biography of Ellen Key, Swedish Social Reformer." PhD diss., University of Connecticut, 1978.

Delap, Lucy. *The Feminist Avant-Garde: Transatlantic Encounters of the Early Twentieth Century.* New York: Cambridge University Press, 2007.

Descouturelle, Frédéric, Bernard Ponton, François Roth, and Hélène Sicard-Lenattier. *Nancy 1909: Centenaire de l'Exposition Internationale de l'Est de La France.* Nancy: Editions Place Stanislas, 2008.

DiCenzo, Maria. "Feminism, Theatre Criticism, and the Modern Drama." *South Central Review* 25, no. 1 (2008): 36–55.

Dickinson, Edward Ross. *Sex, Freedom, and Power in Imperial Germany, 1880–1914.* New York: Cambridge University Press, 2014.

Dodge, E. R., and L. P. Green. *Sixty Years in Kappa Alpha Theta, 1870–1929.* Menasha, WI: George Banta, 1930.

Doty, Madeleine Z. "Women of the Future: In Sweden the Genius." *Good Housekeeping*, August 1918.

Dreiser, Theodore. *A Traveler at Forty.* New York: Century, 1913.

Drennan, William R. *Death in a Prairie House: Frank Lloyd Wright and the Taliesin Murders.* Madison: University of Wisconsin Press, 2007.

Durbach, Errol. *A Doll's House: Ibsen's Myth of Transformation.* Boston: Twayne, 1991.

Dykhuizen, George. "John Dewey and the University of Michigan." *Journal of the History of Ideas* 4, no. 23 (October 1962): 513–44.

Ellis, Anthony L. "Woman in the Modern Drama." *Englishwoman*, April 1909.

Endell, August. *The Beauty of the Metropolis.* Translated by James J. Conway. 1908. Reprint, Berlin: Rixdorf Editions, 2018.

Fici, Filipo. "Frank Lloyd Wright in Florence and Fiesole, 1909–1910." *Frank Lloyd Wright Quarterly* 22, no. 4 (2011).

Fitzwater, Marlin. *Esther's Pillow: The Tar and Feathering of Margaret Chambers.* [Terrace, BC]: CCB, 2011.

Friedman, Alice T. "Frank Lloyd Wright and Feminism: Mamah Borthwick's Letters to Ellen Key." *Journal of the Society of Architectural Historians* 61, no. 2 (June 2002): 140–51.

Friedman, Alice T. *Women and the Making of the Modern House: A Social and Architectural History.* New Haven, CT: Yale University Press, 2006.

Gaffney, T. J. *Port Huron, 1880–1960.* Charleston, SC: Arcadia, 2006.

Galicki, Marta McBride, and Gunther Stamm. "The Villa Koehne in Palm Beach." *Florida Architect* 25, no. 1 (January 1975): 14–15.

Gill, Brendan. *Many Masks: A Life of Frank Lloyd Wright.* New York: G. P. Putnam's Sons, 1987.

Gilman, Charlotte Perkins. "The New Motherhood." *Forerunner* 1 (December 1910): 17–18.

———. "On Ellen Key and the Woman Movement." *Forerunner* 4 (February 1913): 35–38.

———. *Women and Economics: A Study of the Economic Relation between Men and Women as a Factor in Social Evolution.* 1898. Reprint, New York: Source Book Press, 1970.

Goethe, Johann Wolfgang von. "Hymn to Nature." Translated by Mamah Bouton Borthwick and Frank Lloyd Wright. *Little Review* 1, no. 11 (1914): 30–32.

Goldman, Emma. *The Social Significance of the Modern Drama.* Boston: Richard G. Badger, 1914.

Guarino, Jean. *Yesterday: A Historical View of Oak Park, Illinois.* Vol. 1, *Prairie Days to World War I.* Oak Park, IL: Oak Ridge Press, 2000.

Guthrie, William Norman. *Beyond Disillusion: A Dramatic Study of Modern Marriage.* New York: Petrus Stuyvesant Book Guild at St. Mark's in-the-Bouwerie, Manhattan, 1915.

———. *Modern Poet Prophets: Essays Critical and Interpretive.* Cincinnati: R. Clark, 1897.

Hasbrouck, Wilbert R. *The Chicago Architectural Club: Prelude to the Modern.* New York: Monacelli Press, 2005.

Hayden, Dolores. *The Grand Domestic Revolution: A History of Feminist Designs for American Homes, Neighborhoods, and Cities.* Cambridge, MA: MIT Press, 1982.

Hecker, Genevieve. *Golf for Women.* New York: Harper & Brothers, 1902.

Hendrickson, Paul. *Plagued by Fire: The Dreams and Furies of Frank Lloyd Wright.* New York: Knopf Doubleday, 2019.

Herink, Richie. *The Car Is Architecture—A Visual History of Frank Lloyd Wright's 85 Cars and One Motorcycle.* Martinsville, IN: Fideli, 2015.

Herrick, Robert. "Our Predecessors." In *The Cliff Dwellers: An Account of Their Organization, the Dedication and Opening of Their Quarters, Constitution and Bylaws, Officers, Committees, and List of Members*, 23–31. Chicago: Ralph Fletcher Seymour, 1910.

———. *Together.* New York: Macmillan, 1908.

Hertzberg, Mark. *Frank Lloyd Wright's Hardy House.* San Francisco: Pomegranate, 2006.

Hildebrand, Grant. *The Wright Space: Pattern and Meaning in Frank Lloyd Wright's Houses.* Seattle: University of Washington Press, 1991.

Hoffmann, Donald. *Frank Lloyd Wright's Robie House: The Illustrated Story of an Architectural Masterpiece.* New York: Dover, 1984.

———. "Meeting Nature Face to Face." In *The Nature of Frank Lloyd Wright*, edited by Carol R. Bolon, Robert S. Nelson, and Linda Seidel, 85–97. Chicago: University of Chicago Press, 1988.

Holm, Birgitta. "The Greatest Movement the World Has Ever Seen." History of Nordic Women's Literature, January 1, 2012. https://nordicwomensliterature.net/2012/01/01/the-greatest-movement-the-world-has-ever-seen/.

———. "The Third Sex." History of Nordic Women's Literature, January 12, 2012. https://nordicwomensliterature.net/2012/01/20/the-third-sex/.

Holzhueter, John O. "Frank Lloyd Wright's Designs for Robert Lamp." *Wisconsin Magazine of History* 72, no. 2 (1988): 82–125.

Huxtable, Ada Louise. *Frank Lloyd Wright: A Life.* New York: Viking Penguin, 2004.

Jackson, Jeffrey H. *Paris under Water: How the City of Light Survived the Great Flood of 1910.* New York: Macmillan, 2010.

Jacobson, Joanne. "The Idea of the Midwest." *Revue Française d'études Américaines*, nos. 48/49 (1991): 235–45.

Johannesson, Lena. "Ellen Key, Mamah Bouton Borthwick and Frank Lloyd Wright: Notes on the Historiography of Non-Existing History." *Nora: Nordic Journal of Women's Studies* 3, no. 3 (1995): 126–36.

Kahneman, Daniel. *Thinking Fast and Slow.* New York: Farrar, Straus and Giroux, 2013.

Key, Ellen. *Century of the Child.* New York: G. P. Putnam's Sons, 1909.

———. *Liebe und Ethik.* Berlin: Wilhelm Borngräber, 1905.

———. *Love and Ethics.* Translated by Amalie K. Boguslawsky. New York: B. W. Huebsch, 1911.

———. *Love and Ethics.* Translated by Mamah Bouton Borthwick. Chicago: Ralph Fletcher Seymour, 1912.

———. *Love and Marriage.* Translated by Arthur G. Chater. New York: G. P. Putnam's Sons, 1911.

———. *The Morality of Woman: And Other Essays.* Translated by Mamah Bouton Borthwick. Chicago: Ralph Fletcher Seymour, 1911.

———. *The Torpedo under the Ark: "Ibsen and Women."* Translated by Mamah Bouton Borthwick. Chicago: Ralph Fletcher Seymour, 1912.

———. *Uber Liebe und Ehe: Essays* [On love and marriage: Essays]. Berlin: S. Fischer, 1905.

———. *Verk Och Manniskor* [Man and works]. Stockholm: Bonniers, 1910.

———. *The Woman Movement.* Translated by Mamah Bouton Borthwick. New York: Putnam's, 1912.

Kistler, Mark O. "The Sources of the Goethe-Tobler Fragment 'Die Natur.'" *Monatshefte* 47, no. 7 (1954): 383–89.

Kittredge, Charmian. "Cross Saddle Riding for Women." *Out West,* July 1904.

Lane, Barbara Miller. "An Introduction to Ellen Key's 'Beauty in the Home.'" In *Modern Swedish Design: Three Founding Texts,* 19–31. New York: Museum of Modern Art, 2008.

Larson, Erik. *The Devil in the White City: Murder, Magic, and Madness at the Fair that Changed America.* New York: Vintage, 2004.

Lears, T. J. Jackson. *No Place of Grace: Antimodernism and the Transformation of American Culture, 1880–1920.* Chicago: University of Chicago Press, 1994.

Levine, Neil. *The Architecture of Frank Lloyd Wright.* Princeton, NJ: Princeton University Press, 1996.

———. "Frank Lloyd Wright's Own Houses and His Changing Concept of Representation." In *The Nature of Frank Lloyd Wright,* edited by Carol R. Bolon, Robert S. Nelson, and Linda Seidel, 20–69. Chicago: University of Chicago Press, 1988.

———. "The Story of Taliesin: Wright's First Natural House." In *Taliesin 1911–1914,* edited by Narciso G. Menocal, 2–27. Carbondale: Southern Illinois University, 1992.

Lewinnek, Elaine. *The Working Man's Reward: Chicago's Early Suburbs and the Roots of American Sprawl.* New York: Oxford University Press, 2014.

Manson, Grant Carpenter. *Frank Lloyd Wright to 1910: The First Golden Age.* New York: Van Nostrand Reinhold, 1958.

Matthews, Brander. *The Development of the Drama.* New York: Charles Scribner's Sons, 1912.

McCrea, Ron. *Building Taliesin: Frank Lloyd Wright's Home of Love and Loss.* Madison: Wisconsin Historical Society Press, 2012.

Meech, Julia. *Frank Lloyd Wright and the Art of Japan: The Architect's Other Passion.* New York: Harry N. Abrams, 2001.

Menocal, Narciso G. "Taliesin, the Gilmore House, and the Flower in the Crannied Wall." In *Wright Studies,* vol. 1, *Taliesin 1911–1914,* edited by Narciso G. Menocal, 66–82. Carbondale: Southern Illinois University, 1992.

Moi, Toril. *Henrik Ibsen and the Birth of Modernism: Art, Theater, Philosophy.* Oxford: Oxford University Press, 2006.

Moore, Michelle E. *Chicago and the Making of American Modernism: Cather, Hemingway, Faulkner, and Fitzgerald in Conflict.* London: Bloomsbury Academic, 2018.

Nevius, Blake. *Robert Herrick: The Development of a Novelist.* 1962. Reprint, Oakland: University of California Press, 2021.

Newham-Davis, Nathaniel. *The Gourmet's Guide to Europe.* 3rd ed. New York: Brentano's, 1911.

Nissen, Anne D. "From the Cheney House to Taliesin: Frank Lloyd Wright and Feminist Mamah Borthwick." Master's thesis, Massachusetts Institute of Technology, 1988.

Nyström-Hamilton, Louise. *Ellen Key: Her Life and Work.* Translated by Anna E. B. Fries. New York: G. P. Putnam's Sons, 1913.

Purnell, Carolyn. *The Sensational Past: How the Enlightenment Changed the Way We Use Our Senses.* New York: W. W. Norton, 2017.

Rand, Ayn. *The Fountainhead.* Indianapolis: Bobbs-Merrill, 1943.

Regnery, Henry. *The Cliff-Dwellers: A History of a Chicago Cultural Institution.* Chicago: Chicago Historical Bookworks, 1990.

Reitherman, Robert King. "Frank Lloyd Wright's Imperial Hotel: A Seismic Re-Evaluation." In *Proceedings of the Seventh World Conference on Earthquake Engineering Istanbul, Turkey,* vol. 4, 145–52. Istanbul: Turkish National Committee on Earthquake Engineering, 1980.

Remus, Emily A. "Tippling Ladies and the Making of Consumer Culture: Gender and Public Space in Fin-de-Siècle Chicago." *Journal of American History,* December 2014.

Roeck, Bernd. *Florence 1900: The Quest for Arcadia.* Translated by Stewart Spencer. New Haven, CT: Yale University Press, 2009.

Rury, John L. "Schools and Education." Chicago Historical Society, *Encyclopedia of Chicago,* 2005. https://encyclopedia.chicagohistory.org/pages/1124.html.

Saint, Andrew. "Wright and Great Britain." In *Frank Lloyd Wright: Europe and Beyond,* edited by Anthony Alofsin, 121–46. Berkeley: University of California Press, 1999.

Schlereth, Thomas J. "H. H. Richardson's Influence in Chicago's Midwest, 1872–1914." In *The Spirit of H. H. Richardson on the Midland Prairies: Regional Transformations of an Architectural Style,* edited by Paul Clifford Larson and Susan M. Brown, 44–65. Exhibit catalog. Minneapolis: University Art Museum, University of Minnesota, 1988.

Schrenk, Lisa D. *The Oak Park Studio of Frank Lloyd Wright.* Chicago: University of Chicago Press, 2021.

Secrest, Meryle. *Frank Lloyd Wright: A Biography.* Chicago: University of Chicago Press, 1998.

Sheffield, Edith L. "Student Life in the University of Michigan." *Cosmopolitan,* June 1889.

Slotkin, Richard. "Nostalgia and Progress: Theodore Roosevelt's Myth of the Frontier." *American Quarterly* 33, no. 5 (1981): 608–37.

Smith, Kathryn. "Frank Lloyd Wright and the Imperial Hotel: A Postscript." *Art Bulletin* 67, no. 2 (1985): 296–310.

Smith-Rosenberg, Caroll. "The Female World of Love and Ritual: Relations between Women in Nineteenth-Century America." *Signs* 1, no. 1 (1975): 1–29.

Smyth, Katherine. *Wright on Exhibit: Frank Lloyd Wright's Architectural Exhibitions.* Princeton, NJ: Princeton University Press, 2013.

Solomon, Barbara Miller. *In the Company of Educated Women: A History of Women and Higher Education in America.* New Haven, CT: Yale University Press, 1985.

Storrer, William Allin. *The Architecture of Frank Lloyd Wright: A Complete Catalog.* 2nd ed. Cambridge, MA: MIT Press, 1982.

Sutton, Jane. *The House of My Sojourn: Rhetoric, Women, and the Question of Authority.* Tuscaloosa: University of Alabama Press, 2004.

Szuberla, Guy. "Yesterday's City: Miss Chicago and Dad Dearborn." *Chicago History* 35, nos. 1–2 (2007): 44–65.

Titus, W. A. "Historic Spots in Wisconsin." *Wisconsin Magazine of History* 11, no. 3 (1928): 320–27.

Trevelyan, Humphry. *Goethe and the Greeks.* New York: Cambridge University Press, 1981.

Turk, Diana B. *Bound by a Mighty Vow: Sisterhood and Women's Fraternities, 1870–1920.* New York: New York University Press, 2004.

Twombly, Robert C. *Frank Lloyd Wright: An Interpretive Biography.* New York: Harper & Row, 1973.

———. *Frank Lloyd Wright: His Life and Architecture.* New York: John Wiley & Sons, 1987.

Wägner, Elin. *Penwoman.* Translated by Sarah Death. London: Norvik Press, 2009.

Ward, Maria E. *Bicycling for Ladies.* New York: Brentano's, 1896.

Weimann, Jeanne Madeline. *The Fair Women.* Chicago: Academy Chicago, 1981.

Werner, Anja. *The Transatlantic World of Higher Education: Americans at German Universities, 1776–1914.* New York: Berghahn Books, 2013.

Witherspoon, Halliday. *Men of Illinois.* Chicago: n.p., 1902.

Wright, Frank Lloyd. *Ausgeführte Bauten und Entwürfe von Frank Lloyd Wright.* Vol. 1. Berlin: Ernst Wasmuth Verlag, 1910.

———. *An Autobiography.* New York: Duell, Sloan and Pearce, 1943.

———. *An Autobiography.* In *Frank Lloyd Wright Collected Writings: Including an Autobiography,* vol. 2, *1930–1932.* Edited by Bruce Brooks Pfeiffer. New York: Rizzoli, 1992.

———. *Frank Lloyd Wright: An Autobiography.* 1932. Reprint, San Francisco: Pomegranate, 2005.

———. "In the Cause of Architecture." *Architectural Record* 23, no. 3 (March 1908).

———. "In the Cause of Architecture." *Architectural Record* 35, no. 5 (May 1914).

Wright, Gwendolyn. *Moralism and the Model Home: Domestic Architecture and Cultural Conflict in Chicago, 1873–1913.* Chicago: University of Chicago Press, 1980.

Wright, John Lloyd. *My Father Who Is on Earth.* New York: G. P. Putnam's Sons, 1946.

Young, R. T. *Biology in America.* Boston: Richard G. Badger, 1922.

Yusa, Michiko. "Zen-Feminist Raichō in the Context of Meiji Spirituality." In *The Oxford Handbook of Japanese Philosophy,* edited by Bret W. Davis, 613–23. New York: Oxford University Press, 2019.

INDEX

Page numbers in italics refer to illustrations.